ASEAN BUSINESS IN CRISIS

STUDIES IN ASIA PACIFIC BUSINESS
1369-7153

General Editors: Chris Rowley, Paul Stewart and Malcolm Warner

Greater China: Political Economy, Inward Investment and Business Culture
Edited by Chris Rowley and Mark Lewis

Beyond Japanese Management: The End of Modern Times?
Edited by Paul Stewart

Management in China: The Experience of Foreign Businesses
Edited by Roger Strange

**Human Resource Management in the Asia Pacific Region:
Convergence Questioned**
Edited by Chris Rowley

Korean Businesses: Internal and External Industrialization
Edited by Chris Rowley and Johngseok Bae

China's Managerial Revolution
Edited by Malcolm Warner

Managed in Hong Kong: Adaptive Systems, Entrepreneurship and Human Resources
Edited by Chris Rowley and Robert Fitzgerald

Globalization and Labour in the Asia Pacific Region
Edited by Chris Rowley and John Benson

Work and Employment in a Globalized Era: An Asia Pacific Focus
Edited by Yaw A. Debrah and Ian G. Smith

Managing Korean Business: Organization, Culture, Human Resources and Change
Edited by Chris Rowley, Tae-Won Sohn and Johngseok Bae

ASEAN Business in Crisis

Editors

Mhinder Bhopal
Michael Hitchcock

FRANK CASS
LONDON • PORTLAND, OR.

First published in 2002 in Great Britain by
FRANK CASS PUBLISHERS
2 Park Square, Milton Park, Abingdon, Oxon, OX14 4RN

and in the United States of America by
FRANK CASS PUBLISHERS
270 Madison Ave,
New York NY 10016

Transferred to Digital Printing 2005

Website www.frankcass.com

British Library Cataloguing in Publication Data

ASEAN business in crisis. – (Studies in Asia Pacific Business)
   1. International business enterprises – Asia, Southeastern
   2. Asia, Southeastern – Economic conditions – 20th century
   3. Asia, Southeastern – Politics and government – 1945
   I. Bhopal, Mhinder II. Hitchcock, Michael
   338.9´.59

ISBN 0 7146 5263 6 (cloth)
ISSN 1369-7153

Library of Congress Cataloging-in-Publication Data

ASEAN business in crisis / editers Mhinder Bhopal, Michael Hitchcock.
   p.cm. – (Studies in Asia Pacific Business, ISSN 1369-7153)
This group of studies first appeared in a special issue of "Asia Pacific
Business Review" [ISSN 1360-2381], Vol.8, No.2 (Winter 2001)
published by Frank Cass and Co. Ltd.
   Includes bibliographical references and index.
   ISBN 0-7146-5263-6 (cloth)
   1. Financial crises – Asia, Southeastern – 2. International
finance. 3. Asia, Southeastern – Economic conditions. 4. ASEAN.
I. Bhopal, Mhinder, 1958– II. Hitchcock, Michael. III. Series.
IV. Asia Pacific Business Review. v.8, no.2, 2001 (Supplement)
   HB3812 .A84 2002

                    2002001626

This group of studies first appeared in a special issue of
Asia Pacific Business Review [ISSN 1360-2381], Vol.8, No.2 (Winter 2001)
published by Frank Cass and Co. Ltd.

Contents

Introduction:
The Culture and Context   MHINDER BHOPAL and
of the ASEAN Business Crisis   MICHAEL HITCHCOCK   1

The Causes of South East Asia's
Economic Crisis: A Sceptical Review
of the Debate   ANNE BOOTH   19

The Economic Crisis and Law Reform
in South East Asia   ANDREW HARDING   49

The Internet, Email, and the
Malaysian Political Crisis: LEN HOLMES and
The Power of Transparency   MARGARET GRIECO   59

Malaysian Unions in Political Crisis:
Assessing the Impact of the Asian
Contagion   MHINDER BHOPAL   73

Tourism and Total Crisis in
Indonesia: The Case of Bali   MICHAEL HITCHCOCK   101

The International Expansion of
Thailand's Jasmine Group:
Built on Shaky Ground?   PAVIDA PANANOND   121

Downsizing the Thai Subsidiary
Corporation: A Case Analysis   TIM G. ANDREWS   149

Conclusion: ASEAN Economic
and Institutional Development   MHINDER BHOPAL and
in Perspective   MICHAEL HITCHCOCK   171

Notes on Contributors   183

Abstracts   185

Index   189

1

Introduction:
The Culture and Context of
the ASEAN Business Crisis

MHINDER BHOPAL and MICHAEL HITCHCOCK

The flotation of the baht on 2 July 1997 and the subsequent run on
the Thai currency is widely regarded as the trigger for what rapidly
became known as the 'Asian Crisis'. The contagion spread and by
21 July a seven per cent drop in the value of the rupiah heralded
the start of the downturn in Indonesia. Dynamic Malaysia also
succumbed, and to prevent the ringgit from plummeting any
further Prime Minister Mahathir introduced exchange controls.
The crisis rapidly assumed global proportions and by 17 November
it was clear that South Korea was in serious trouble. These events
heightened tensions within South East Asia and provoked
considerable commentary on and analysis of the region.

By 2000 much of Asia was on the way to recovery, though
Indonesia remained strife-ridden, and it would not be unreasonable
to ask why this collection merits attention. There is already a
burgeoning literature on the crisis and the serious analyst may ask
how much more needs to be added. Our view is that the multidisciplinary approach offered by the authors of this volume offers
some additional insights into what is largely seen as an economic
and political phenomenon. It particular, we stress the cultural
context of the crisis and in particular the specific characteristics of
business and politics in the South East Asian region. We also cover
some novel areas – information technology, tourism and trades
unions – that have not hitherto been central to the debates arising
out of the crisis. It is also our view that the crisis was of such
magnitude that the discussions concerning its causes and outcomes
remain relevant.

In analysing the causes and consequences of the crisis it is
helpful to distinguish between triggers and underlying causes. The

run on the Thai baht was clearly the trigger that set off this catastrophic chain of events, but what were the fundamental causes and why it is that not all countries had recovered by 2000 has not been resolved. Indonesia, for example, the largest of the South East Asian countries affected, was still in serious trouble by late 2000. Singapore and Taiwan, despite being buffeted by the financial turbulence, were not dragged into the abyss by their troubled neighbours. Newly liberated from British colonial rule, Hong Kong struggled with its first serious economic setback in living memory.

This collection represents different disciplinary perspectives – of management, economics, politics, sociology and social anthropology. The contributors are not solely concerned with the economic ramifications of the Asian crisis, though economics provides the springboard for these discussions. There are three general essays, but in the main coverage is largely limited to the Association of South East Asian Nations (ASEAN) and particular reference is made to Thailand, Malaysia and Indonesia.

ASIAN VALUES

For Thailand, Malaysia and Indonesia, real gross domestic product growth of 5.9 per cent, 10 per cent and 8 per cent respectively in 1996 plummeted to –10.8 per cent, –7.6 per cent and –13.2 per cent in 1998 (source: World Bank, 2001). Although Thailand and Indonesia were on the way to recovery by 2000, one of the main outcomes of the crisis was the realization that the Asian economies were not invulnerable. The strong growth of countries like Thailand, Malaysia and Indonesia in the 1980s and 1990s had been accompanied by a great deal of euphoria. A major preoccupation of economists and political scientists had been why these economies were growing so robustly, and a variety of explanatory frameworks began to be debated. Perhaps one of the most contentious was the idea that the 'miracle' economies of Asia had found a unique to route to development that involved eschewing the universalism inherent in Western models of economic and cultural modernization in favour of home-grown approaches that had been devised in distinctive Asian contexts (Wee, 1997). The crisis has served to rapidly demystify such explanations and reassert the rationalism of 'Western', essentially Anglo-Saxon, approaches to economic development as indicated by the rapid move from a focus on the supposed 'virtues' of the Asian model to the 'vices' of Asian nepotism, cronyism and corruption.

In Asia much of the debate over the virtues of Asian values was led by politicians, especially Singapore's former premier Lee Kuan Yew. To a lesser extent Western politicians followed suit, though some Western academic analysts similarly utilized 'culturalism' to account for rapid East Asian economic development (Lodge and Vogel, 1987; Min Chen, 1995). The following sections explore the exterior and interior applications of the values dimension with particular reference to what became known as the 'Singapore school', whose chief architect was former prime minister Lee Kuan Yew.

The Singaporean prime minister's calls in the 1980s and 1990s for Asians to look to their own cultures for inspiration, identity construction and affirmation were not unlike those of the early independence leaders of the 1950s and 1960s. Sukarno, for example, encouraged the newly independent Indonesians to look to their own traditions, and went as far as to encourage leading experts on Javanese batik cloth to devise more nationalistic designs (Hitchcock and Wiendu Nuryanti, 2000: xxix). The combination of political sponsorship and rapid South East Asian economic growth led to increasing interest in and analysis of the so-called Asian model. Within this context there emerged what is popularly referred to as the 'Singapore school', which held that Asian societies were different from those of the West because of their distinctive value systems.

The idea that 'Asian values' could somehow account for the increasing prosperity of the region gained in popularity and received ringing endorsements from senior politicians, most notably Malaysia's Prime Minister, Mahathir Mohamed. Suharto's government in neighbouring Indonesia was also technically a supporter of the 'Singapore school', though the president himself appeared to be more circumspect. Indonesian academics may have grumbled that 'Asian values' as advanced by politicians represented a gross simplification of the rich heritage of Asia, but Mahathir's stirring speeches on the supremacy of the Eastern moral code were rapturously received in Jakarta.

Growth of Asian Values and Confucianism

A full account of this long-running debate lies beyond the scope of this contribution; the intention here is to outline some of the main features that are relevant to the discussion of the crisis. Perhaps one of the most controversial aspects of the debate, and one which might explain the reservations expressed by certain Indonesian academics and the incorporation of the wider notion of 'Asian' by political leaders, was the role played by Confucianism in what might be regarded as a sinocentric explanation of growth. The teachings of Kong Fu Zi (Confucius), who is variously described as a teacher, provincial administrator and civil servant (circa 551–479 BC), became the basis of a vast philosophical system known as Confucianism. This codified system of thought was not confined to China, but strongly influenced neighbouring states such as Vietnam and Korea that were drawn into China's orbit. Confucian teachings were also taken abroad by Chinese migrants, particularly across the *Nanyang* (Southern Sea) to South East Asia and thus these values are encountered wherever the Chinese have settled.

In his studies of the relationship between the spirit of economic life and the ethics of ascetic Protestantism, Weber made comparisons with the Asian world religions. In particular, he argued that the Confucian-influenced government of pre-revolutionary China had only fiscal and mercantilist interests and no 'commercial policy' in the modern sense (from Weber, 1977: 440). As Singapore's economy developed and overtook that of its former colonial ruler, Britain, in Gross National Product (GNP) per capita terms, Weber's observation became one of the brickbats of the 'Singapore school'. With politicians such as Lee Kuan Yew looking to distinctly Asian ways of regulating and organizing Singapore society, interest in Confucianism revived, leading to the foundation of new institutes. The combination of economic development and Confucian revival was interpreted as a rebuttal of Weber's position, despite the fact that he never argued that economic behaviour was 'determined solely by religion' (Ibid: 268). On a broader front while such analysis may have served to build positive identities in Chinese-dominated societies, it also served theoretically to explain the rise of Chinese business (see Gomez, 1999), and point to the relative impenetrability, or 'closure', of Chinese business in countries such as Malaysia, Thailand and Indonesia, where the Chinese are numerically in a minority but economically strong.

Economic Growth and Social (Dis)integration

Irrespective of the explanatory power of Confucianism as a significant variable in Asian economic growth, the leaders of the emergent Asian economies were concerned with the moral education of children. Many educationists believed that economic success was somehow linked to self-discipline, and the idea that children should be taught moral values was widely adopted. Korean children, for example, were expected to master set texts on moral values before moving on to study 'national ethics'. In Taiwan children were taught moral education for 40 minutes a week, and in Hong Kong moral education spread through the curriculum. To ensure that the message was not lost in translation, Singaporean children were provided with moral education in their own language. In Indonesia students had to master the state moral code – 'five principles' (*pancasila*) – in order to progress through the education system.

The idea that a state education system should inculcate moral values is not new, but what was distinctive was the view that education should nurture and protect the values of the Pacific Asian societies as they were transformed though development. Simply put, these newly industrialized countries desired the benefits of Western prosperity without what their leaders saw as the attendant ills of Western morality. Former Prime Minister Lee Kuan Yew warned that 'If Western values are adopted, cohesion will be threatened and the country will go downhill'

In tandem with the debate on social order, this discourse was applied to the industrial domain, especially with regard to the early 1980s promotion of Japanization with its attendant implications for industrial culture and values. This potentially served two purposes. It aimed to create the right conditions for the application of emerging 'best management practice' in what were multinational corporation (MNC)-dependent economies while simultaneously mitigating the potential strains from the growth of a large urban workforce which was the natural consequence of successful industrialization (Wadd, 1988; Sing, 1994). This was evident in Malaysia's 'Look East' policy which was summarized by Prime Minister Mahathir of Malaysia as

> emulating the rapidly developing countries of the East in the effort to develop Malaysia. Matters deserving

attention are: diligence and discipline in work, loyalty to
the nation and to the enterprise or business ... priority of
group over individual differences, emphasis on
productivity and efficiency and high quality, upgrading
efficiency (quoted in Jomo 1989)

Asian Cultural Heterogeneity

While 'Asian values' are something of a misnomer since the
societies in question possessed a multiplicity of moral codes, this
did not stop politicians from engaging in discussion of some core
elements of Asian identity, however heterogeneous that may be (see
Anwar, 1996). Confucianism may have been the dominant moral
code of Vietnam and latterly Singapore, but the nature of
Confucianism and its relevance for contemporary analysis and
understanding has been disputed (see Kim, 1994; Cable, 1995).
Furthermore, Indian values, specifically Buddhism, held sway in
much of mainland South East Asia. Maritime South East Asia was
different again, with the majority of the population in Malaysia,
Indonesia and Brunei subscribing to Islam, whereas the Philippines
were predominantly Catholic. Despite these differences, the idea
that Western values posed a threat acted as a cohesive force, though
each country tackled the perceived problem in its own way.
Malaysia, for example, tried to incorporate Islamic values into its
bureaucratic structures and opted to teach students both Western
and Islamic legal codes. Anti-Chinese sentiment in Malaysia,
however, led to an under-emphasis on Confucianism and elevation
of Japan as a role model, a strategy made possible owing to the
antagonism between Japan and China. Indonesia's state philosophy
placed emphasis on religious tolerance and attempted to reconcile
the beliefs of the Muslim majority, roughly 85 per cent of the
population, with those of the substantial Hindu and Christian
minorities. In Thailand, children were taught that Buddhism was a
central pillar of the kingdom.

Culture and Identity

Given these differences, it would be absurdly reductionist to
suggest that 'Asian values' represented a homogenous response to
the growth of a world system based on Western values. It would
also be misleading to conceive of Asian values in purely religious
terms in the manner of Huntingdon's (1996) 'civilizational clash'

since the identities of the countries involved in this debate were much more complex. Indonesia's sense of nationhood, for example, was based on a reaction to Western intrusion on one hand and an absorption of some key European concepts on the other. Indeed, it has long been noted that some parts of Malaysian urbanized elites of all ethnic groups had a commonality by virtue of a strong British influence via education and colonial history (Saravanamutta, 1983); similar effects of colonial history on the ruling elites in Singapore have also been noted (see Sing 1991). Unlike Korea and Taiwan, which were colonized by Japan and have Japanese influences, Singapore and Malaysia have been strongly influenced by Western values. However, as part of national projects it is not unsurprising if attempts are made to differentiate the nation as sharply as possible from its former colonial status, or to resurrect such status in attempts to re-forge identities (Kim, 1995). Thus, while one might have expected the Indonesian nationalists to draw a sharp distinction between Indonesian and European cultural heritage (Holtzappel, 1996: 64), which would have been in accordance with the official view, in practice the evolution of the Indonesian nation state owed much to European inspiration. The Indonesian national philosophy of 'five principles', which was devised during the early years of independence, was taken from Old Javanese sources (Holtzappel, 1996: 103), but Indonesian nationalism per se was born out of the Herderian brand of nationalism in which the nation's founders are its people (Hubinger, 1992: 4), though the Indonesian nationalists in the 1950s intermittently denied any debt to the West.

Nonetheless, the differentiation and distancing between the 'West' and the 'East' seemed to serve domestic and overseas interest and contributed to distilling the distinctive features of Asian and Western management (see below), as well as providing a listing of characteristics for state action in the (re)construction and modification of culture. An example of this kind of codification, which verges on being stereotypical, is outlined in Table 1.

Managing Through Cultures

Some common themes can be detected in the management debate, which resonate with the Asian values discourse in Asia, and, despite the risk of simplification, they are worth outlining here. First, there is the respect for authority, namely that superiors, whether in the

TABLE 1
ASIAN AND WESTERN MANAGEMENT CHARACTERISTICS

Asian management	Western management
Communitarianism	Individualism
High Duty Consciousness	Property Rights
Community Need	Competition to meet customer need
Powerful State	Limited State
Holism and Interdependence	Scientific Specialization

Source: Min Chen (1995) summarizing Lodge and Vogel (1987).

familial or public domains, should be deferred to. Second, there is an emphasis on the long view and that future benefits should not be sacrificed for short-term gains. Third, there is the cultural preference for saving face and the avoidance of embarrassment, the antithesis of the direct speech that is often considered praiseworthy in the Western context. Fourth, there is the desire for harmony, in particular the avoidance of clashes and instability. Fifth, there is the stress on reciprocity, the desirability of sharing favours and mutual benefits. Above all there is the notion that it is the group that takes precedence and not the individual, and that each person is obliged to place obligations above individual rights.

The notion of Asian cultural values raises important and contentious issues over identities and differences. For instance, while it is clear that Asia is a constructed region with no real coherence and possibly greater diversity than any other region in the world, the elites within East and South East Asia have utilized the notion of a cultural essence for domestic, regional, political and industrial purposes as exemplified in debates over Asian values, and East Asian trade blocks. Economic growth provided a confidence to assert such an identity in an global system in which East and South East Asia became increasingly important (Wee, 1997). This assertion served to create a distance from the Western 'other' while simultaneously promoting the form, if not the substance, of a coherent 'self'. Such assertions arose at a time of concern over 'Western industrial decline' and an erosion of Western confidence. East Asian success has been an important anchor for neo-liberals in their attribution of decline to the fragmentation of social and industrial order arising from cultural values. In this sense the Asian values debate has served to explicitly and implicitly underpin the need for societal and industrial restructuring which emphasizes commitment, leadership, entrepreneurship and super-ordinate goals to ensure survival in an increasingly competitive world that was approaching the 'Pacific century'.

With the onset of the Asian crisis, however, the confidence associated with growth was supplanted with the uncertainty of decline. The issue of values was again invoked but in a different context, with Prime Minister Mahathir blaming the 'West' for the Asian crisis (see *Time*, September 1998; Jomo, 1998). In his opening speech to the United Malay National Organization's national conference of 1998 he argued: 'We are pushed to become a backward weak race which is re-colonized and having to serve others'. In the context of decline rather than growth, Andrews in this collection explores how a discourse of cultural identity can be utilized not for the creation of order but to resist change by representing change as culturally alien at the micro organizational level. On a different note, Hitchcock advances the view that effects of the crisis were highly variable and that tourism on the Indonesian island of Bali remained relatively unscathed. He argues that although advocates for Bali's tourism industry offered cultural explanations, namely the essentially peaceful nature of the island's inhabitants, this was a best a partial explanation. During the crisis the island had become something of a haven for Chinese fleeing persecution in the major Indonesian cities, as well as a safety-net for the Jakarta conglomerates with interests in tourism who were anxious to protect their assets. Many of the latter included family members of the deposed Indonesian premier, Suharto, though the critical scrutiny of business practice that accompanied reform elsewhere in Indonesia was not as marked in Bali, possibly because of local fears about the negative impact of political unrest on the all-important tourism sector. Both Hitchcock's and Andrews' essays allude to the need to differentiate the notion of culture as explanation from analyses that perceive culture as a resource.

While such a debate in the West and East served to (re)produce stereotypical notions, the cultural focus on Asia has tended to neglect the quite significant differences in not only culture but also in political structure. Indeed, the relative socio-cultural and political homogeneity in East Asia has been argued to have enabled the political consolidation necessary for strong developmental states (Chowdhury and Islam, 1993), whereas the more heterogeneous South East Asia has been politically more fragmented, giving rise to factional and political accommodation by state structures which has resulted in their relatively lower levels of state autonomy (Henk *et al.*, 1995). The inherent political competition resulting from difference of interest has been largely contained by state control and regulation of the mass media, particularly in Malaysia (Milne and Mauzy, 1999: 113–15). However, the political tensions which unfolded in Indonesia and Malaysia in the wake of the crisis demonstrated the potential of the Internet to transcend the heavy infrastructure of traditional mass media in opening up the political discourse. The contribution by Grieco and Holmes, using the case of Malaysia, identifies and explores the significance of the Internet in opening up the very political space that has arguably been closed in the instrumental developmentalism pursued by state elites.

The link between Asian values and the rise of Pacific Asia in the late twentieth century remains contentious, not least because they appear to be more concerned with nation-building than economic prosperity per se. 'Asian values' also provided politicians with an alternative to Western liberalism and an opportunity to shape the current political agenda. In promoting these values, politicians were able to use history to justify contemporary social relations and parallels may be drawn with the 'invented traditions' outlined by Hobsbawm and Ranger (1983) in their seminal volume on nationalism. To account for the success of Pacific Asia solely in terms of local virtues also risks ignoring other factors such as globalization and world financial shifts. Despite these reservations it is worthwhile exploring whether or not an examination of these values can shed light on aspects of the crisis, and this is particularly the case with regard to management.

ASIAN MANAGEMENT

The crisis is significant in so far as it dents narrow forms of analysis verging on the monistic, and promotes wider debates about the management of economies that occurred in the neo-liberal decade of the 1980s. This period also saw an intensification of the forces of globalization, particularly financial globalization, which was unleashed not just as a promoter of growth but also as a market-based disciplinary mechanism. In addition to being drawn into the world capital markets, the ASEAN nations have been affected by a variety of other globalizing forces, namely involvement in the international labour system, the interaction of nation-states and ascription into the international military order. Globalization may be characterized by the intensification of economic and social relations across the world, linking distant localities so that experiences in one location are influenced by events taking place far away in another and vice versa (Giddens, 1991, 64). Different analysts have associated the onset of the world capitalist system with different periods; Wallerstein (1976), for example, links it to the sixteenth century, whereas Giddens has argued that the first truly global experience occurred in the twentieth.

The countries that comprise ASEAN were by and large drawn into the orbits of the European mercantile powers in the sixteenth century, though it is helpful to link the onset of global social relations in the region with the period of 'high colonialism', roughly 1870 to 1940 (Scholte 1996: 24). With the exception of Thailand, the South East Asian nations were linked to this earlier version of globalization via European colonization: The Philippines (Spain and USA), Singapore, Brunei, Malaysia and Myanmar (Britain), Indonesia (The Netherlands), Vietnam, Laos and Cambodia (France). The point is that the Asian crisis was not the region's first experience of global turbulence – the 1930s and the Second World War being two notable examples – but was arguably the first crisis that might be attributed to distinctive Asian causes.

South East Asia's rapid growth in the wake of the newly industrializing economies (NIEs) sparked some serious study of the causes of the growth. This was not only to draw lessons for the less developed economies of the world but also to serve ideological debates about the role and interrelationship between states, markets and firms in the West. While these debates were couched in terms of different kinds of capitalism, the underlying comparative models being Anglo-American in contrast to the insider models of Rhenish and Japanese capitalism (Dore, 1994; Hutton, 1996). To this may be added those models that lie between the market and the state, and in particular those based on international production involving a high degree of state direction, the prime example being South Korea (Evans, 1995; Rowley and

Bae, 1998). In this sense the crisis re-ignited older and deep-seated debates about the efficacy of the global market economy and the nature, function and orientation of states in this order. Many on the right, having initially sung the praises of the market orientation and cultural characteristics of Asian growth, became highly critical of the political business practices, nepotism, inefficient allocative mechanisms and 'backward' business practices that were seen as the cause of the crisis. Others argued that the crisis was not one of fundamentals, nor one that was generic across Asia. Indeed not only were countries different from one another, but the crisis was generated by the unregulated flow of global capital that did not sufficiently understand the particular structures of Asian economies. Instead, financial decisions were influenced by a herd-like instinct that threatened the stability of the world economy (see Booth in this volume).

A second more critical strand focuses on the omission within the battle of positions, by concentrating on the murkier side of Asian growth. Much discussion of the Asian model, while addressing many organizational issues, has tended to ignore or neglect the wider geopolitical landscape within which Asian economic growth occurred. Such arguments have, for example, tended to emphasize the significance of the Cold War in providing major contracts to support military intervention in Vietnam and Korea. This also helped to reduce Asian expenditure on arms on one hand and encouraged a general US commitment to stimulate growth in the East Asian capitalist economies as an antidote to Communism on the other (Bello and Rosenfeld, 1992; Iriye, 1994). While these factors alone may not account for East Asian development, as Chowdhury and Islam have argued, the exigencies of the Cold War helped bolster growth in Korea, Japan, Taiwan and Singapore, while simultaneously tolerating the suppression of labour (see Ogle, 1990) and neglect of Japanese atrocities in China in the 1930s (Chang, 1997). There has been an attendant growth in a critical literature documenting the internal cost of East Asian development in social and cultural terms (Bello and Rosenfeld, 1992; Deyo, 1989). This literature, rather than focusing on the cultural and organizational attributes, has pointed to the use of cheap female labour in the export strategies of the Asian economies, along with long hours of work, poor conditions of health and safety and a general suppression of organized labour. It has been argued that the dash for growth, in what became known as 'authoritarian developmental states', has been accompanied by a widespread neglect of the environment and, in most countries, the marginalization and suppression of political opposition. This literature, perhaps, provides a vital social historical context for our appreciation of the potential consequences of social dislocation and the political constraints on policy responses that accompanied the financial crisis of 1997.

FROM ASIAN VALUES TO CRONY CAPITALISM

Despite the enormous disparities between the states in question, in terms of both cultural outlook and political disposition, the term 'developmental state' took root and the Asian model entered the literature in a number of related social science disciplines, especially economics, politics and management. How far the phenomenon of the developmental state in Asia was culturally and historically specific, if indeed such a general model had an adequate explanatory value, remains beyond the scope of this introduction. But what is of interest here are the ways in which the model was revisited in both the popular media and academic press in the wake of the Asian Crisis. Even before the outbreak of the crisis the so-called Asian model had its critics, and their publications were approached with renewed interest by commentators.

One of the most frequently cited authorities was Lingle (1998), whose polemical riposte to the Asian model appeared just at the time of the crisis. Lingle had earlier come to public attention as the author of an article in the *International Herald Tribune* that criticized the handling of forest fires by ASEAN politicians, and was alleged to have made reference to Singapore's compliant judiciary. Lingle argued that Asian leaders were more concerned with saving face than solving the problem of the haze smothering Malaysia, Indonesia and Singapore. He argued that no European government would stand for this lack of action, nor be hampered by Asian values from criticizing one another. Lingle was soon after forced to flee the country as a Singapore court found him guilty, along with other defendants, of contempt of court on 17 January 1995.

One of the first to invoke Lingle on the crisis was Samuel Brittan in a *Financial Times* commentary provocatively entitled 'Asian model, RIP' on 4 December 1997. The article is worth noting not so much for its distinctive analysis, but the way that it urges Europeans and Americans not to be panicked by the supposed Asian threat. The article also treats Lingle as an authoritative source of what went wrong in Asia and goes on to discuss the suppression of criticism in public life, the rise of the 'one family state' and the other attendant ills of the maintenance of Asian values. 'Harsher critics,' he writes, 'talk of "crony capitalism"'. However, in Malaysia the issue of corruption, nepotism and cronyism had been exposed prior to the crisis. This material was not only available in the public domain of academic analysis through the works of Malaysian political economists such as Jomo and Gomez, but was also the subject matter of pre-crisis inter-factional political manoeuvring within the ruling party. Bhopal argues that factionalism and division was prevalent prior to the crisis, and accusations of corruption, nepotism and cronyism existed prior to the crisis, and indeed this was a rallying cry to continue the efforts of oppositional mobilization and consolidation which had been occurring in pre-crisis Malaysia.

Despite the ubiquity of the term 'crony capitalism' in commentaries on the Asian crisis, it is often difficult to pin down precisely what authors mean. The fact that the term is alliterative, pejorative and easy to remember may have widened its appeal, but it is by no means certain that it can be applied generally in the Asian context. Citing Krugman (1998), Pincus and Ramli (1998: 724) use the term of 'patrimonial' ('crony capitalism') to describe and explain relations between government and big business. Hill (1999) discusses the thesis that a combination of corruption and poor government in Indonesia helped to bring about the crisis. According to the thesis, a partially liberalized economy combined with cautious macro-economic management can yield impressive rates of growth, especially when sustained by private capital inflows and international investment agencies, hopeful of ongoing reforms and keen to enlarge their lending portfolios. Such a strategy may, however, cover up deeper problems and the export sector, often burdened with inefficiencies, may falter. In this collection, Panond explores one aspect of this debate. She outlines the growth of Thai telecommunications firms and shows how this was accomplished through the involvement of bureaucrats, government, military and private interests. Panond then evaluates the sustainability of such a strategy in the context of crisis and downturn.

Large uneconomic projects, often selected on the basis of cronyism, do not provide a sufficient flow of funds to service debts; and a complex web of vested interests inhibits the government from acting decisively in a crisis (Hill 1999: 51). Such a model may well explain how aspects of the crisis evolved in Indonesia after the capital markets had reacted to the fall of the Thai baht, but cannot necessarily be applied elsewhere as a root cause of the crisis. Pincus and Ramli (1998: 732) maintain that the intensity of the Indonesian crisis cannot be explained by external factors alone and argue that 'deeply entrenched patrimonial state structures increased the likelihood of collapse'. The corruption and nepotism of the Indonesian regime may have been exposed as a result of the intense international and domestic scrutiny that came in the wake of the crisis, but does not explain the onset of the crisis in the first place. Moreover, as Hitchcock shows here, many of the so-called nepotistic networks remained in place well after the fall of the government that was most widely regarded as corrupt, partly for pragmatic reasons. Booth argues that the crisis, particularly in Indonesia, was in part due to the marginalization of otherwise very capable government technocrats in the economic and finance ministries of the region.

In all these debates, what has been significant is how the level of generality has been progressively reduced in recognition of the fact that Asia is diverse. In view of the continent's varied geography, history and culture it is difficult to conceive of 'Asia' as a valid analytical unit. The use of the term 'Asian' when analysing the economies and management of this vast region not only blurs important cultural differences, but suggests that the coverage is more general than it really is. The burgeoning literature on 'Asia' tends to overlook South East Asia and what we end up with is essentially an analysis of Japan, South Korea, Hong Kong, Taiwan and Singapore. Furthermore, the societies subjected to intensive analysis (Redding, 1990) comprise countries that either had Chinese majorities (Taiwan, Singapore and Hong Kong) or had been profoundly influenced through contact with China (Japan and Korea). It would be misleading to suggest that differences between the historical, organizational, political and economic circumstances of these countries have been completely overlooked, but it is reasonable to suggest that the overall balance is weighted in favour of overly generalized analysis (see Min Chen, 1995; Whitley,

1992). The fact is that the debate about Asia in the context of Asian growth has tended to ignore the fact that South East Asia is qualitatively different from East Asia, in terms of its peoples, cultures, language and scripts, as well as contemporary and ancient historical influences. What this volume does is to concentrate on the comparatively neglected countries of Malaysia, Indonesia and Thailand, the very countries that were at the heart of the Asian crisis. We stress the point that the onset of the crisis, and possible causes, were not necessarily Asian nor East Asian but primarily South East Asian and ASEAN. It is our view that the term 'Asian crisis' is itself something of a misnomer – given Asia's economic, cultural and political complexity, not to mention size – and that the term 'ASEAN crisis' might be more appropriate, albeit with a number of caveats.

We do not focus necessarily on the big issues but on the consequences in particular areas, and we eschew grand analysis in favour of more specific and detailed, and above all contexualized, commentary. This approach is in keeping with our attempt to appreciate the local but in the context of the global rather than to let the global supersede the nuanced reality of local dynamics. Corporate restructuring directed at encouraging foreign investment in closed local companies was seen as an essential ingredient in the region's recovery. The opening-up of companies to foreign ownership would, it was argued, speed up the restoration of the region's economic fortunes and help reduce corruption and inefficiency. The worst affected countries, Thailand and Indonesia, have found it difficult to follow this prescription for recovery, not least because cash-strapped politicians, particularly in Indonesia, have found it necessary to continue protecting favoured corporations (Vatikiotis, 2000: 76). More recently, it would appear that the IMF is unhappy with this lack of reform and that there are fears that there may be a recurrence of the 1997 crisis.

REFERENCES

Anwar, Ibrahim (1996), *The Asian Renaissance*. Singapore: Time Books International.
Amsden, Alice H. (1989), *Asia's Next Giant: South Korea and Late Industrialisation*. Oxford and New York: Oxford University Press.
Bello, W., and Rosenfeld, S. (1992), *Dragons in Distress: Asia's Miracle Economies in Crisis*. London: Penguin.
Brittan, S. (1997), '"Asian model", R.I.P.', *Financial Times*, 4 Dec., p.24.

Cable, V. (1995), 'Coming to terms with the Asian miracle', *Demos*, pp.2–5.

Chang, Iris (1997), *The Rape of Nanking: The Forgotten Holocaust of World War II*. New York: Basic Books.

Chen, Min (1995), *Asian Management Systems: Chinese, Japanese and Korean styles of Business*. London: Routledge.

Chowdhury, A., and Islam, I. (1993), *The Newly Industrialising Economies of East Asia*. London: Routledge.

Deyo, F. (1989), *Beneath the Miracle: Labor Subordination in the New Asian Industrialism*. Berkeley: University of California Press.

Dore, R. (1994), 'Japanese Capitalism, Anglo-Saxon Capitalism' in N. Campbell and F. Burton (eds), *Japanese Multinationals: Strategies and Management in the Global Kaisha*. London: Routledge.

Evans, P. (1995), *Embedded Autonomy: States and Industrial Transformation*. Princeton, NJ: Princeton University Press.

Giddens, A. (1991), *The Consequences of Modernity*. Cambridge: Polity Press.

Gomez, T. (1999), *Chinese Business in Malaysia: accumulation, accommodation and ascendance*. Richmond, Surrey: Curzon Press.

Henk, T., Ramaswamy, E., Chhacchi, A., and Hendricks, M. (1995), 'Three Highly Differentiated Trajectories' in T. Henk (ed.), *Globalization and Third World Trade Unions: The Challenge of Rapid Economic Change*. London: Zed books.

Hill, H. (1999), *The Indonesian Economy in Crisis*. Singapore: ISEAS.

Hitchcock, M., and Wiendu Nuryanti (2000), 'Introduction', in M. Hitchcock and Wiendu Nuryanti (eds) *Building on Batik: The Globalization of a Craft Community*. Aldershot: Ashgate, pp.xxii-xxxi.

Hitchcock, M., King, V.T., and Parnwell, M.J.G. (1997), 'Introduction', in M. Hitchcock and V.T. King (eds), *Images of Malay-Indonesian Identity*. Kuala Lumpur: Oxford University Press, pp.63–107.

Hobsbawm, Eric, and Ranger, Terence (eds) (1983), *The Invention of Tradition*. Cambridge: Cambridge University Press.

Holtzappel, Coen (1996), 'Nationalism and Cultural Identity', in M. Hitchcock and V.T. King (eds), *Images of Malay-Indonesian Identity*. Kuala Lumpur: Oxford University Press, pp.63–107).

Hubinger, V. (1992), 'The Creation of Indonesian National Identity', *Prague Occasional Papers in Ethnology* 1, pp.1–35.

Huntington, Samuel (1996), *The Clash of Civilizations and The Remaking of World Order*. New York: Simon & Schuster.

Hutton, W. (1996), *The State We're In*. London: Vintage.

Iriye, Akira (1994), 'The United States and Japan in Asia', in G. Curtis (ed.), *The United States, Japan, and Asia*. New York: W.W. Norton.

Jomo, K.S. (1989) *Mahathir's Economic Policies* (2nd ed.). Kuala Lumpur: INSAW.

Jomo, K.S. (1998), 'Malaysian Debacle: Whose Fault', *Cambridge Journal of Economics*, Vol.22, pp.707–22.

Kamata, S. (1983), *Japan In The Passing Lane: An Insider's Account of Life in a Japanese Auto Factory*. London: Allen & Unwin.

Kim Kyong-Dong (1994), 'Confucianism and Capitalist Development in East Asia', in L. Sklair (ed.), *Capitalism and Development*. London: Routledge.

Krugman, P. (1998), *What happened to Asia?* Cambridge, MA: MIT, mimeo.

Lingle, Christopher (1988), *The Rise and Decline of the Asian Century: False starts on the Path to the Global Millennium*. Seattle, WA: University of Washington Press, 1998.

Lodge, G.C. and Erza F. Vogel (1987), *Ideology and National Competitiveness*. Boston: Harvard University Press.

Milne, R.S. and Mauzy, D. (1999), *Malaysian Politics Under Mahathir*. London:Routledge.

Min-Chen (1995), *Asian Management Systems*. London: Routledge.

Ogle, G. (1990), *South Korea: Dissent Within the Economic Miracle*. London: Zed Books.

Pincus, J., and Romli, R. (1998), 'Indonesia: From Showcase to Basket Case', *Cambridge Journal of Economics*, Vol.22, pp.723–34.

Redding, G. (1990), *The Spirit of Chinese Capitalism*. Berlin: Walter de Gruyler.

Rowley, C., and Bae, J. (eds) (1998), *Korean Business: Internal and External Industrialization*. London: Frank Cass.

Saravanamutta, J. (1983), 'The Look East Policy and Japanese Economic Penetration in Malaysia' in S. Jomo (ed.), *The Sun Also Sets*. Kuala Lumpur: INSAN.

Scholte, Jan Aart (1996), 'Identifying Indonesia' in M. Hitchcock and V.T. King (eds), *Images of Malay-Indonesian Identity*. Kuala Lumpur: Oxford University Press, pp.21–44.

Sing, L. (1991), 'Features of Japanese Direct Investment and Japanese-Style Management in Singapore' in S. Yamashita (ed.), *Transfer of Technology and Management to the ASEAN countries*. Tokyo: University of Tokyo Press.

Sing, L. (1994), *Japan's Role in Asia: Issues and Perspectives*. Singapore: Times Academic Press.

Time (1998), 'Malaysia in Crisis', *Time*, 14 Sep., pp.16–24.

Vatikiotis, M. (2000), 'Going Backward', *Far Eastern Economic Review*, 19 Oct., pp.76–9.

World Bank (2001) Online at http://wbln0018.worldbank.org/eap/eap.nsf/General/8BACD5416E7C79538525696700582520?OpenDocument

Wallerstein, Immanuel (1976), *The Modern World System: Capitalist Agriculture and the Origins of the European World Economy in the Sixteenth Century*. New York: Academic Press.

Weber, M. (1977), *Essays in Sociology*. Trans., ed. and intro. by H.H. Gerth and C. Wright Mills. London: Routledge & Kegan Paul.

Wee, L (1997), 'Buying Japan: Singapore, Japan and an "East Asian" Modernity', *Journal of Pacific Asia*, Vol.4, pp.21–46.

Whitley, R. (1992), *East Asian Business Systems*. London: Sage.

2

The Causes of South East Asia's Economic Crisis: A Sceptical Review of the Debate

ANNE BOOTH

'If anyone had predicted a year ago that Indonesia, South Korea and Thailand would have to go cap in hand to the IMF, they would have been thought mad.'

– East Asian Economies Survey, *The Economist*,
7 March 1998, p.5.

To many people, both in the region and elsewhere, the crisis which struck South East Asia in the latter part of 1997 seemed like a bolt from the blue, a meteor crashing from outer space onto what had seemed to many experts to be the most dynamic and successful part of the world economy. As the crisis deepened, it became clear that both the economic and the political consequences for the three worst affected South East Asian countries would be severe. There has been an explosion of literature (which continues unabated) as a range of commentators from various parts of the world give their views on why the crisis happened and what lessons can be learned from it. But to those economists whose main interest is the study of long-term economic development in the ASEAN economies, much of this work has been rather disappointing. One of the reasons for this disappointment, it has to be admitted, is that many of the international pundits who have been speaking or writing on the South East Asian crisis since late 1997 have only a slender grasp of South East Asian economic history, and indeed in many cases have had no previous engagement with the region. Often they appear to have been using the events in Thailand, Indonesia or Malaysia simply to prove their own theories of economic crises or disprove rival theories. While there may be little harm in this kind of academic activity, much of it is of dubious benefit to those policy-makers now struggling to deal with the aftermath of the crisis, or to improve economic institutions so that similar cataclysms cannot occur again.

It would be beyond the scope of a survey article to examine in depth the reasons for the severity of the crisis in Indonesia, Malaysia and Thailand, but it is worth pointing out that, even after three years, there still appear to be important differences of opinion among the foreign observers, and among experts within ASEAN, as to why the crisis occurred. One division, made by foreign commentators such as Corsetti (1998) and Noland (2000) is between those writers who see the origins of the crisis in fundamental weaknesses and policy inconsistencies *within* the afflicted economies, and those who see the crisis as mainly due to external contagion and speculative panic. But within these two camps there are also significant divisions. In the 'internal causes' camp there are those who blame weak financial regulation, those who blame 'premature' liberalization of the financial system, those who see the fundamental problem in the growing corruption, nepotism and cronyism in the political systems of the worst affected economies, and those who point to a sharp decline in the role of technocrats in economic management. Among those who blame external causes there are those who point to the malign effects of international currency speculators, and those who claim that the real villain was the International Monetary Fund whose interventions in both Thailand and Indonesia were determined by a dogmatic adherence to a particular package of economic policy reforms which in fact aggravated the domestic economic problems in these economies.

A key argument of this contribution will be that the crisis in South East Asia was due to a number of causes, often interacting with one another, and that these causes varied between countries. It is now obvious that within South East Asia the impact of the crisis on real output differed considerably across countries; this fact alone should deter any serious commentator from blaming a single cause, such as foreign speculation, domestic corruption, or openness to international capital flows. The most open economy in the region, Singapore, escaped the worst effects of the crisis, as did the Philippines, widely considered to be one of the most corrupt. In this essay I will try to establish why Indonesia, Thailand and Malaysia were the worst affected, at least in terms of real declines in output.[1] In doing this, I will try to explain the ways in which domestic policy weaknesses interacted with external factors, including (in Thailand and Indonesia) the behaviour of the International Monetary Fund. But first, it is necessary to examine the extent to which warning signals predicting the crisis were already evident in the worst affected economies before July 1997, and why these signals were ignored.

WAS THE CRISIS PREDICTED?

In 1993 the World Bank included four ASEAN economies (Indonesia, Malaysia, Singapore and Thailand) among its 'Asian miracles' (World Bank, 1993) and in 1996 it was still confidently predicting that the growth would continue.

> Although looking into the future is always a risky business, some things are likely to be good bets. Rapid growth is likely to continue in East Asia, and the pace of change experienced by these economies should continue to be very impressive. East Asian economies are committed to an open and cooperative approach in the evolution of economic relations among themselves and with the rest of the world, and will use market-based and competitive means to achieve their goals (World Bank 1996: 126).

But in fact by the latter part of 1996, this type of buoyant optimism was already tempered with a growing concern about economic trends in the ASEAN region. In what turned out to be a startlingly prescient article, the *Economist* of 24 August 1996 drew parallels between the Mexican economy in the run-up to the crisis of late 1994 and emerging trends in Thailand, Malaysia, Indonesia and the Philippines.[2] One obvious similarity was the large balance-of-payments deficits as a percentage of GDP in both Malaysia (9.7 per cent) and Thailand (7.7 per cent), compared with 7.8 per cent in Mexico in 1994. Although the deficit was larger in Malaysia as a percentage of GDP than in Thailand, a much higher proportion was funded by long-term inflows of foreign direct investment. In Thailand by contrast the balance-of-payments deficit net of FDI inflows was still very large in 1996; at 7.5 per cent of GDP, it was higher than in Mexico two years earlier. In other words almost all of the large balance of payments deficit in Thailand was funded by short-term capital inflows. By 1996–7, Thailand had a much higher ratio of short-term debt owed to international banks than any other country in Asia (Khoman, 1998: Figure 3).

Several other worrying trends had emerged in Thailand by the end of 1996.[3] After over a decade of very rapid export growth, in 1996 commodity export earnings hardly grew at all, and earnings growth from invisibles such as tourism also slowed. There were several reasons for the slowdown; one was the appreciation of the baht against other regional currencies induced by the policy of pegging the baht to the US dollar. Another was the sharp increase in real wages which had occurred since the early 1990s. This together with a severe shortage of skilled and semi-skilled workers, due in turn to government neglect of the post-primary education system, induced many manufacturers to re-locate their plants to other parts of the region where unskilled labour was cheaper (such as China, Vietnam or Bangladesh) or where skilled workers were more readily available (Hong Kong, Singapore or Malaysia). There was also concern about over-supply in the commercial and residential property market, especially in Bangkok. More broadly it was felt that the era of rapid growth was coming to an end and that the economy faced an uncertain future. A *Financial Times* survey summed up the situation at the end of 1996 as follows:

> Over the past year, it has become painfully obvious that Thailand can no longer produce the growth rates to which it has become accustomed; an average of 8 per cent a year for 10 straight years, on the back of government monopolies, asset inflation, cheap labour, tariff protection and illegal activities (*Financial Times*, 5 December 1996).

In other parts of the region, there appeared to be less cause for concern, at least on the economic front. After a long period of economic stagnation, the Philippines economy had begun to recover during the Ramos administration. This recovery was attributed to the 'significant reforms of the real side of the economy in the 1980s', which were aimed at equalizing incentives across different sectors of the economy (Noland, 2000). In addition, in 1993–95 the Ramos administration was able to implement a number of reforms which increased the efficiency of the financial sector. In both Indonesia and Malaysia the economic boom which had begun in the latter part of the 1980s showed few signs of slowing down. Although the political situation in Indonesia was attracting some negative comment by early 1997, with a number of anti-Chinese and anti-Christian riots in various parts of Java and serious disturbances in West Kalimantan, there was still considerable confidence in the strength of the Indonesian economy. Solomons (1997: 56) argued that 'sound economic fundamentals' meant that the Indonesian economy continued to grow at a solid pace in spite of the political storm-clouds. He stressed the strong economic growth in 1996 (GDP growing by almost eight per cent), a 'manageable balance of payments deficit of around four per cent of GDP', declining inflation (6.5 per cent per annum in 1996), strong investor confidence, symbolized by high levels of inward foreign investment, and an apparent determination on the part of President Suharto to limit the growth of government expenditure. All these economic signals, according to Solomons, 'have set investors alight'. Kenward (1999: 73) writing well after the effects of the crisis were obvious in Indonesia, concurred that before July 1997, 'virtually all of the broadest macro indicators were very reassuring'.

Solomons's views were widely shared in the Asian region, and as Thailand's problems became more obvious and more widely discussed in mid-1997, there appeared to be widespread agreement that 'Thailand's maladies are painful, but probably not contagious'.[4] But at the same time, several commentators stressed that there were lessons to be learnt from Thailand's plight. Underinvestment in public infrastructure and education, together with the appreciation of the baht against most other Asian currencies, were the obvious reasons for the export slowdown. The liberalization of the capital account of the balance of payments in the early 1990s, and especially the launching of the Bangkok International Banking Facility in 1993, were expected both by the government, and by the politically powerful Thai banking sector, to turn Bangkok into a dynamic regional financial centre to rival Singapore and Hong Kong (Lauridsen, 1998: 1578–9; Vajragupta and Vichyanond, 1998: 5–9; Alba et al., 1998: 48–9; Brown 2000: 168–9). These policies induced many Thai businesses and financial institutions to borrow abroad in dollars or yen at lower rates of interest. The exchange rate risk was perceived to be minimal because of the policy of keeping the baht tightly pegged to the dollar had been pursued successfully for over a decade. Although part of the foreign borrowing went into investment in export-oriented manufacturing industry, a considerable share went into sectors producing non-traded goods, especially real estate. Even investment that went into the industrial sector was often used to expand capacity in sectors such as steel and petrochemicals where both domestic and international markets were becoming glutted.

WHY WERE THE WARNINGS IGNORED?

How was it that so many experts, including the important rating agencies, were convinced that 'sound fundamentals' would prevent the flotation of the baht from having a serious effect even on the domestic Thai economy, let alone on those of its ASEAN neighbours? Surely there must have been serious problems in all these economies which simply were not being picked up in the indicators which the pundits habitually consulted? Goldstein (1998) has argued that changes in the sovereign credit ratings produced by agencies such as Moody's have performed quite badly as predictors of serious financial crises, at least compared with his regression model based on a range of monetary and real indicators. But he acknowledges that his model failed to predict the crisis in Indonesia. One reason for this, put forward by Kenward (1999: 90), was that data on key indicators such as growth in private sector capital inflows were very weak in the Indonesian context.

Goldstein's model suggests that current-account indicators were among the best crisis predictors, and there can be little doubt that in both Thailand and Malaysia the current-account deficits were large enough, relative to GDP, to be ringing alarm bells by mid-1996. One explanation why the alarms were not heeded was certainly the decline in the political influence of technocrats in the early and mid-1990s; I return to this point below. But another reason lay in the influence of what some commentators have termed the 'new view' of the balance of payments. As expounded by economists such as Corden (1994: Chapter 6), this view held that it was not the size of the current-account deficit that mattered but its causes. A current-account balance, whether positive or negative, is the net result of savings and investment decisions both public and private. If the government in a particular country habitually runs a large budget deficit and if this deficit is not matched by private savings, then a current account deficit will result. If this is financed by borrowing abroad as happened in a number of Latin American countries, then the probable outcome would be a debt crisis, especially if the loans were at variable rates, and world interest rates were to rise. But what if the government budget were in balance or even in surplus, but a balance of payments deficit were to emerge as the result of a sharp increase in domestic investment by the private sector? Such investment could be directly financed by inward investment, or it could be financed by a domestic investor who funds the investment through a foreign loan. In these cases the domestic investment is tightly tied to an inward capital flow, and the current account deficit (if there is one) can be seen as the net result of such investment decisions. If the private investment decision was based on sound judgement about the productivity of capital in that particular economy, then the current-account outcome should not be a matter of policy concern to the government. If the investment decision turned out to be unsound, then the cost would be born by the investor, whether domestic or foreign, and the bank which lent the money. There would be no cost to the government or to other private actors in the economy.

In the latter part of the 1980s and early 1990s a number of economies, both in ASEAN and elsewhere, ran substantial current-account deficits when government budgets were balanced or in surplus. This 'new' view of the current account became quite influential, in ASEAN as elsewhere (Montes 1998a, Chapter 3; Montes 1998b: 59–65). In the view of many commentators, if the balance-of-payments deficit was financed by (in fact caused by) large inward flows of direct investment, as in Indonesia or Malaysia, where was the problem? Foreign firms formed a judgement about the profitability of investment in these economies and invested accordingly. If their decision proved wrong, they and their shareholders and their bankers (in Japan shareholders and bankers are often one and the same) would bear the cost. Even where the balance-of-payments deficit was financed by portfolio inflows, doctrinaire supporters of the 'new view' argued that there was no problem (see e.g McLeod, 1997). Foreigners invested in Indonesian equities, or lent directly to Indonesian firms, because returns adjusted for the risk of exchange-rate depreciation, were estimated to be high. If governments continued to implement policies which led to high growth and high profitability of private investment, then there was little risk of sudden and massive withdrawal of capital.

Some analysts recognized that there were problems with the 'new view'. Most obviously there is the very real possibility that individual investors might find they have made errors of judgement in their projections of rates of return. If this happened for a few small investments it would hardly matter; the costs would be born by the investor and by whomever had lent to that investor. But if some large, high-profile investments were to turn sour for whatever reason, could this not lead to a loss of confidence, which in turn could trigger large-scale capital flight? Obviously withdrawal is easier, although not costless, for portfolio investors but foreign companies have not infrequently closed plants which they perceive to be unprofitable in many parts of the world. And foreign bankers can refuse to roll over short-term loans to corporate clients suddenly perceived to be high-risk borrowers.

It now seems clear that this is what happened in Thailand, Malaysia and Indonesia in varying degrees in 1997–8. It is also clear that the 'new view' of the balance of payments, to the extent that it was influential in ASEAN, probably induced a sense of false complacency in at least some policy-makers. It is certainly valid to argue that a current-account deficit may not be a legitimate cause for government policy intervention if it is the result of high levels of private investment. But it hardly follows that the ASEAN countries were correct in taking a relaxed view of sustained current-account deficits, even where they were largely covered by inward flows of direct investment. At the very least such deficits should have encouraged policy-makers to take other warning signals more seriously. In the Indonesian context, these included the high level of foreign borrowing by the Indonesian corporate sector, much of which financed investment in the non-traded goods sectors, together with the rapid growth of politically motivated lending by Indonesian banks to domestic firms. There is plenty of evidence in both Indonesia and Thailand that economists in the universities, in independent think tanks and in government were concerned about these problems by the mid-1990s. Why was their concern not translated into policy action?

THE DECLINE OF TECHNOCRATIC INFLUENCE

The emergence of the technocrat in South East Asia over the last three decades has been a much discussed feature of public policy-making throughout the region. By the late 1960s, 'every government in Southeast Asia was authoritarian to some degree, and economic planning agencies were playing significant roles in most of them' (Bresnan, 1993: 72). These agencies needed economists, statisticians and demographers and (to a much lesser extent) other social scientists who could easily interact with similarly trained people in the international and bilateral development agencies who controlled the flows of aid, so important to most regimes in the region. Foreign governments and foundations made generous funding available to train young Indonesians, Malaysians, Thais and Filipino graduates in Western universities, especially in the USA. As these graduates returned, often with doctoral degrees, they moved into senior positions not just in planning agencies, but in central banks, ministries of finance, other government departments and university research centres. Some were appointed to cabinet positions, usually as ministers of planning or finance, although in Indonesia, such technocrats also became at various times ministers of agriculture, health, education, trade, and research. The Indonesian reliance on technocrats was indeed exceptional, but successive administrations in Thailand, Malaysia and the Philippines also appointed economists with foreign (usually American) graduate training to cabinet posts. In virtually no case did these appointees have to go through any form of electoral process.

To some foreign observers, this reliance on technocrats suggested that the ASEAN countries were following the 'East Asian' model of the strong developmental state, derived from the experience of Japan, South Korea and Taiwan. This model emphasizes the high degree of autonomy enjoyed by key decision-makers, especially in the bureaucracy. As Johnson (1995: 68) has argued in the context of Japan, the government 'displays the usual qualities of an Asian kleptocracy only in its ruling party, but the party's functions in the Japanese system are to reign, not to rule. The latter is entrusted to an elite officialdom.' Can we find any evidence of such insulated bureaucracies 'ruling' in South East Asia? How autonomous were the central banks? Certainly the Bank

of Thailand has enjoyed a considerable, albeit fluctuating, degree of
independence over several decades and its technocrats were crucial
in maintaining a stable monetary and fiscal policy regime through
Thailand's years of accelerated growth (Warr and Bhanupong,
1996; Phongpaichit, 1992). In Thailand, Indonesia and Malaysia,
technocrats in the ministries of finance also had considerable
success in insulating key areas of macroeconomic policy-making
from overt political interference (Jomo et al., 1997). In Thailand
and Indonesia, for example, the administration of duty drawback
schemes, crucial to the rapid growth of a number of export-
oriented industries, were placed in the ministries of finance to
minimize corruption and malpractice.[5]

But at the same time some authors have claimed that policy-
makers in the fast growing economies of South East Asia have
always been ready to listen to influential business lobby groups,
who in their turn have been catalysts of policy reform, and active
in promoting structural adjustment measures. In the case of
Thailand, both Doner and Laothamatas (1994) and Rock (1995)
argue that the successful implementation of a series of structural
adjustment measures in the years from 1980 to 1985 was due in
large measure to the government's successful attempts to build
effective alliances between technocratic advisers (usually academic
economists with strong neo-classical sympathies), key politicians,
and business groups. While, as Phongpaichit (1996) points out, it is
difficult to fit Thailand, with its notoriously weak planning
apparatus, into the strong developmental state model, it is also
wrong to assume that the government did nothing to facilitate
industrial expansion. Interventions in both capital and labour
markets were crucial and often carried through at the instigation
of, and with the full cooperation of, powerful industrial groups.

On the basis of the development experience of Malaysia,
Thailand and Indonesia in the 1980s and early 1990s, it has been
suggested that the states of South East Asia comprise an
intermediate case between the strong developmental states of
North East Asia (Singapore would certainly be included in this
group) and the notorious 'klepto-patrimonial' regimes of Africa
such as Nigeria or Zaire (Macintyre, 1994). Their governments did
not appear to be hopelessly captured and corrupt, but on the other
hand they were frequently beholden to sectional interest groups,
and tainted by nepotism and cronyism. Nevertheless the Malaysian,

Thai and Indonesian governments clearly were capable of coherent policy formulation and implementation in the face of external shocks, and were able to maintain the momentum of growth over several decades. In this they resemble Taiwan and South Korea to a greater extent than regimes in other parts of the developing world. What then went wrong? A leading Thai economist has argued that the power of the technocrats over macroeconomic policy in Thailand was strongest when army governments were in power:

> whenever the army's power waned, the power of the technocrats would go into eclipse. Because of the need for patronage on the part of the elected politicians, technocrats began to have an adversarial relationship against them, and naturally sought the army as allies to push their case and to protect them (Siamwalla, 1997: 6–7)

Siamwalla goes on to argue that the 'quality and competency of the Thai civil service has been declining, precipitously during the last decade', and this inevitably affected the formulation and implementation of macroeconomic policies. The Bank of Thailand, usually considered among the more independent of the Asian central banks, and certainly a bastion of probity within the Thai financial system, was also the object of increased political interference; partly as a result of this and partly because salaries were so much better in the private sector, many highly qualified employees left (Lauridsen, 1998: 1580–1). Those that remained were, in the words of Phongpaichit and Baker (1998: 126), 'tempted and intimidated into collusion with the world of crony politics'. Finally in a desperate attempt to maintain the baht peg, they pledged virtually all the country's foreign reserves in forward purchases of the baht. When the baht was floated on 2 July 1997, it was clear that Thailand would be forced to seek a standby facility from the International Monetary Fund, and comply with the conditions the IMF imposed.

In Indonesia also, the power of the economic technocrats who had been so influential from the very beginning of Suharto's new order regime, appeared to be on the decline by the early 1990s. A key turning-point was the announcement of the cabinet after Suharto's re-election for a sixth term as president in 1993; to many observers the role of the Minister of Research and Technology, Dr

Habibie, seemed stronger and that of the economists much weaker
(Hill, 1999: 74–5). Dr Habibie was well-known for his scepticism
about 'orthodox' economics and his enthusiasm for spending large
sums on ambitious technology projects such as the State Airplane
Enterprise in Bandung. He also enjoyed a close relationship with
President Suharto, and during the years from 1993 to 1997 had
some highly publicized battles with the Minister of Finance, Mar'ie
Muhammad, over his spending plans. But however great his
influence with the president was, it was also becoming increasingly
clear that an ageing president with almost three decades of service
behind him was paying less and less attention to any member of his
cabinet (Nasution, 2000: 155). By far the most influential people
were his immediate family and a small group of their business
associates. Cabinet ministers challenged the wishes of the first
family and their courtiers at their peril.

Suharto made a last-ditch attempt to use his technocrats to stave
off economic disaster in the aftermath of the Thai devaluation, but
ultimately to no avail. In fact it appears that the technocrats,
especially in the Ministry of Finance, used the opportunity of the
first IMF agreement to insert conditions concerning deregulation
of the 'real' economy, especially the abolition of state and private
monopolies and other perquisites of the Suharto family. Indonesian
economists have argued that such measures were 'voluntarily
proposed' by the technocrats to increase the credibility of the
package, both to the Indonesian public and to the international
markets (Soesastro and Basri, 1998: 16).[6] Needless to say, Suharto
was having none of this, and so what the technocrats feared in fact
came true. Both domestic and international confidence collapsed,
and with it the rupiah. Companies that had borrowed abroad and
not hedged their borrowings were unable to service their loans. By
early 1998 much of corporate Indonesia was in effect bankrupt.

WAS FINANCIAL SECTOR LIBERALIZATION TO BLAME?

Many international commentators have tended to blame
imperfections in the financial system for the severity of the crisis in
both South Korea and South East Asia. The IMF argued that many
Asian financial systems suffered from 'weak management and poor
control of risks, lax enforcement of prudential rules and inadequate
supervision, and associated relationship and government-directed

lending practices that had led to a sharp deterioration in the quality of banks' loan portfolios' (IMF, 1998: 3).[7] Critics of the IMF have argued that many of these problems were the result of too rapid liberalization of the financial system, which in turn was actively encouraged not just by the IMF but also by a range of other bilateral and multilateral development agencies for at least a decade prior to the crisis.[8] The financial development of Malaysia, Indonesia and Thailand has been extensively researched in recent years, not least by economists working in the IMF and the World Bank. Until 1997 a principal finding of this research was that the deregulation and liberalization of the financial sector had been an important factor contributing to rapid economic growth (see e.g. World Bank. 1993: 203ff). But the pace and sequencing of financial sector reform differed considerably within ASEAN, and between the economies most affected by the crisis of 1997–8.

In discussing financial liberalization, it is important to distinguish between removing controls on the inward and outward flow of capital ('opening the capital account') and liberalizing the domestic financial system. Many recent studies of economic reform in developing countries have argued that opening the capital account should come after reforms intended to make the domestic financial system more efficient (see e.g. McKinnon, 1993: 7–8). Thailand and Malaysia broadly followed this sequence, but Indonesia did not. In their study of the Indonesian experience, Cole and Slade (1996: 3) point out that 'Indonesia initiated some financial reform measures in the late 1960s and early 1970s, well before such notions became fashionable, and it has followed a sequence of reforms that was the reverse of recently prescribed patterns'. From 1970 onwards, Indonesia abolished most controls on outward capital flows, although inward flows, especially of direct foreign investment, remained subject to considerable government regulation, which was reduced gradually in the late 1980s and early 1990s. By the early 1990s, Indonesia had become well-known as an economy with unusually high inward and outward flows of capital; in 1995 the volume of daily foreign exchange transactions was estimated to be between $4.6 and $5 billion dollars, almost twice the volume of transactions in Thailand and six times that in Malaysia (Kuroyanagi and Hayakawa, 1997: Table 6).[9]

But in spite of early liberalization of capital flows, the domestic Indonesian banking system remained highly regulated and dominated by a small number of state-owned trading banks until the 1980s. In 1983 ceilings on interest rates were removed and other measures taken to improve the efficiency of the banking system, but the most sweeping reforms occurred in October 1988 when the government removed many restrictions on private banks and made it easier for foreign banks to operate in the domestic economy. The result of these reforms was a dramatic expansion in the role of private banks relative to those of the state banks; by 1996 the state banks accounted for only 40 per cent of all bank loans compared with over 80 per cent in 1980 (McLeod, 1999: 274–5). Numbers of private banks proliferated and competition for new depositors became more intense. Real interest rates also rose over these years, and the ratio of broad money (coins, notes, demand and time deposits) to GDP increased (Cole and Slade, 1996: 10–27; Chant and Pangestu, 1994: 230–50).

After 1991, it became clear that the rapid growth in the private banking sector was leading to problems. One of the largest private banks, Bank Duta, lost hundreds of millions of dollars as a result of foreign currency speculations by one employee. It was rescued through a massive injection of capital from a foundation controlled by the Suharto family. Another large private bank, Bank Summa, which was connected to a large industrial group, ran into problems in 1992, and finally had its license revoked in 1994 (Chant and Pangestu, 1994: 257–62). Were these episodes just minor accidents, inevitable in a process of rapid growth and diversification of the financial sector? Or were they symptoms of a deeper malaise? Some independent commentators pointed to the dangers of a proliferation of private banks, many of them offshoots of conglomerates whose core business was far removed from finance, and whose managers were usually inexperienced in banking.

Cole and Slade (1996: Chapter 10) expressed concern over the mounting evidence of cronyism in the financial sector and the increasing politicization of major investment decisions, and predicted that, like most other developing economies, Indonesia would at some stage face a financial crisis whose handling would provide 'an important test of how sound a structure has been created'. Two years later, they wryly conceded that 'these cautionary assessments proved much too moderate' (Cole and Slade, 1998: 62). The rapid collapse of the Indonesian banking system in late 1997 and early 1998 necessitated huge liquidity supports from the central bank, and the eventual nationalization in August 1998 of several of the worst affected banks. By early 2000, it was estimated that the total cost of government bonds needed to recapitalize the banking system would be 51 per cent of GDP, and that the interest payments on these bonds would be a considerable burden on the government budget for years to come (Fane, 2000: 37–42). Cole and Slade were in no doubt that the problems in the Indonesian financial system were essentially political and argued:

> The failure to put together an effective initial response and the ultimate severity of the Indonesian financial crisis must be understood and explained as the consequence of the lengthy process of politicisation of economic and financial activity within Indonesia, and the concomitant erosion of any effective prudential supervision over financial institutions by regulatory authorities, coupled with imprudent behaviour by many foreign lenders and investors (Cole and Slade, 1998: 65).

Other writers have argued that the fundamental mistake made in Indonesia was to attempt 'to implement a radical programme of financial liberalization in the context of deeply entrenched patrimonial state structures' (Pincus and Ramli, 1998: 732). While this type of argument has some force, it is important to bear in mind that the state-dominated banking system which developed in Indonesia over the first four decades of independence was itself riddled with inefficiencies and dubious lending practices. Much of the lending was either to state enterprises or to politically well-connected individuals. The liberalization set in train in 1983, and further extended with the PAKTO reforms of 1988, was intended not just to increase domestic savings but also to increase competition for customers between banks and thus to improve the quality of lending by making it easier for private individuals to get access to loans for viable projects. Such lending did increase greatly, bringing undoubted benefits to many millions of Indonesians (McLeod, 1999: 288). It must also be borne in mind that the problem of 'connected lending' was certainly worse in the state banks than in the private sector and after the crisis the state banks accounted for a disproportionate number of non-performing loans (Pardede, 1999: 26). Had there been no financial liberalization in the late 1980s and early 1990s, the problem of non-performing loans in the state sector could well have been even worse.

It can thus be argued that it was politically invoked regulatory failure rather than 'premature' financial liberalization which precipitated the crisis in the Indonesian financial sector. In Malaysia and Thailand, although neither country followed the same rather eccentric liberalization sequence as Indonesia, there were also signs of increasing financial sector vulnerability by the mid-1990s, which the regulatory agencies were either unwilling or unable to tackle. In Malaysia, where a modern financial system had begun to develop in the late colonial era, the official approach to financial liberalization since 1980 had been 'gradual and cautious', involving a process of 'structural deregulation and prudential reregulation' (Yusof et al., 1994: 276). Reform of the capital account was modest, and the central bank (Bank Negara Malaysia) had considerable autonomy in exercising its regulatory function (Athukorola, 1998: 91). But some signs of vulnerability were evident by the mid-1990s; lending to the real-estate sector accounted for around 30 to 40 per cent of total lending, a much higher proportion than in South Korea or Indonesia and about the same as Thailand (Reisen, 1998: Table 4; Noland, 2000: Table 2). Bank Bumiputera, which had powerful political backing and whose role was to lend to indigenous Malays, had already received massive liquidity support from the cash-rich state petroleum enterprise, which in turn aggravated the problem of moral hazard in other banks with powerful political connections (Gomez and Jomo, 1997: 60–66)

In Thailand, like Malaysia, the government approach to both opening the capital account and to deregulation of the domestic financial sector was slow and cautious, at least until the latter part of the 1980s. The Thai banking system was dominated by a few large domestic banks, with state-owned banks playing a smaller role than in Indonesia. The entry of foreign banks was tightly controlled and their share of total assets was small. Beginning in 1988, the government adopted policies which were designed to make the domestic financial sector more competitve, and also removed most controls on capital inflows and outflows (Lauridsen, 1998: 1578–9; Vajragupta and Vichyanond, 1998: Chapter 3). The establishment of the Bangkok International Banking Facility was designed to turn Bangkok into an important regional financial sector. As has already been explained, these changes took place in the context of a rapid decline in the authority and competence of the key regulatory agencies in Thailand. By 1996, there was clear evidence of growing vulnerability in the financial sector, especially as a high proportion of loans were to the property sector, which had become glutted both in Bangkok and in other parts of the country.[10] After the crisis, the non-performing loan ratio increased to nearly 50 per cent, and by early 2000 the debt restructuring process was still far from completed (Pichit, 2000: 301).

The striking exception to the story of financial deregulation in the context of inadequate regulatory supervision was the Philippines. There, the supervisory role of the central bank was strengthened in 1993–95, and tougher capital adequacy requirements imposed on commercial banks (Intal et al., 1998: 154; Noland, 2000). Although the Philippine financial sector was hardly free of the problems which had emerged elsewhere in the ASEAN region, the banking system did survive the sharp depreciation of the peso which occurred in late 1997 and early 1998. The non-performing loan ratio remained under ten per cent in 1998, and while real output contracted the extent of the decline was not nearly as severe as in Indonesia, Thailand or Malaysia.

Thus I would argue that the evidence from the worst affected economies of South East Asia does not support the argument that 'premature' financial liberalization precipitated the crisis. The process of liberalization proceeded quite differently in the three worst affected economies, and in the Indonesian case in particular, the impact of the financial crisis on the banking system would likely have been even more severe without the reforms of the 1988–91 period. Certainly the liberalization of the capital account in Thailand and the establishment of the BIBF did accelerate the inflow of capital, at least some of which went into the speculative and high-risk sectors of the economy. But with stronger prudential regulation this need not have been the case. Neither is it correct to argue, as critics of the IMF such as Stiglitz (2000) have done, that financial liberalization was forced on unwilling ASEAN countries by the IMF and the USA. All the evidence indicates that the processes of financial reform in ASEAN countries in the 1980s and 1990s were home-grown and indeed brought about by powerful vested interests, especially in the financial sectors, who thought they would benefit.

WHAT WAS THE ROLE OF FOREIGN SPECULATORS?

When the consequences of a massive outflow of capital from the afflicted ASEAN economies became clear in late 1997, many commentators in the region argued that their currencies were being 'attacked' by foreign speculators. Particular anger was directed at hedge funds which were thought to be using their massive weight in international markets to push prices of stocks and currencies down, making huge profits in the process. The most vocal critic among leading politicians was Dr Mahathir, the Prime Minister of Malaysia. His views attracted considerable attention in the international press, and they certainly reflected a wider sense of disillusionment, even betrayal, which many Asian politicians, civil servants, business people, academics and journalists felt about their treatment at the hands of the international markets. Why did these markets turn so savagely against a group of economies which had been their darlings, praised by international development agencies, major financial institutions, the rating agencies and many other experts for doing practically everything right? True, there may have been policy mistakes, and some corruption in government decision-making, but surely these problems were not sufficiently serious to provoke the ferocious onslaught of late 1997 and early 1998? There must have been other malign forces at work, whose main aim was to destroy the 'Asian miracle' and discredit the politicians who had done so much to bring it about.

While such a reaction is understandable, it ignores a fact which soon became obvious to many observers in Thailand, Indonesia and Malaysia in late 1997 and early 1998. Many of those selling assets denominated in baht, rupiah or ringgit and putting their funds into dollars were not foreign speculators but domestic citizens. As Krugman (1999) has pointed out, investors who panic during any crisis 'are more likely to be respectable bankers and wealthy domestic residents than nefarious rootless cosmopolitans'. Whatever the reason for the panic, once it sets in many people are motivated above all by a desire to preserve the value of their assets if they possibly can. If the currency seems to be in free fall and the government apparently powerless to reverse the situation, then a rush into dollars or some other 'safe' currency is inevitable. Krugman came to the conclusion that such a situation justifies the imposition of capital controls, at least as a temporary expedient until the government can take other actions to restore investor confidence. Defenders of Malaysia's controversial policy of imposing capital controls in September 1998 claim that it did help to boost domestic confidence in the financial sector while at the same time maintaining social cohesion in the face of a sharp decline in real output (Abidin, 2000: 194–5).

Whatever the verdict of history will be on the Malaysian policy, one trend emerged very clearly in the first part of 1998, even before the Malaysian controls were imposed. Several eminent economists with impeccable scholarly credentials began to question the benefits for developing countries of unrestricted access to global capital markets. Indeed the idea that some 'sand in the wheels' of international financial markets was needed to curb huge speculative movements in capital had been around at least since the late 1970s, when Professor Tobin had suggested a tax on international financial transactions (see Eichengreen, Tobin and Wyplosz, 1995, for a overview of the issues). The currency crises which erupted in Latin America and the Western Europe in the early 1990s all provoked further discussion of the costs and benefits of free and unregulated global capital markets. By early 1998, the then chief economist at the World Bank, Joseph Stiglitz, was arguing that there may be a case for government interventions to control capital flows; he suggested that the Chilean imposition of a reserve requirement on all short-term capital inflows could be emulated in other parts of the world (Stiglitz, 1998). On the day the *Financial Times* carried Professor Stiglitz's article, the paper editorialized: 'The case for early and complete freedom for international capital flows has, unquestionably, been damaged. The world's leaders must now ask themselves how to maximise the benefits of capital flows to developing countries, while minimising both the number of panics and the damage they do' (Financial Times, 1998).

Other eminent international economists including Jagdish Bhagwati, a long-time advocate of the benefits of free trade for developing countries, joined in the chorus (Bhagwati, 1998). Almost inevitably, these writers became involved in a wider debate, which gathered force in late 1997 and early 1998 as the crisis worsened and its real effects became more obvious. This debate concerned the role of the Bretton Woods institutions, and especially of the International Monetary Fund.

THE BEHAVIOUR OF THE IMF

One of the more extraordinary consequences of the Asian crisis has been the barrage of criticism directed against the International Monetary Fund (IMF). Criticism of the IMF and its role as a lender of last resort for the global economy is not new but never has the organization had to endure so many sustained attacks from such a range of critics. Indeed by late 1997 it was almost universally argued that the IMF's actions in Thailand, Malaysia and Indonesia were aggravating what was already a bad situation; some observers were going much further and claiming that it was actions of the IMF that precipitated the crisis.

Foremost among the American critics of the IMF has been Jeffrey Sachs of Harvard University; his views have been given wide coverage in the international media and through the Internet. In the Indonesian context, his arguments are as follows. There was no economic reason for the collapse of confidence in the rupiah in late 1997; unlike Thailand export growth had stayed strong in 1996, the current-account deficit was much smaller relative to GDP, the budget was in overall surplus, credit growth was not excessive, foreign liabilities of the commercial banks were substantially below those in Thailand and in South Korea and there had been no spectacular corporate bankruptcies, again in contrast to South Korea and Thailand. The Indonesian government in fact responded to the crisis more sensibly than other countries in the region, although some mixed signals were sent about government willingness to curb investment projects in which the Suharto family were heavily involved. In fact in October 1997, Indonesia did not seem an obvious candidate for an IMF programme. The first of the IMF programmes signed at the end of October did stabilize the rupiah, but in early November the rupiah again slid alarmingly, and it was at this point that Indonesia began to look worse than its neighbours (Radelet and Sachs, 1998).

The reason for the collapse, according to this view, was panic, induced in part by government actions such as the closure of 16 banks in early November (see also Soesastro and Basri, 1998: 17). This inevitably triggered a run on the entire domestic banking system by depositors who feared that they would lose their savings. Radelet and Sachs (1998) admitted that political factors were also responsible for much of the panic and indeed 'the economic and political issues have fed off each other, adding a whole new dimension to the dynamics of the panic'. They also conceded that the very severe drought aggravated the problem by causing serious food shortages in some areas. But they appear to imply that the IMF was responsible for at least aggravating the panic if not for initiating it in the first place, and thus for provoking an unnecessary real contraction in the Indonesian economy.[11]

An alternative view, which I find more persuasive, sees the IMF as essentially responding to events rather than provoking the crisis. According to this argument, the financial sector's problems reflected deeper problems of nepotism and corruption, which by the mid-1990s permeated the entire government system. It was these problems, rather than the lack of deposit insurance, that triggered the bank runs in late 1997, which in turn necessitated huge injections of liquidity support from Bank Indonesia. In fact depositors had no reason to fear that they would lose their money after the bank closures in late 1997; the government had already announced in September 1997 that in the event of any bank closures small depositors would be immediately reimbursed. And there were precedents in recent memory; when Bank Summa was closed in 1992, small depositors were immediately repaid in full and large depositors got their money back as the bank's assets were sold (Djiwandono, 2000: 61). The real reason for the bank runs was the much broader collapse of confidence in the entire economic and political system.[12] As the crisis deepened it became clear that the administration, and the elderly autocrat who led it, were more concerned with protecting family and cronies than with the health of the economy. Years of 'crony capitalism' had taken a severe toll not just in terms of public confidence but also in terms of the regime's ability to respond to a serious economic crisis. The behaviour of the IMF in the latter part of 1997 may not have been well judged or especially skilful, but to blame it or any other external power for what happened is to miss the central point. The Suharto regime finally collapsed because of its severe internal problems, and because of policy mistakes and wilful negligence, whose cumulative impact finally destroyed the credibility of the regime both at home and abroad.

Many other IMF critics have emerged over the past two years, in the context of Thailand as well as in Indonesia. Some have argued that their policy prescriptions in Thailand and, to begin with at least, Indonesia, appeared to have been drawn from the experience of previous crises in Latin America, even though the causes of the currency falls in South East Asia were very different. Thus the IMF imposed conditions relating to budget surpluses on both Thailand and Indonesia, even though everyone agreed that irresponsible government spending was not the cause of the problem in either country.[13] Other criticisms relate to the secrecy under which the IMF operates (even though it urges greater transparency on its client governments) and its bias in favour of Western governments and financial institutions (Jomo, 1998: 18–21, and Stiglitz, 2000). Some of these criticisms may well be true, although the IMF has relaxed some of its conditions in Thailand in response to Thai government requests, while in Indonesia it had little choice but to accept a budget deficit projected to reach 6.5 per cent of GDP in 1998–99.[14]

But even if some of the criticism of the IMF, especially in the Indonesian context, is not very persuasive, there can be little doubt that the crisis there and in other parts of the region has dealt a severe blow to the prestige and the credibility of the Bretton Woods institutions. If neither the IMF nor the World Bank could predict the crisis in countries which had been among their largest borrowers for decades, or come up with sensible policy measures once the crisis hit, then what is the point of having them? Have they both become expensive anachronisms, intellectually as well as geographically remote from their most important clients? Indonesia has been one of the World Bank's largest borrowers for over three decades, and the World Bank has maintained a large resident mission in Jakarta since the late 1960s. It is difficult to believe that neither it nor the IMF were aware of the political problems which were all too obvious to many observers by 1996. Why did they not have contingency plans in place for the kind of crisis which erupted in late 1997 and early 1998?

WHAT ABOUT KKN?

Before trying to answer that question, we must return to the vexed issue of the role of corruption, collusion and nepotism (KKN is the widely used Indonesia acronym) in precipitating the crisis, not just in Indonesia but in other parts of ASEAN. One rather unexpected feature of the large 'crisis literature' that has emerged over the past three years is that a number of authors, whose views on the causes of the crisis otherwise differ quite markedly, appear to agree that corruption was not an important factor. Those writers who view the behaviour of the IMF, or of foreign speculators, as the main reason for the severity of the crisis obviously tend to play down the role of domestic weaknesses, including corruption. Others try to make a distinction, however implausibly, between regulatory failure and the more obvious manifestations of KKN. For example Johnson (1998: 654) argued that 'throughout the region, the current crisis was caused much more by under-regulation than by corruption or any other side effects of an overly close relationship between business and the government'. In the Indonesian context writers such as McLeod (1998: 46) and Hill (1999: 68–9) take the view that widespread corruption in Indonesia has been compatible with strong growth for several decades, and it is therefore implausible to argue that it was corruption which precipitated the crisis in 1997–8. Hill points out that other countries which ranked almost as high as Indonesia in the international corruption league tables (including China and India) largely avoided the crisis, and anyway it is at least arguable that Indonesia was less corrupt in the latter part of the 1990s than in 1980. In similar vein, Chang (2000: 780) argues that the widely used corruption index compiled by Transparency International suggested that corruption was perceived to be on the decline in all the Asian countries most affected by the crisis. Chang continues:

> [C]ronyism did play a role in the generation of the crisis in the Asian countries, but it is unlikely to have been more than a minor factor. Cronyism has been a permanent feature of these countries at least in certain sectors during the last few decades, and there is little evidence that the changes in its form and extent that did occur in some of these countries (notably Korea and Thailand) were so significant as to create a crisis.

My own view is rather different. I would argue that it is almost impossible to estimate the absolute extent of corruption in a given country, let alone make sensible comparisons either across countries or over time. What most of the widely used indicators try to do is measure *perceptions* of corruption, usually on the part of national or international businesspeople. Such exercises can be useful as a guide for international investors, but they do not tell us much about what citizens *within* developing countries think about standards of public morality and governance.[15] In recent years there have been some attempts to monitor changes in opinion on such issues in the more 'democratic' countries in ASEAN such as Thailand and the Philippines, although several governments are still hostile to such exercises. The extreme antagonism felt by Suharto and his key national security advisers to any form of independent public opinion monitoring was well known; the governments of both Singapore and Malaysia have also been quite hostile to any independent opinion polling by local media.

If we know little about changing perceptions of political corruption in most part of South East Asia, we can perhaps infer something about changing public tolerance for corrupt behaviour on the part of senior political figures. As populations in countries such as Thailand, Indonesia and Malaysia have become better educated and more mobile, migrating to urban areas and abroad to find work, they have inevitably become more aware of the behaviour of senior political figures and more critical of such behaviour. This in turn has meant that behaviour which might have been accepted as normal, or even admirable, by a poor, illiterate and largely rural population in the 1960s, has been subjected to increasingly hostile scrutiny by a younger generation ambitious not just to better themselves materially but also to live in a society where public services are delivered in a reasonably efficient and equitable fashion.

It seems plausible to argue that confidence in the ability of governments to handle the economic crisis collapsed very rapidly in Thailand, Malaysia and (especially) Indonesia among the great majority of the urban middle classes, who controlled most of the wealth, precisely because they had become convinced that their governments were controlled by corrupt and self-serving people whose only motivation was to increase their own personal wealth and that of their families and cronies. It is thus academic to debate whether the actual level of corruption (however measured) was better or worse in 1997 than in 1980 or 1990. By 1997, many millions of Thais, Indonesians and Malaysians had reached the point where they no longer had any confidence in the ability of their leaders to handle a severe financial crisis, and to put the national interest ahead of their own. Many citizens decided that they too would act to preserve their own wealth regardless of the effect on others. The result was massive capital flight, collapsing currencies, bank failures and corporate bankruptcies.

Why did many international observers, including of course the World Bank and the International Monetary Fund, fail to appreciate the changing public tolerance for corruption, cronyism and nepotism in countries such as Thailand and Indonesia in the early and mid-1990s? In their defence it can be pointed out that both the IMF and the World Bank did draw attention in their country economic memoranda to the declining influence of technocrats in government decision-making, to abuses in at least some parts of the government bureaucracy and to the possible consequences of inadequate regulation of the financial sector. But in retrospect it is clear that most commentators failed to link these developments to the broader changes in public opinion which were occurring among the urban middle classes in many parts of the ASEAN region. It was indeed difficult for even the most perceptive observers to appreciate these changes in the absence of any independent monitoring of public opinion. In addition, many foreign economists, including those working in the resident missions of the international agencies, had most contact with senior civil servants who were themselves beneficiaries of KKN, and who had little interest in changing the system.[16]

Since 1997, there have been many official statements by senior figures in the Bretton Woods institutions about the importance of 'good governance' at the corporate and government level, and a spate of publications has appeared on these issues.[17] No doubt this emphasis will continue, although whether it will prevent more financial crises in the future remains to be seen. Economic historians argue that financial crises are almost inevitable in the early stages of capitalist development, and indeed continue to afflict even the most developed economies, although their real costs diminish with greater economic maturity.[18] Destabilizing speculative movements of capital across international boundaries will continue as long as countries operate independent currencies and exchange-rate policies. Some economists are convinced that only currency boards or 'dollarization' will prevent more financial crises in South East Asia and elsewhere.[19] Individual ASEAN economies will have to think carefully about the costs and benefits of such policies as they plan their recovery strategies. But they should not overlook what seems to me to be a crucial lesson of the 1997–98 crisis. Public confidence in economic management is crucial, and where political, bureaucratic and corporate leaders have squandered that confidence through selfish and irresponsible behaviour, they can hardly expect their fellow citizens to put the national interest ahead of their own interests when the economy runs into choppy waters. In Singapore and Taiwan, where public confidence in the probity of the political leadership remained high, there was little panic and the real impact of the crisis was correspondingly less. At the other extreme, in Indonesia, public confidence in the Suharto regime by 1997 was already fragile, and this fragility interacted with the economic problems (including imprudently high levels of corporate foreign borrowing and inadequate regulation of the financial sector) to produce a crisis from which the economy and the polity have yet to fully recover.

ACKNOWLEDGEMENTS

This is a revised version of a paper given to the ASEASUK Seminar on the South East Asian Crisis, University of North London, June 1999. I have benefited from the comments of seminar participants, and of two referees.

NOTES

1. See World Bank (2000), Table 1.1 for details of real changes in GDP between 1996 and 1999 in the main East Asian economies.
2. The article drew especially on the work of Morris Goldstein at the Institute for International Economics in Washington. Goldstein (1998) discusses further which early warning indicators are most likely to predict financial crises.
3. See Ghosh, Sen and Chandrasekhar (1996), Warr (1997), Warr (1998), Lauridsen (1998) and Brown (2000) for further analyses of Thailand's economic problems. The first two papers were published before the crisis broke.
4. 'Let This be a Lesson', *Far Eastern Economic Review* (1997: 71).
5. Cole and Slade (1996), Chapter 10, examine the role of technocrats in policy-making in Suharto's Indonesia. Yoshihara (1994), Chapter 18, contrasts the performance of the bureaucracy in Thailand and the Philippines after 1960, and concludes that in Thailand government interventions were far more pro-market and supportive of rapid capital formation in the private sector than in the Philippines, especially in the martial law era.
6. For a very similar argument in the context of South Korea, see Wade (1998: 12).
7. See Booth (2000a) for similar views from other Washington-based commentators.
8. See e.g. Chang (1998: 84), who argues that it was no coincidence that India, China and Taiwan, which did not implement sweeping financial sector liberalization, survived the crisis in good shape compared with Thailand, Malaysia and Indonesia.
9. Nasution (2000: 153–4) points out that Indonesia survived early liberalization of the capital account mainly because until the early 1990s there were 'few reputable companies that had access to international financial markets'.
10. It has also become clear that there was insufficient disclosure of financial information before loans were given to many clients. Dollar and Hallward-Driemeier (2000: 14)

report the findings of a Thai survey which indicated that only 40 per cent of clients were required to provide audited account statements before receiving bank credit. Only 60 per cent of respondents, many of them foreign firms, said that their loans were backed by collateral. There is every reason to believe that the situation was even worse in Indonesia.

11. Corbett and Vines (1999: 88–9) also blamed the 'IMF and the Washington policy community' for the way they 'comprehensively trashed' the draft budget for 1998–9 which was presented to the Indonesian parliament by an obviously ailing President Suharto in early January 1998. In fact the draft budget was considered by most observers within Indonesia and in the Asian region to be quite unrealistic in its assumptions about real growth, inflation and the exchange rate. Although the IMF certainly made no secret of its unhappiness with the document, it seems a grotesque exaggeration to claim that it was the IMF's expression of unhappiness which triggered the collapse of the rupiah in late Janury 1998, rather than the continuing doubts within Indonesia about Suharto's desire to implement any reform which damaged the interests of his family. Soesastro and Basri (1998: 26–8) give a much more balanced assessment of the role of the IMF over this period.

12. Many Indonesians who did not convert their savings into dollars removed them from national banks and put them into rupiah accounts in branches of foreign banks; this 'flight to safety' further damaged the already fragile national banks (Djiwandono 2000: 61–2). Similar reactions occurred in Kuala Lumpur and Bangkok.

13. This point has been reiterated by virtually everyone writing on the Asian crisis, but Corsetti (1998: 29) makes an important qualification, drawing on the work of Diaz-Alejandro (1985) in the context of Chile. In Chile, although budget deficits were small or zero in the early 1980s, massive use was made of 'off-budget' liquidity support, channelled through the central bank, to bail out failing banks. This was also true in the context of Indonesia where similar use was made of off-budget 'liquidity credits' to assist state enterprises including state banks throughout the 'new order' period. It was the huge increase in liquidity credits to the banking system in late 1997 and early 1998 which triggered the inflationary surge in Indonesia in mid-1998.

14. In fact, for reasons set out in Booth (1999), the Indonesian government found it impossible to run as large a government deficit as both the World Bank and the IMF had approved in fiscal year 1998–9.

15. It has to be admitted that a number of people have tried to compile quantitative indicators of 'good governance' which are not just based on subjective evaluations of corruption; see for example Kaufmann, Kraay and Zoido-Lobaton (2000: 10–13). These efforts also seem to me to be largely useless as a measure of public opinion about corruption or governance in any given country.

16. This was much more the case in Indonesia than in Thailand, where independent university researchers and think-tanks such as the Thai Development Research Institute have done an excellent job in educating foreigners about trends in the economy, and about their social and political ramifications.

17. See e.g. World Bank (2000), Chapter 5. The June 2000 issue of the IMF publication *Finance and Development* contained several papers on corruption and governance issues.

18. See Kindleberger (1988, 1989) and the essays in Kindleberger and Lafargue (1982) for more detailed discussion of these points. Booth (2000) looks at the Indonesian crisis in the light of the historical lessons from Europe and Latin America.

19. A prominent exponent of the view that central banking and a national currency has been a disaster in Indonesia is Steven Hanke; see *Wall Street Journal*, 29 June 2000. Schuler (1999) gives a rather more balanced view of the costs and benefits of dollarization in the Indonesian context.

REFERENCES

Abidin, Mahani Zainal (2000), 'Malaysia's Alternative Approach to Crisis Management', in *Southeast Asian Affairs 2000*. Singapore: Institute of Southeast Asian Studies.

46 ASEAN BUSINESS IN CRISIS

Alba, Pedro, *et al.* (1999), 'The Role of Macroeconomic and Financial Sector Linkages in East Asia's Financial Crisis', in Pierre-Richard Agenor, Marcus Miller, David Vines and Axel Weber (eds), *The Asian Financial Crisis: Causes, Contagion and Consequences.* Cambridge: Cambridge University Press.

Athukorala, Prema-chandra (1998), 'Malaysia', in Ross H. McLeod and Ross Garnaut (eds), *East Asia in Crisis: From being a miracle to needing one?* London: Routledge.

Bhagwati, Jagdish (1998), 'The Capital Myth', *Foreign Affairs*, Vol.77, No.3 (May/June), pp.7–12.

Booth, Anne (1999), 'Survey of Recent Developments', *Bulletin of Indonesian Economic Studies*, Vol.35, No.3 (December), pp.3–38.

Booth, Anne (2000a), 'Southeast Asia: Towards a Sustained Recovery', *Southeast Asian Affairs 2000.* Singapore: Institute of Southeast Asian Studies.

Booth, Anne (2000b), 'The Indonesian Crisis of 1997/99 and the Way Out: What are the Lessons of History?', *Economic Papers* (Economic Society of Australia), Vol.19, No.2, pp.21–43.

Bresnan, John (1993), *Managing Indonesia: The Modern Political Economy.* New York: Columbia University Press.

Brown, Rajeswary A. (2000), 'Sino-Thai Corporate Profligacy and the Financial Turmoil of 1997', *South East Asia Research*, Vol.8, No.2, pp.147–84.

Chang, Ha-Joon (1998), 'The Role of Institutions in Asian Development', *Asian Development Review*, Vol.16, No.2, pp.64–95.

Chang, Ha-Joon (2000), 'The Hazard of Moral Hazard: Untangling the Asian Crisis', *World Development*, Vol.28, No.4, pp.775–88.

Chant, John, and Pangestu, Mari (1994), 'An Assessment of Financial Reform in Indonesia, 1983–90', in G. Caprio, I. Atiyas and James A. Hansen (eds), *Financial Reform: Theory and Experience.* Cambridge: Cambridge University Press, pp.257–62.

Cole, David C., and Slade, Betty F. (1996), *Building a Modern Financial System: The Indonesian Experience.* Cambridge: Cambridge University Press.

Cole, David C., and Slade, Betty F. (1998), 'Why has Indonesia's Financial Crisis Been So Bad?', *Bulletin of Indonesian Economic Studies*, Vol.34, No.2 (August), pp.61–6.

Corbett, Jenny and Vines, David (1999), 'The Asian Crisis: Lessons From the Collapse of Financial Systems, Exchange Rates and Macroeconomic Policy', in Pierre-Richard Agenor, Marcus Miller, David Vines and Axel Weber (eds), *The Asian Financial Crisis: Causes, Contagion and Consequences.* Cambridge: Cambridge University Press.

Corden, W. Max (1994), *Economic Policy, Exchange Rates and the International System.* Oxford: Oxford University Press.

Corsetti, Giancarlo (1998), 'Interpreting the Asian Financial Crisis: Open Issues in Theory and Policy', *Asian Development Review*, Vol.16, No.2, pp.18–63.

Diaz-Alejandro, Carlos (1985), 'Good-bye Financial Repression, Hello Financial Crash', *Journal of Development Economics*, Vol.19, Nos.1/2, pp.1–24.

Djiwandono, J. Soedradjad (2000), 'Bank Indonesia and the Recent Crisis', *Bulletin of Indonesian Economic Studies*, Vol.36, No.1, pp.47–72.

Dollar, David, and Hallward-Driemeier, Mary (2000), 'Crisis, Adjustment and Reform in Thailand's Industrial Firms', *World Bank Research Observer*, Vol.15, No.1, pp.1–22.

Doner, Richard, and Laothamatas, Anek, 'Thailand: Economic and Political Gradualism' in Stephan Haggard and Steven B. Webb (eds), *Voting for Reform.* New York: Oxford University Press, 1994.

The Economist (1996), 24 Aug., pp.67–8.

The Economist (1998), East Asian Economies Survey, 7 March, p.5.

Eichengreen, Barry, Tobin, James, and Wyplosz, Charles(1995), 'Two Cases for Sand in the Wheels of International Finance', *Economic Journal*, Vol.105, pp.162–72.

Fane, George (2000), 'Survey of Recent Developments', *Bulletin of Indonesian Economic Studies*, Vol.36, No.1, pp.13–46.

Far Eastern Economic Review (1997), 'Let This be a Lesson', *Far Eastern Economic Review*, 12 June, p.71.

Financial Times (1996), Thailand survey, *Financial Times*, 5 Dec. 1996.

Financial Times (1998), (editorial), *Financial Times*, 25 March 1998.

Ghosh, Jayati, Sen, Abhijit, and Chandrasekhar, C.P. (1996), 'South-East Asian Economies: Miracle or Meltdown?', *Economic and Political Weekly*, 12–19 Oct., pp.2766–80.

Goldstein, Morris (1998), 'Early Warning Indicators of Financial Crises' in W. Hunter, G. Kaufman and T.H. Krueger (eds), *The Asian Financial Crisis: Origins, Implications and Solutions*. Boston, MA: Kluwer Academic Publishers.

Gomez, Terence, and Jomo, K.S. (1997), *Malaysia's Political Economy: Politics, Patronage and Profits*. Cambridge: Cambridge University Press.

Hill, Hal (1999), *The Indonesian Economy in Crisis*. Singapore: Institute of Southeast Asian Studies.

IMF (1998), *World Economic Outlook*. Washington, DC: International Monetary Fund, May.

Intal, Ponciano, *et al.*, (1998), 'The Philippines', in Ross H. McLeod and Ross Garnaut (eds), *East Asia in Crisis: From Being a Miracle to Needing One?* London: Routledge.

Johnson, Chalmers (1995), *Japan: Who Governs? The Rise of the Developmental State*. New York: W.W. Norton.

Johnson, Chalmers (1998), 'Economic Crisis in East Asia; the Clash of Capitalisms', *Cambridge Journal of Economics*, Vol.22, No.6, pp.653–61.

Jomo, K.S., *et al.* (1997), *Southeast Asia's Misunderstood Miracle: Industrial Policy and Economic Development in Thailand, Malaysia and Indonesia*. Boulder, CO: Westview Press.

Jomo, K.S. (1998), 'Introduction' in K.S. Jomo (ed.), *Tigers in Trouble: Financial Governance, Liberalisation and Crises in East Asia*. London: Zed Books, 1998.

Kaufmann, Daniel, Kraay, Aart, and Zoido-Lobaton, Pablo (2000), 'Governance Matters: From Measurement to Action', *Finance and Development*, Vol.37, No.2, pp.10–13.

Kenward, Lloyd R. (1999), 'Assessing Vulnerability to Financial Crisis: Evidence from Indonesia', *Bulletin of Indonesian Economic Studies*, Vol.35, No.3, pp.71–96.

Kindleberger, Charles (1998), *The International Economic Order: Essays on Financial Crisis and International Public Goods*. New York: Harvester Wheatsheaf.

Kindleberger, Charles (1989), *Manias, Panics and Crashes* (second edition). London: Macmillan.

Kindleberger, Charles, and Laffargue, Jean-Pierre (eds) (1982), *Financial Crises: Theory, History and Policy*. Cambridge: Cambridge University Press.

Khoman, Sirilaksana (1998), 'The Asian Financial Crisis and Prospects for Trade and Business with Thailand', *Thammasat Review*, Vol.3, No.1, pp.64–86.

Krugman, Paul (1999), 'Capital Control Freaks: How Malaysia Got Away With Economic Heresy', *Slate: The Dismal Science* (online at www.slate.com/Dismal/99-09-27/Dismal.asp).

Kuroyanagi, M., and Hayakawa, Y. (1997), 'Macroeconomic Policy Management and Capital Movements in Four ASEAN Countries: Indonesia, Malaysia, the Philippines and Thailand', *EXIM Review*, Vol.17, No.1, pp.65–120.

Lauridsen, Laurids S. (1998), 'The Financial Crisis in Thailand: Causes, Conduct and Consequences?', *World Development*, Vol.26, No.8, pp.1575–91.

Macintyre, Andrew (1994), 'Business, Government and Development: Northeast Asian and Southeast Asian Comparisons', in Andrew Macintyre (ed.), *Business and Government in Industrializing Asia*. Ithaca, NY: Cornell University Press.

McKinnon, Ronald M. (1993), *The Order of Economic Liberalization: Financial Control in the Transition to a Market Economy*. Baltimore, MD: Johns Hopkins University Press.

McLeod, Ross (1997), 'Policy Conflicts in Indonesia: The Impact of the Current Account Deficit Target on Growth, Equity and Stability', *ASEAN Economic Bulletin*, Vol.14, No.1 (July), pp.32–45.

McLeod, Ross (1998), 'Indonesia' in Ross H. McLeod and Ross Garnaut (eds), *East Asia in Crisis: From Being a Miracle to Needing One?* London: Routledge.

McLeod, Ross (1999), 'Control and Competition: Banking Deregulation and Re-regulation in Indonesia', *Journal of the Asia Pacific Economy*, Vol.4, No.2, pp.258–96.

Montes, Manuel (1998a), *The Currency Crisis in Southeast Asia*. Singapore: Institute of South East Asian Studies.

Montes, Manuel (1998b), 'Banking on Contagion: The Southeast Asian Currency Crisis', in

C.H. Kwan, Donna Vandenbrink and Chia Siow Yue (eds), *Coping with Capital Flows in East Asia*. Singapore: Institute of South East Asian Studies.

Nasution, Anwar (2000), 'The Meltdown of the Indonesian Economy: Causes, Responses and Lessons', *ASEAN Economic Bulletin*, Vol.17, No.2, pp.148–62.

Noland, Marcus (2000), 'How the Sick Man of Asia avoided Pneumonia: The Philippines in the Asian Financial Crisis', Working Paper 00-5, Washington, DC: Institute for International Economics.

Pardede, Raden (1999), 'Survey of Recent Developments', *Bulletin of Indonesian Economic Studies*, Vol.35, No.2, August, pp.3–39.

Phongpaichit, Pasuk (1992), 'Technocrats, Businessmen and Generals: Democracy and Economic Policymaking in Thailand', in Andrew J. MacIntyre and K. Jayasuriya (eds), *The Dynamics of Economic Policy Reform in South-east Asia and the South-west Pacific*. Singapore: Oxford University Press.

Phongpaichit, Pasuk (1996),'The Thai Economy in the mid-1990s', *Southeast Asian Affairs 1996*. Singapore: Institute of Southeast Asian Studies.

Phongpaichit, Pasuk, and Baker, Chris (1998), *Thailand's Boom and Bust*. Chiang Mai: Silkworm Books.

Pichit Likitkijsomboon, 'The Thai Economy: Stabilisation and Reforms', in *Southeast Asian Affairs 2000*. Singapore: Institute of Southeast Asian Studies.

Pincus, Jonathan, and Ramli, Rizal (1998), 'Indonesia; From Showcase to Basket Case', *Cambridge Journal of Economics*, Vol.22, No.6, pp.723–34.

Radelet, Steven, and Sachs, Jeffrey (1998), 'The Onset of the East Asian Financial Crisis', *Harvard Institute for International Development*, 30 March (processed).

Reisen, Helmut (1998),'Domestic Causes of Currency Crises: Policy Lessons for Crisis Avoidance', *Technical Papers No.136*. Paris: OECD Development Centre, June.

Rock, Michael (1995), 'Thai Industrial Policy: How Irrelevant was it to Export Success?', *Journal of International Development*, Vol.7, No.5, pp.759–73.

Schuler, Kurt (1999), 'Dollarising Indonesia', *Bulletin of Indonesian Economic Studies*, Vol.35, No.3, December, pp.97–114.

Siamwalla, Ammar (1997), 'Can a Developing Democracy Manage its Macroeconomy? The Case of Thailand', *TDRI Quarterly Review*, Vol.12, No.4 (December), pp.3–10.

Soesastro, Hadi and Basri, M. Chatib (1998), 'Survey of Recent Developments', *Bulletin of Indonesian Economic Studies*, Vol.34, No.1 (April), pp.3–54.

Solomons, Jay (1997), 'What Political Risk?', *Far Eastern Economic Review*, 20 Feb., p.56.

Stiglitz, James (1998), 'Boats, planes and capital flows', *Financial Times*, 25 March.

Stiglitz, James (2000), 'What I learned at the world economic crisis', *New Republic*, 17 April.

Vajragupta, Yos and Vichyanond, Pakorn (1998), *Thailand's Financial Evolution and the 1997 Crisis*. Bangkok: Thai Development Research Institute.

Vatikiotis, Michael (1997),'High Hopes', *Far Eastern Economic Review*, 20 Nov., p.24.

Wade, Robert (1998), *The Asian Crisis: Debt Deflation, Vulnerabilities, Moral Hazard, or Panic*. New York: Russell Sage Foundation, May.

Warr, Peter (1997), 'The Thai Economy: From Boom to Gloom?', *Southeast Asian Affairs 1997*. Singapore: Institute of Southeast Asian Studies.

Warr, Peter (1998), 'Thailand', in Ross H. McLeod and Ross Garnaut (eds), *East Asia in Crisis: From Being a Miracle to Needing One?* London: Routledge.

Warr, Peter G., and Nidhiprabha, Bhanupong (1996), *Thailand's Macroeconomic Miracle: Stable Adjustment and Sustained Growth*. Washington, DC: World Bank.

World Bank (1993), *The East Asian Miracle: Economic Growth and Public Policy*. Washington, DC: World Bank.

World Bank (1996), *Managing Capital Flows in East Asia*. Washington, DC: World Bank.

World Bank (2000), *East Asia: Recovery and Beyond*. Washington, DC: World Bank.

Yoshihara, Kunio (1994), *The Nation and Economic Growth: The Philippines and Thailand*. Kuala Lumpur: Oxford University Press.

Yusof, Zainal Aznam *et al.*, 'Financial Reform in Malaysia', in G. Caprio, I. Atiyas and James A. Hansen (eds), *Financial Reform: Theory and Experience*. Cambridge: Cambridge University Press.

3

The Economic Crisis and Law Reform in South East Asia

ANDREW HARDING

In mid-1997 an unprecedented economic crisis hit South East Asia and continued for about two years. Its effects are still, in late 2001, being felt, and in that sense the crisis is not yet over; recovery has been slow and uncertain (Mya Than, 2001; Lasserre and Schutte, 1999). The crisis has been described as an economic one, and undoubtedly the economic problems and indicators bear this out; nonetheless the crisis was no mere economic downturn, such as has occurred before in the region, and both its roots and its consequences are clearly seen to be political and institutional in nature (Booth, 1999). The present landscape of South East Asian legality and its defects has been emphasized in both the analyses and prescribed solutions of the crisis. The problem of finding the correct response of the legal systems of the region is still acute: so far the principal remedial measures have been short-term, and institutional and legal reforms have been very slow in coming (Tan, 1999). This is largely because law reform requires the answering of many complex, prior, and political, not just legal, questions (Tey Tsun Hang, 1999).[1] The effect of the crisis has been different in the various countries affected, and there is probably no single batch of remedies that is valid for the entire region. Nonetheless the lessons to be learned are broadly similar and in my view the legal systems will have to respond strongly and much more speedily if the position is to improve; the economic and political crisis is also at root a legal one. Here the imperatives of commerce and investment roughly correspond to those of democracy and the rule of law, thus bringing together the law-and-economic-development debate and the law-and-governance debate.

Singapore is the one country in the region to emerge relatively (though not of course entirely) unscathed from the crisis. The Prime Minister of Singapore, Goh Chok Tong, has listed the reasons for this:

- a huge current account surplus;

- a strong and well-regulated financial sector;

- clean government; and

- a reliable legal system

- banking prudence, and non-incurring of large foreign loans (*Straits Times*, May 1998).

The rule of law can be seen as relevant to most of these factors.

The Senior Minister in Goh's government, Lee Kuan Yew, put forward the following regional prescriptions, commenting that *institutions* in the region have not developed to keep pace with the changes coming with rapid economic growth and globalization:

- strengthening of institutions of government;

- improvement of corporate governance, leading to soundly managed banks and companies;

- a professional civil service;

- an effective central bank;

- criminalization of corruption for receivers and givers of bribes;

- improvement of the flow and disclosure of economic information, leading to greater transparency and an end to rumour-created reactions by markets;

- a general opening of protected economic sectors; and

- political continuity (*Straits Times*, February 1998).

These contributions amount virtually to a description of Singapore's model for economic development. The list of desiderata also clearly implies a crucial link between law and economic development, which is now (though not at all times in the past) generally accepted. It is also an implicit criticism of the other South East Asian countries. Singapore's own adjustments have been fairly limited, and are a measure of its comparative immunity from the prevailing contagion: a measured *deregulation* of the financial sector and tax incentives to *encourage* fund management, bond markets and unit trusts and the building up of reserves, at a time when other countries are having greatly to *increase* regulation (*Straits Times*, February 1998). By way of contrast with the rest of the region, Singapore's economy actually *grew* by 1.3% in 1998. In November 1998 the Singapore government instituted a package of measures designed to increase competitiveness: US$10.5bn worth of measures to cut business costs, measures to reduce prices, together with job-shedding and wage cuts. As Prime Minister Goh Chok Tong put it in his New Year address in January 1999, 'Our banks have been prudent. Our private sector has not incurred large foreign debts' (*Straits Times*, January 1999).[2]

Lee's prescriptions carry implications for legal reform, in that each of them requires careful underpinning by law if it is to be successful. It is therefore to be expected that the adoption of purely interim economic measures (such as the withdrawal of banking licences in Thailand and Indonesia) will lead to more fundamental legal reforms over the next few years: it needs to be demonstrated not only that the right decisions are being made by the right people, but that the institutions, control mechanisms, and legal remedies are in place to ensure that the right decisions continue to be made by the right people. In other words extemporizing solutions to the crisis may in some respects be successful, but in the long term only fundamental institutional changes will prevent economic instability.

Having good laws provides a basis for renewed growth; it will not guarantee success, but without reform it is hard to see how anything like the growth rates of 1987–97 can be restored. However, as matters stand, most states in the region are weak in precisely those areas where Singapore is strong; and unfortunately they have a great deal of catching up to do. I do not mean to suggest that Singapore's system can simply be copied: indeed its highly statist legal system appears to set it apart from the general direction being set by Thailand, Philippines and Indonesia. The whole point of Singapore's success is that the institutions and the legal culture have been built up over 30 years in a deeply premeditated fashion (Carter, 2001). The other countries need (or at least needed at the time) a much quicker fix in the short term as well as much deeper reforms in the longer term, because they are not starting from the same position as Singapore. Still, there is obviously much to be learned from Singapore's experience: its central bankers have been advising the Central Bank of Thailand how to improve its performance and its management of the banking sector, and the latter has purged those responsible for the mistakes of 1997.

Thailand is coping with fundamental political restructuring. It was recognized that economic reform would not be possible without a new constitution, designed to create greater accountability, more democracy, less corruption, and less risk of military intervention. The timing was perfect: the crucial parliamentary vote came at the height of the crisis, and parliamentarians were frightened into passing the constitution without amendment (in the process actually reducing their own powers) by a combination of economic necessity and, somewhat ironically, military backing for the reforms with an implicit threat of the 18th military coup since 1932 (Harding, 2001). The resulting document is remarkable for having probably more checks and balances even than the US Constitution. The constitution creates no less than eight new courts and other judicial or watchdog bodies, in addition to revamping many existing ones, including the Supreme Court and the legislature.[3]

Whether such an elaborate structure designed to outflank politicians and the military will actually deliver the Thai state into the hands of technocrats, lawyers and democrats, and as a result restore Thai economic fortunes, remains to be seen. The government, at the virtual insistence of the IMF, proceeded with the urgently required bankruptcy law, passed in February 1999,[4] and improved banking regulation, while also moving to reduce the power of the military. A Financial Restructuring Authority is designed to provide for better redistribution of assets, and there are to be no corporate bail-outs. The Board of Investment has renewed its efforts to attract foreign investment (Thailand Board of Investment, 2001).[5] In addition, 58 non-bank finance houses were closed. Recovery seems to be on the way, but whether this will be a strong recovery probably depends on the resolution of underlying legal and institutional problems.

Lee Kuan Yew's point about transparency is highly relevant in relation to Thailand. It is remarkable that Thailand's foreign reserves were allowed to dwindle from $30 billion to about $1.5 billion in a kind of Leeson-style meltdown without anyone outside the Central Bank, even the Finance Minister, being told the facts. The point has been repeatedly made in South East Asia that a free press is essential to the kind of transparency that might have alerted people to the impending crisis during the early part of 1997. Singapore itself has followed this logic by requiring banks to issue quarterly statements of capital and non-performing loans. It is interesting to note that none of the other countries affected by the crisis has put in place similar rules. Press freedom is now more apparent in Thailand and Indonesia than in Singapore or Malaysia.

Indonesia presents of course a more extreme case. Even more fundamental reform of the constitutional and legal systems is required, but there seems much less chance that these will be delivered without a greater change than is represented by the swearing in of three new Presidents in the last three years. Again bankruptcy law provides a good example. In Thailand the aim is to make the rather ancient bankruptcy law more effective and available in conditions in which bankruptcy proceedings take far too long, bridging loans are not permitted, and it is generally easier to write off the debt. In Indonesia the need is to make bankruptcy proceedings available and effective at all. The current position, indicated by a presidential decree signed in April 1998, is the complete replacement of the Dutch-style bankruptcy law of 1905. The implication is that the existing legal system is simply incapable of delivering law. What replaces the 1905 regime is a new Commercial Court, which decides whether the stricken company proceeds to straight bankruptcy or to a moratorium on debts.

Consider the following conditions:

1. In mid-1999, 96% of Indonesian companies were technically bankrupt but very few indeed (the precise number is disputed) had been declared such by the courts.

2. One bank operated for two years without a licence.
3. Two others defrauded their customers of one billion *rupiah* without punishment.
4. Two others were plundered by their owners, again without punishment.
5. Some law firms will not litigate because that very act implicates them in corruption.

The only remedy seemed to be to sweep everything aside and start afresh (Manring, 1999). Since this could not be done effectively at speed, the new bankruptcy law and the new court, echoing the relatively successful creation of an Administrative Court in 1990 (Bedner, 2001) but building on the old law, seemed an attractive option. In the long term Indonesia has to develop a greater respect for law and legal institutions (Lindsey, 1997) and could learn from Singapore and Malaysia in this respect. Fundamental reform of the legal system will have to embrace the law schools as the wellsprings of judicial and legal competence and independence for the future. The IMF reform package recognizes Indonesia's weakness in these respects, and a thorough reform of the judicial system is possible. The new regulations on government procurement are also to be welcomed, but are said to have been undermined in the drafting process (*Financial Times*, April 1998). Forty banks are under official supervision. Parallel with legal reform must go reform of the administrative system, designed to create greater devolution, competence, independence, and also democratic control. Whether these things will occur depends on the will and the competence of the political leaders in the new democratic order. The recent laws on regional autonomy (Bell, 2001), which have created considerable confusion with regard to important economic functions such as foreign investment decisions and the regulatory powers of regional governments, and which also create new opportunities for corruption at the local level while seen as necessary for political integration, have resulted in a flight of capital.[6]

Malaysia presents a less extreme but still problematical case. Like Singapore it has institutional and legal strengths, but it has also suffered from wild investment decisions, cronyism, and lack of regulation of the financial sector. It has not gone to the IMF, partly because it has less need to but partly for political reasons: any IMF package would involve the dismantling of the entrepreneurial sector of subsidized *bumiputera* companies, which would present a large political problem and erode political support for the United Malay National Organization (UMNO) leadership. Instead, the government, on what is still stated to be a temporary basis, pegged the *ringgit* to the US dollar, instituted currency exchange controls, and did away with restrictions on equity participation, so that the '30%-*bumiputera*' rule no longer applies (at least until 31 December 2003) and non-Malays and foreigners can participate; the government has indicated that this rule is replaced by an aim of 30% *bumiputera* ownership of the entire economy. On 1 September 1998 the Malaysian government announced capital controls, pegging the *Ringgit* and preventing offshore trading in it, and its Deputy Prime Minister, Anwar Ibrahim, who had been arguing for more regulation and reform, was sacked (Tey Tsun Hang, 1999). Although Malaysia is still regarded as an attractive locus for foreign investment, the environmental problems and the water shortages, partly another result of wild investment decisions, are beginning to render it less so; and likewise so are the political uncertainties over the continuing elective dictatorship of the Mahathir clique and the suppression of the reform movement.

Taking bankruptcy yet again as a test, Malaysia has effective bankruptcy laws on the common-law pattern, as does Singapore, and has the legal infrastructure to implement them. The problem is simply that the government considers it cannot afford to allow certain companies to go under. Thus, although the (now deposed) Finance Minister Anwar Ibrahim spoke shortly before his fall in September 1998 of 'no more subsidies', this was so much in flat contradiction of the logic of the Malaysian economic system that one did not believe it would happen, and so far, indeed, it has not: witness the huge bailout for Renong, an UMNO-linked company. The waiving of stock market rules for another UMNO-linked engineering company UEM indicates that nothing has changed. The only effective measures that have been taken are the rescheduling of a number of mega-projects such as the Bakun Dam, and the Multimedia Super Corridor, and the extending of liability for insider trading under amendments to the Securities

Commission Act. The policy of forcing mergers among financial institutions has not so far proved practicable. Malaysia's problems are perhaps not as deeply seated as those of Thailand or Indonesia, but it is still far from the desirable position occupied by Singapore. The general view is that absent legal reform, Malaysia's measures will not prove sustainable or healthy in the longer term.

The remedies to the present ills are therefore relatively clear, at least in outline. However, their implementation creates several difficulties. The necessary curb in public spending, exacerbated by loss of revenue from earnings and corporation tax, is causing social unrest across the region. Unemployment is hitting hard; even Singapore is being affected, having to cut wages and lay off thousands of workers. This is not offset by any legal provision for social protection, in which South East Asia is weak. In this way the region's strength in nation building and its social stability, which have formed the basis of its economic development over the last 30 years, are once more thrown into question. For this reason, the governments of South East Asia have to consider the social as well as economic effects of the reforms. This is not an argument for inaction, but for rebuilding the region's legal systems in a careful and sensitive way. 'McDonaldization' of law, by which I mean unthinking adoption of western commercial laws, may cause many more problems than it solves; this is an important and difficult balance which South East Asian governments now have to achieve: how to satisfy the economic and IMF imperatives without destroying the social fabric.

Recovery demands not just the appearance of legality but its reality. It demands greater and more consistent regulation of banks and other private sectors, and more rationality and legitimacy in both public and private investment. It demands a transfer of power with greater opportunities for legislatures and courts to call to account the inefficient and the corrupt. Ultimately nothing short of a complete overhaul will be enough to make a difference. Thailand has a head start in this, having commenced its reforms before the economic collapse. Singapore has found other, instrumentalist, methods of creating favourable conditions, but these are probably not easily repeatable elsewhere. For the rest, there can be no going back to pre-1997 ways. There must be new laws, but the gap between written law and social and economic reality will have to be narrowed.

I suggest this can only be done if independent and competent courts back up the economic and legal reforms, and this is accompanied by a revolution in legal and corporate culture (See Tim Andrews, this volume). The problem is that, although many of the causes of the crisis were attributable to lack of a proper legal/ regulatory infrastructure and culture, legal reform operates over a much longer cycle than economic recovery can and needs to. Thus, while legal reform is still certainly necessary in the long term, it may be that other measures are more likely to have desirable short-term effects. The worrying point is that the long-term issues are not really being adequately addressed in most South East Asian countries.

NOTES

1. A good example of this is the Anwar Ibrahim trial in Malaysia.
2. Hedge funds have however been subjected to greater regulation (Chew, 1999).
3. Others include the Election Commission, the Supreme Court's Criminal Division for Persons Holding Political Positions, the Ombudsman, the State Audit Commission, the National Human Rights Commission, the Constitutional Court, and the Administrative Courts.
4. Bankruptcy Act (No4) BE 2541, w.e.f. 10 April 1998.
5. In 1999, a new Act, the Foreign Business Act, B.E. 2542, was passed which supersedes the earlier Alien Business Law 1972. The Act is designed to attract foreign investment.
6. A report based on the year to October 2001 indicates a 90% reduction. At the same time there is a dispute over the takeover of a cement factory by the provincial government of West Sumatra, which has been criticized by the World Bank and central government.

REFERENCES

Bedner, A. (2001), *Administrative Courts in Indonesia: A Socio-Legal Study*. Kluwer Law International: The Hague.

Bell, G. (2001), 'The New Indonesian Laws Relating to Regional Autonomy: Good Intentions, Confusing Laws', *Asia-Pacific Law and Policy*, Vol.2, accessed at www.hawaii.edu/aplpj/2/1.html.

Booth, A. (1999), *The Causes and Consequences of South East Asia's Economic Crisis*. London: SOAS.

Carol G.S. Tan, (1999), 'Economic Recovery and the Recovery of Law in South East Asia', in P. Davidson (ed.), *Trading Arrangements in the Pacific Rim: ASEAN and APEC*. New York: Oceana Publications.

Carter, C. (2001), *Eyes on the Prize: Law and Economic Development in Singapore, 1959–1999*. The Hague: Kluwer Law International.

Chew, M. (1999), 'The Spectre of Hedge Funds: Regulatory Responses to Speculative Activity in Singapore and Hong Kong', *Singapore Journal of International and Comparative Law*, Vol.3, pp.82–107.

The Financial Times, 3 April 1998.

Harding, A.J. (2001), 'May There be Virtue: "New Asian Constitutionalism in Thailand"', *Australian Journal of Asian Law*, Vol.3, pp.24–48.

Lasserre, P. and Schutte, H. (1999), *Strategies for Asia-Pacific: Beyond the Crisis*. London: Macmillan.

Lindsey, T. (ed.)(2001), *Law and Society in Indonesia*. London: Macmillan.

Manring, T.A. (1999) 'Debt Restructuring in Indonesia', *Singapore Journal of International and Comparative Law*, Vol.3, pp.58–81.

Mya Than (2001) ASEAN Beyond the Regional Crisis: Challenges and Initiatives (2001). Singapore: ISEAS.

Straits Times Overseas Edition, 16 May 1998.

Straits Times Overseas Edition, 2 January 1999.

Straits Times Overseas Edition, 28 February 1998.

Straits Times Overseas Edition, 28 February 1998. Budget speech by Finance Minister Richard Hu.

Tey Tsun Hang, (1999) 'Malaysia: The Fierce Politico-Legal Backlash', *Singapore Journal of International and Comparative Law*, Vol.3, pp.1–25.

Thailand Board of Investment (2001), 'Investing in Thailand - Business and Investment Information', accessed at www.boi.go.th.

4

The Internet, Email, and the Malaysian Political Crisis: The Power of Transparency

LEN HOLMES and MARGARET GRIECO

The dilemma posed by the widespread use of new communication channels for the development and success of Malaysian business has become apparent: the 'unmuzzling' of the Internet necessary for the success of any modern economy has, in the case of Malaysia, been accompanied by the widespread and effective use of the Internet for political challenges and resistance to Government. Bob Paquin of the *Ottowa Citizen* newspaper provides a succinct analysis of both situation and dilemma under the title 'Malaysia unmuzzled: Internet ensures information flow in turbulent times':

> The Malaysian government of Mahathir Mohamad may have silenced former deputy premier Anwar Ibrahim – convicted last month of corruption and sentenced to six years in prison – but thanks to the Internet and other electronic media channels, Mr Anwar's message of reform continues to be heard throughout the country. The fact that Malaysian citizens have been able to obtain relatively unbiased news on the Anwar trial and the 'reformasi' campaign exemplifies the increasing difficulty governments have in managing the flow of information within their borders – even when they control the major print and broadcast media. Within days of Anwar's arrest, offshore Web sites sprouted by the dozen offering a combination of news, analysis and essays, and serving as repositories for press statements and letters from prison from Mr. Anwar himself. ...
>
> Ironically, the fact Malaysians are in a position to make use of digital media reports is due in large part to the government's efforts to transform the country into a kind

of information technology mecca. Over the last few years, fuelled by a decade of double-digit growth, Malaysia has been witness to a series of bold investments in its infrastructure, including the construction of a cross-country highway, the world's tallest building, a state-of-the-art airport, and a soon-to-be-completed new capital city. The jewel in Prime Minister Mahathir Mohamad's crown, however, was to be the Multimedia Super Corridor, a swath of land hewn out of the jungle, and transformed into the world's latest Silicon Valley upstart. Until the Asian financial crisis hit, the project was going surprisingly well. Bill Gates and Microsoft were among those promising to build R & D facilities, locate regional headquarters and produce goods within this wired village.

The financial crisis and the Anwar trial changed all that. The trees have been levelled and some of the data pipes have been installed, but most of the potential investors have delayed or cancelled their plans for the region. Nonetheless, the emphasis on an IT future, coupled with years of increased consumer spending, has created a widely shared taste for the latest in technological gadgets, including Internet connectivity and VCDs. (*Ottawa Citizen*, 17 May 1999)[1]

Malaysian government and Malaysian business had seen the advantages of global communication technologies for external trade and internal organization: the consequences for the support and upholding of sustained political resistance such as is now found in the *reformasi* movement had been dramatically underestimated or ignored.[2]

The Internet, aligned to the suite of new electronic technologies such as CD ROMs, videotapes, digital cameras, email and in combination with modern telephonic capabilities, has enabled the external world to be brought in to the middle of the Malaysian political arena at the press of a button. The access of the external world to the centre of Malaysian political space and the access of Malaysian activists, and indeed the less-active citizenry, to global views on the Malaysian political and economic crisis has created a new electronic space for political and commercial interaction. External business can at the touch of a button identify areas of discord and uncertainty in Malaysian political and economic life: interests which are being suppressed internally can signal out the extent of their disenchantment and willingness to confront the existing order. As the Paquin article indicates, the new online visibility of Malaysia's difficult political circumstance has an immediate economic effect: and negative economic effects have their impact in increasing political disenchantment.

The transparency of Malaysia's difficulties has been enhanced by the unmuzzling of the Internet, a transparency which has negative economic and business consequences. The situation is not, however, easily reversed since the remuzzling of the Internet would have direct negative economic consequences. Asian management and Asian government, in this case Malaysia, face a dilemma. In times of stability when the citizenry is compliant, the Internet plays the ready role of efficiently organizing societal resources and enlarging trade and business opportunities (Singapore would be a good example of such a state), but in times of crisis, the Internet serves to amplify the visibility and transparency of conflicts for the external observer. Where the external observer is an investor, the consequences are clear and business can suffer. Within this article, we examine more fully this particular dilemma of Asian management and Asian government.

In exploring this dilemma we encounter another: the proliferation of Malaysian websites dedicated to political challenge and social reform. The invitation that these sites make to those outside Malaysian politics to participate in moving such political challenge and social reform forward has the consequence of enabling the access of outside interests into this complex political space. At present, Malaysian reformist constituencies find mainstream support for their activities from the external global arena. There are, however, circumstances in which, through the very same medium, the Internet, external forces which are hostile towards the *reformasi* agenda can hijack or alter the path of change in a different direction to that sought by the *reformasi* movement. It is a dilemma: to open a call for support and to open a medium for establishing solidarity and participation can result in the initiative being taken over. Already there are examples on *reformasi* chat lines and pages of contributions which are negative about the *reformasi* cause. Disinformation can as easily be broadcast over the electronic forms as accurate information. This is not to suggest that to date the Internet has not proved a major weapon in the

Anwar/*reformasi* confrontation, but rather to suggest that the tool has its limits and the original user of the tool may not remain the permanent controller.

We might reasonably expect the Malaysian government to begin to make use of the Internet in 'spinning' the current political problematic and that it will aim its materials at many of the same audiences in a bid to retain trade and investment. Indeed, in some ways we already have some indication of such a trend: the search engine for Malaysia 'broadcast' from California appears to have no political content whatsoever in it, suggesting that is 'moderated' in such a way as to keep it clean,[3] although the main MalaysiaNET site did, for a time, carry supportive material on Anwar and a statement from Alvin Toffler to the effect that it is important that super-communications highways should not become vehicles for repression. A quick review of the contents of the first page of the MalaysiaNET website gives us a feel of the politico-commercial debate around the technology, at the time of the Asian Crisis:

> Welcome to MalaysiaNET
> MalaysiaNET, is a wholly owned project of Infogroup Corporation Ltd., to promote E-commerce on the information highway in Southeast Asia. The main principles of this site are the introduction of e-commerce, a free search engine. a free web-based e-mail service, the promotion of freedom of expression and the free flow of information via the Internet.
> November 17, 1998
> Statement from Mr Alvin Toffler
> Although in my recent correspondence with Prime Minister Mahathir and in published articles I have sharply criticized the imprisonment in Malaysia of former Deputy Prime Minister Anwar Ibrahim and my friend Munawar Anees, I have not yet formally resigned from the International Advisory Panel of the Malaysian Multi-Media Supercorridor as reported in the press.
>
> I do not believe that this visionary project, which is important for the future of the Malaysian people and serves, in part, as a model and challenge to other countries, can flourish in the present climate of political repression.
>
> I am sure other members of the panel, including the heads of many giant software, computer, and telecommunications companies, share this view.

And I do not agree, as Prime Minister Mahathir has argued in response to my appeals, that the MMSC project is purely a business matter and has nothing to do with politics. The 'cyberlaws' that he promised investors – complete freedom of access to information, and other Third Wave freedoms, are, in fact, clearly political.

The creation of an Asian Silicon Valley is itself inherently political.

That is why I hope that even at this late date a calm and just resolution can be found to the conflict between those calling for reform in Malaysia and a once visionary Prime Minister, who in the past has prevented ethnic conflict, marginalized religious fanaticism and helped replace rubber, tin and timber with semiconductor chips as his country's key export.

If Anwar and Anees are not released from prison unharmed as soon as possible, I will resign, as, I suspect, will other members of the panel on whose investments the project depends.

Alvin Toffler, November 17, 1998

For the latest information on the Former Deputy Prime Minister, Dato Seri Anwar Ibrahim, please click here.

Online Resumé & Vacancy Request – Update Service

If you are based in Malaysia or any other member states of the Association of Southeast Asian nations, you may click here to post at no cost your resumé or job vacancy request in to our AseanJOB Database.

Copyright: Infogroup Corporation Ltd.

For feedback please e-mail erwan@malaysianet.net

[Thailand] – [Malaysia] – [Singapore][4]

In this short first section, we have identified a number of dilemmas clustered around the widespread use of the Internet in Malaysia and on Malaysian issues. We wish to close the first section by commenting on the emergence of this electronic political-commercial dynamic in what is conventionally termed a developing country. The complexity of these new political forms is worthy of a sustained critique. This article does not attempt a comprehensive analysis of these new forms but the following sections do provide a sampling of some of the complex technical, social, political and commercial dynamics involved.

THE PRISON NOTEBOOKS: AN ELECTRONIC CHALLENGE
ON HEGEMONY

The tradition of communicating with the world from the solitary status of political imprisonment has a long and distinguished history. Imprisonments for social and religious reasons have also produced their high literary forms, from Bunyan's *Pilgrim's Progress* to Wilde's *The Ballad of Reading Gaol*. It can be seen in the work of Genet and par excellence in the work of Gramsci (*The Prison Notebooks*). The imprisoned have issued their challenges in high forms to the existing social order. Reducing the individual to the solitary state has often resulted in the most critical and cutting challenges to existing hegemonies. Anwar, when he placed his letters from prison on the Internet through the offices of a second party,[5] most surely shaped his action within this tradition.

> I have chosen the path of societal reform and, in so doing, I often have had to sacrifice that just balance I have always wanted to maintain between contemplation and action. Through ABIM, student and youth movements, and later in government, I have tried to generate public awareness (taw'iyya) of the crucial importance of ensuring al-adl wal-ihsan (justice and virtue/equity) in all human affairs. It is true that I have often been conciliatory, and at times I have been criticised by colleagues and Islamists and social activists and the opposition, who insisted that not all of such compromises could be rationalized in the name of hikmah, or wisdom. (In fact, I intimated to you some time ago of my growing disenchantment and frustrations at the excesses of the government, Dr. Mahathir's abhorrence of criticism, his mega-enterprises and delusions of grandeur.) However, I had to draw the line when transgressions went beyond acceptable boundaries, when corruption had become pervasive and rampant, when religious laws and ulamas were belittled and abused, when public funds were plundered to enrich families and cronies, and when there was travesty of justice and the rule of law trampled. I have highlighted some of these issues in my earlier letters from prison, such as *From the Halls Of Power to the Labyrinths of Incarceration*. (I had wanted to use 'Labyrinth of Solitude,' but it's a novel by Octavio Paz).

Of course, I am paying a high price for sticking to my convictions. Nor am I alone in facing the rage of an ageing dictator. Unfortunately, my family and friends have to suffer along with me. Some have been arrested, tortured, or otherwise harassed by the Special Branch. My experience in detention in 1974 taught me that it would be totally unacceptable merely to survive as a conformist while having to endure corruption and oppression. Alternatively, having to pursue a reform agenda as a competent critic is certainly challenging and beset with obstacles. Nonetheless, it is beyond my worst expectations   that Dr. Mahathir could act in such a desperate, despicable manner – to allege that I am guilty of acts of treason (foreign agent), sexual misconduct, corruption, even explored the possibility that I was involved in a complicity to murder. And the fitnah and mihnah continue unabated, with vilification by the government-controlled media. Since you left, the Inspector General of Police, Tan Sri Rahim Nor, has resigned and Dr Mahathir has relinquished his role as Minister of Home Affairs. But I intend to proceed with a civil suit against him and the IGP for the physical assault, for being stripped naked, and the inhuman treatment under police custody. A lesson must be learnt. Citizens cannot be subjected to brutal physical abuse and ridicule.

Nevertheless, like you, I have no regrets. I'm trying to keep myself busy – with prayers and du'a, tadarrus and reading. How else could I be expected to finish *The Complete Works Of Shakespeare*, Will Durant's *Study of Philosophy*, *The Penguin History of the World*, works of Plato and Aristotle etc. etc.? My old copy of Abdullah Yusuf Ali's translation of the Quran is most valuable because of my earlier short notes and references from Ibn Kathir, al-Qurtubi, Sayyid Qutb and Maulana Maududi's tafsirs. Because of the limited number of books permitted at any given time, my hadith collection is confined to Riadh us-Salihin for the present.

So, as you can observe, I have not overlooked the importance of education and the intellectual tradition in bringing about reform. I recall my last IIIT meeting with al-Marhum Ismail al Faruqi in Virginia, which featured a debate on 'Ibn Khaldun and Change', based on Ernest Gellner's *Muslim Society*. Al-Marhum Ismail had a way to compel me to read the relevant texts before such meetings. Such encounters undoubtedly helped to further enhance my love for scholarly discourse and rekindle my passion for literature, which I have tried to share with the public even in dry budget speeches in Parliament in the hope of introducing the great minds to the uninitiated. Thus, while trying to justify the need for reform or the reduction of taxes, for instance, I used to slip in quotes from Ibn Khaldun. I concur with Mortimer Adler in his attempt to popularize philosophy. Thus Asian sages and reformers feature regularly in my speeches and writings, including Kung Fu Tze, Wang An Shih and the author of *Kurikural*. The Asian Renaissance series (of conferences) beginning with Jose Rizal whom I consider a precursor to the Asian renaissance, was a great success.[6]

What is significant about Anwar's imprisonment is that, for the first time, mass access to his contemporaneous writings from prison was immediately enabled online. The power to instantaneously communicate the immediacy of punishment, torture and imprisonment has never previously existed. In terms of political communication, it is an unanalyzed and untheorized new event: and it is a particularly distinctive feature of the Asian crisis.

Under traditional circumstances, imprisoned leaders were separated from their peoples: their living images were rarely available. In the period of video film and the mass instantaneous broadcasting capabilities of interactive visual materials, a leader with a strong social network surrounding him/her is able to 'capture' and release the leader's image through electronic forms There is a new potential for leaders to remain in the eye of their peoples, as we have also seen on a lesser scale in Burma. Video clips of Anwar and his full writings from prison are available on the Internet.[7] In order to ensure that government can not simply bring down this material by closing a single Anwar site, the website developers have ensured that there are a number of mirror sites with different geographical homes.[8]

In pre-Internet times, newspapers would simply be closed down if they were friendly to the opponents of government and their stock of photographs which supported their views would be destroyed. The development of the Internet means that the physical visual image no longer needs to be held in a place where it can so easily be destroyed: visual images which act as confirmatory evidence can be transmitted outside national border and held in an electronic location where they can be readily accessed but cannot be destroyed.

In researching this essay, we have spent considerable time on the Internet looking at the way in which individuals and situations are being portrayed in order to elicit the desired sympathy with the *reformasi* cause. We have come across a number of very interesting new forms of communication designed to generate solidarity with the *reformasi* cause and weaken the respect for and allegiance to the government of the day. A particularly skilled form is that of the 'Rogues' Row'⁹ which provides photographs of key government and business personalities and subtitles which poke fun at these figures. The Rogues' Row provides information on corruption and other relevant issues arising from the Asian crisis. At the level of the Internet user this will develop a familiarity with those usually held in very high regard and will debunk the sacred character associated with national leaders. In the case of one rogue, the simple act of passing the computer mouse across the 'rogue's face' contorts the face into something recognizably nasty and moreover something which is moving toward the Internet user.¹⁰ Similarly, in the Flash (multimedia animation) opening to the freemalaysia website,¹¹ a picture of Hitler is briefly displayed then replaced by one of Mahathir. Clearly, people very skilled in the technology have been at work ensuring that the Internet delivers a form of social caricature which reduces respect for the national leaders. The contrast between the dignity of Anwar's prison letters and those national leaders 'imprisoned' on Rogues' Row (the term used is 'inmates') invites sympathy for Anwar. The opposition is of course highly constructed: this is not to argue that Anwar is not worthy of support, nor is to argue that the information contained upon the 'rogues' is incorrect, but simply to indicate that the images are not simply a natural ordering but are highly manipulated. The practice of 'virtual imprisonment' represents a reversal of apparent social power through the use of the electronic mode and invites the understanding that the present set of on-the-ground power relations is open to being overtaken.

The technology allows new forms for framing social reality: and the way in which such social reality is framed will have its impact on external audiences and coalition formation both in international politics and global business. An important feature of the new technology in framing the social and political understanding of new and emergent political and social realities is the ability to provide comprehensive archiving of the chronology and character of social events and processes. In the case of the Anwar confrontation in Malaysia, comprehensive archiving has indeed been undertaken and is accompanied by online ready search facilities which enable new entrants to this electronic political space to track the process and development at will, on their own and in detail.[12] Furthermore, the technology enables the ready transmission of calendars of new activities; obtaining information no longer depends on social group membership.[13] Historically, those wishing to destroy political organization could track a political membership of an organization back along information routes; the best known example of such a process was in the colonial struggle in Algeria, and formed the material for the classic film *The Battle of Algiers* (Pontecorvo, 1965). With new technology, the possession of information gives no such inevitable clue to social and political contacts. Similarly, the availability of such an archive of materials enables the ready refreshing of political memory and provides instantaneous advocacy resources. In the case of Malaysia, it is clear that the density and range of Internet materials will increasingly play a role in the structuring of political understanding: electronic advocacy is a feature of a new political age in which the national can be rendered global through the establishment of inexpensive virtual political spaces in the form of websites.

The complexity of the Internet and email structure surrounding Anwar, in which his own prison letters and video productions play a key and core role, is unrivalled by any of the social or business Malaysian websites currently online. The role of new communications technology in globalizing Malaysian organization is at its most pronounced in the political sector. The parodying of business leaders on the Malaysian political websites will of course present its dilemmas for international business. Under-the-counter deals or 'gentlemen's agreements' are no longer likely to remain matters between two parties: the potential for global observation and display of suspect deals is now an actuality.

The Internet, and its related technology, email, not only enable political organizations to make use of the same distribution and information channels as global business, they also enable the better use and substantial amplification of other communications technologies. Websites typically carry information on other communication modes such as telephone numbers and mailing addresses: through the Internet location information can be readily obtained, with important consequences for international advocacy. The ease of access through the Internet to telephone contacts and mail addresses enlarges the number of reliable modes of communication open to the individual: the search capabilities as well as the connection capabilities of the technology have enabled the social movement around Anwar to make a very real challenge to the existing hegemony.

DEMONSTRATING MASS INTEREST AND COMMITMENT: CLIENT-COUNTING TECHNIQUES

The needs of commerce and business have seen the development of extensive client feedback and client participation systems. The development of commercial websites which enable clients to order online, to share information with other product users (forums) and to assist business in the fine-tuning and improved design of products has its political consequences. Within the high-income countries of the West, consumers have begun to use the inter-client communication capabilities to put pressure on business to reform and transform. The ability to raise online well-organized consumer lobbies is a feature of modern economic life. Within the high income countries, older persons, a group which very often experiences mobility constraints and has traditionally been fragmented in terms of political and social action, have begun to use the technology to effect; the American Association of Retired Persons provides a clear demonstration of this new political form.[14]

These very same feedback systems have become important in the politics of Malaysia. At present, there are a number of sites that carry email addressed to or about Anwar: these forums are an important vehicle for the development of solidarity and interestingly, many of the sites operate in both the local language and English. That these 'chat rooms' have become a major location for Internet activity conducted in one's own language is an indication that the domination of the Internet by English is no means certain: the willingness to provide text translated from local language into English on these sites as a mechanism for internationalizing the discourse indicates the extent to which perfectly parallel discourses can be provided in either language medium. This clearly is a new political form – a form which may indicate the extent to which global business could move away from English dominance on the Internet in favour of English as an international facilitating mode rather than the sole mode.

But presence in the chat-room, no matter which language is being operated, is often concerned with issues of individual visibility. While prominent and external figures are often ready to sign their names to statements of support, the lone individual can court unwanted and significant levels of repression by revealing her or his identity in a political chat room or forum. Consequently, the Anwar Chat room which was hosted on the MalysiaNet website[15] warned users 'do not log in with email address'. That chat-room facility has now been removed, but the facility to post material anonymously is offered by other sites, e.g. Seachange Malaysia.[16]

The contributors to chat-rooms now have a new option in the development of solidarity; they can make a contribution to the Anwar campaign simply by clicking on sites or contributing anonymously to a major open and public debate without exposing themselves politically or socially. Such safe options have consequences for the development of solidarity: individuals can nudge incrementally towards fuller action. But more importantly, many of the various websites and forums have had counters attached to their sites. Each click on a site or addressing of an email is counted: the level of interest and potential support is measured by the traffic through the various websites. Indeed, within electronic technology, the measurement of potential markets by user traffic on websites has become formalized and there are now sites which carry information on the number of hits across a range of sites.[17] The success of the Malaysian websites as measured by user traffic is readily visible from the Counter.com site – as at 12 June 1999, the number of hits given for Reformasi Nasional was 7,771,809, presumably since the commencement of the site.

The client-counting techniques of business and commerce become the solidarity-measuring techniques of political and social change. Not only do such statistics measure solidarity, but they encourage further social action by revealing the strength of support a social movement has already gained. Of course, counters on low-use sites will have a similar dynamic though in the opposite direction. Internet users will be discouraged from joining social and political action which registers low interest as measured by a low count. There is, of course, a capability for technically manipulating these statistics: similarly, it is possible to ensure that the recording of the statistics is placed in the hands of a respected and authoritative agency.

In the same way that client-counting, client forums and other client feedback mechanisms developed in the commercial sector have been taken up in the promotion of the *reformasi* social movement, so too have other tricks and electronic techniques of the commercial trade. One such form is that of sending electronic postcards in support of Anwar.[18] This form requires the individual sending the card to identify him- or herself. This entails the taking of a greater risk than anonymous email or simply clicking on websites for information, but limits that risk by permitting the individual to specify who the recipient of the postcard will be. It is beyond our competence in this article to calculate the level of electronic communication which has been involved in the Anwar campaign, but clearly it is of sizeable proportion and indicates the extent to which global technologies designed for business are now producing new political forms that threaten the old rules and establishment under which business was conducted.

CONCLUSION: POLITICAL CHALLENGE AND THE ESTABLISHMENT OF ELECTRONIC COMPETENCE

It is clear that, before the advent of the Anwar campaign, Malaysia had already experienced substantial developments in the use of global communications technologies. It was a society which demonstrated beyond all doubt that electronic technology is critical in the development of trade and commerce for the developing world. E-commerce was a vehicle which could reduce many of the disadvantages experienced historically by economies outside the high-income country club.

This article has shown the astuteness and skill with which the social movement around Anwar has made use of the Internet in its search for international and internal coalitions and partners in placing pressure on the government of Malaysia. In line with Freireian precepts (Freire, 1972), the relevance of the technology to the struggle to expose corruption is paramount: in the struggle for change new competences and skills have been learnt and innovative adaptation of business and commerce tools by the Anwar social movement have become the order of the day. The political websites carry advice on how to get free email, information on ways of contributing towards the struggle at differentiated levels of exposure and the overall up-technicizing of political action has been largely promoted by the opposition. They have captured a tool of government's economic policy and through its use subverted an established order. It is a dilemma for Asian management, as Alvin Toffler's contribution so vibrantly demonstrates.

NOTES

1. For the full Paquin article go to http://members.xoom.com/Gerakan/unmuzzle_internet.html
2. See, for example, Reformasi News, www.geocities.com/Tokyo/Flats/3797/ berita.htm; also www.cyberway.com.sg/~nassir/index.html
3. See www.malaysia.net/links.
4. www.malaysianet.net/Anwar_Ibrahim/anwar_ibrahim.html (accessed 12 June 1999; link no longer functioning)
5. http://members.tripod.com/~Anwar_Ibrahim/prison/stupid_plot.htm
6. Anwar's letters from prison: http://members.tripod.com/~Anwar_Ibrahim/prison/abu_suleyman.htm
7. http://members.xoom.com/Gerakan/
8. For a listing of over 50 official Anwar Ibrahim online websites which show this mirror dynamic see the Lycos website: http://pages.whowhere.lycos.com/sports/vr4/.
9. www.freemalaysia.com/rogues/samsudin.htm
10. www.freemalaysia.com/rogues/vincent_tan.htm
11. www.freemalaysia.com
12. http://members.xoom.com/_XOOM/Gerakan/archive.html; see also http://members.tripod.com/~Anwarite/
13. www.members.xoom.com/_XOOM/Gerakan/announcements/events.html
14. American Association of Retired Persons: www.aarp.org
15. www.malaysianet.net/index.shtml
16. www.geocities.com/seachange_2000/contrib.htm
17. See, for instance, www.TheCounter.com/stats/toplists/
18. http://cardforanwar.hypermart.net/

REFERENCES

Bunyan, John (1984), *The Pilgrim's Progress*, edited with an introduction by N.H. Keeble. Oxford : Oxford University Press.
Freire, P. (1972), *Pedagogy of the Oppressed*. Harmondsworth: Penguin.
Gramsci, Antonio (1992), *Prison Notebooks*, Vol.1., edited with introduction by A.B. Joseph. New York: Columbia University Press.
Pontecorvo, Gillo (1965), *La Battaglia di Algeri* [*The Battle of Algiers*] (film).
Wilde, O. (1966), *Complete Works of Oscar Wilde*, ed. Vyvyan Holland. London: Collins.

5

Malaysian Unions in Political Crisis: Assessing the Impact of the Asian Contagion

MHINDER BHOPAL

The Asian economic crisis led to the rupture of underlying pre-crisis pressures and tensions in Malaysia, the effects of which are still being felt even as the economy recovers. The 'crony capitalism' attribution of the crisis by economic commentators and internal opponents created significant pressure on the incumbent political leadership and has given rise to a new rupture in the heart of the Malaysian political centre. In the field of industrial relations the events are testing and, potentially, (re)forging the relationship between the state and labour, which has been assumed to be one based suppression arising from the economic imperatives of the dependent state (Kuruvilla and Arudsothy, 1995). Due to the depth of the political crisis, and its impact on regime opening, the post-1997 period will be seen, in retrospect, as one of the 'critical junctures' in the actual or potential development of Malaysia's trade union movement. This contribution, focusing on the 'peak' Malaysian labour body, the Malaysian Trade Unions Congress (MTUC), outlines the historical tensions and resulting institutional 'sedimentation' which has informed the 'strategic choice' of the actors (see Poole, 1986) in their response to the economic crisis and ensuing political ruptures. It is argued that while Malaysian trade unionism has been historically hampered by ethnicity in a number of ways, these factors are beginning to melt away. Although the new opportunities for action are opening, the unfolding response of the Malaysian labour movement to the economic and political crisis needs to be viewed in the context of ethnic identities and the relatively limited impact of the crisis on Malaysian labour.

TRADE UNIONS AND POLITICAL STRUCTURE

Dependency theory argues that multinational companies (MNCs) in search of low labour costs and weak labour organization lead to the suppression of trade unionism owing to the dependent states' relative powerless vis-à-vis multinationals. This situation is reinforced by inter-state competition to provide an attractive site for inward investment (see Southall, 1988). Leaving aside the issue as to whether MNCs are as footloose as suggested by dependency theory, the assumption that states act as agents of capital to deliver labour subordination tends to omit the diversity and internal dynamics of local context (Deyo, 1989; Southall, 1988). Valenzuela (1992) suggests that the dependent state could adopt at least three labour strategies which, while favourable to capital, may reflect labour and political considerations. Each strategy gives rise to its own particular tensions which not only provide potential opportunities for 'action' but insert dynamism into the theorization of labour in dependent states. First, the dependent state can attempt to sponsor and incorporate the labour movement in an attempt to create a cooperative and populist movement accepted by workers. Such a strategy may become unstable where concession-making is undermined by the contradictions between capital, labour and the state.

Second, where the state is unable to accommodate unions, it may seek to incorporate peak labour movements to control autonomous action by unions. However, this may raise questions of union legitimacy and give rise to a challenge to the 'official' labour movement. Finally, where there are unbridgeable differences between political parties and the labour movement, the state may pursue a policy of control based on fragmentation and decentralization. The attempt to expose the union movement to the 'market mechanism' may be associated with an attempt to weaken market power by constraining and limiting workers' ability to organize and mobilize via restrictive legislation. The aim of such fragmentation is not only to prevent the labour movement from exerting economic pressure but also to prevent it from becoming a platform for political opposition to the regime. In this case the state's lack of support for labour could undermine regime legitimacy unless the labour movement is marginalized in political and economic discourse.

The above indicates, but does not fully elaborate, that trade unions and labour are not merely passive. Unions can support or challenge state strategies, and, like their relations with employers, this action cannot be read in a deterministic manner not assumed to be consistent over time. States undergo many tensions in the development process, and workers' organizations are not necessarily passive bystanders to unbridled state strategy. 'Third World' unions are actors with the potential for action and reaction, and their response will be shaped by a variety of economic, political, social and ideological factors internal and external to the union and the union movement. These factors include the level, type, extent and intensity of industrialization; the relationships that the state has with unions; the relationship unions have with other progressive or reactionary forces; the ideology which shapes union practice or worker consciousness; workers' consciousness and experience of struggle (Southall, 1988). Also significant is the composition and characteristics of union membership, the accountability of leadership and the extent of worker democracy and union commitment to shop-floor and progressive political struggle.

While providing comprehensive coverage of the factors affecting trade union action, Southall arguably underemphasizes the significance of individual 'actors'. Few business and industrial relations scholars have utilized ethnicity as an explicit variable in their theorizing. Ethnicity, like gender, has been absent from management texts. This may be explained by the fact that such subjects create too much organizational complexity to be encompassed by the universalist offering of normative rationalist literature (see Clegg *et al.*, 1999). On the other hand, issues of gender and ethnic identity have often been written off as 'false consciousness' and possibly seen as diversionary to analysis based on the labour process (see Mohapatra, 1997), although this is not always the case in micro studies of the labour process and in explanations based upon labour market segmentation. This is despite the fact that analyses of plural multiethnic societies, where the political and social spheres are articulated and expressed in ethnic terms, indicate that there can be strong feelings of ethnic identity in some social formations (Fenton, 1999). Indeed, the value accorded ethnic cleavages, particularly with regard to the pressure for solidarity, has been argued to overshadow and obscure intra-ethnic class differences (see Jesudason, 1989), although this may need to be compensated by perceptions of enhanced group worth or promises of deferred returns. While ethnicity can be used as a resource for political (de)mobilization and boundary (re)definition between ethnic groups (Fenton, 1999) it can also be used in attempts at retention or challenge to intra-ethnic political control (Singh, 1998). Identities are not solely constructed in ethnic terms and can also be constructed in terms of gender, class or occupational grouping (Allen, 1994). Thus individuals or sub-groups with a perceived common ethnic identity may not, in all circumstances, have a primary loyalty to their ethnic group or their leaderships, and identification, where it exists, may be instrumental or opportunistic. The significance of ethnicity is not solely one of identity and culture but also one of politics and economy, and fractures and divisions arising from non-ethnic identities can be played out within ethnic boundaries. Indeed the objective of actors *may* be to work within the discourse of ethnic identity to achieve particular non-ethnic ends.

PRE-CRISIS TRADE UNION DEVELOPMENT AND POLITICAL ECONOMY

The 1996 the Peninsular Malaysia population of 20 million consisted of 61 per cent Malays, 30 per cent Chinese, eight per cent Indians and one per cent others (Gomez and Jomo, 1997). Ethnicity has been the prime organizing principle and basis of electoral mobilization and competition in Malaysia, and this has resulted in the main incumbent and opposition parties being, largely, organized on an ethnic basis. In this context, parties purporting to be 'multiracial' are perceived to be ethnically dominated resulting in the de facto ethnicization and reinforcement of such a political discourse. Many of Malaysia's problems arise from the manner in which the multiethnic nature of the population has been utilized in the political discourse. Academic analysts have seen the discourse of ethnicity as functional in obscuring more fundamental structures of class domination and inter-ethnic elite accommodation (see Hua Wu Yin, 1983; Yun Hing Ai, 1990; Gomez, 1999). The question of whether ethnicity is a problem per se or one that is utilized to maintain political dominance retains a fulcrum position in much analysis. The ruling multiethnic coalition has controlled Malaysia since its independence in 1957. Throughout this period the coalition itself has been dominated by the United Malay National Organization (UMNO), which was formed in 1946 in reaction to British attempts to downgrade the position of Malay rulers and extend citizenship rights to non-Malays (Milne and Mauzy, 1999). Since that time UMNO has both created, and ridden on the back of, Malay nationalism in an attempt to link the party symbiotically with notions of Malay identity (see Singh, 1998). While UMNO has, in effect, ruled uninterruptedly, there have been internal challenges to the incumbent leaderships throughout its short history (see Means, 1991; Milne and Mauzy, 1999), and these challenges have been articulated in terms of (re)asserting or (re)defining the 'Malay interest'.

Structures of ethnic economic, political and cultural segmentation have served to contain the potential of challenge from cross-ethnically organized workers (see Jomo and Todd, 1994), and until the past two decades this was made easier by the relatively low levels of Malay participation in waged labour. For instance, the late-1940s state suppression of the first wave of the militant Chinese Communist-controlled Malaysian labour movement was possible due to the absence of Malays and internal political divisions within the Chinese community. Control of the state-sponsored Indian union movement of the 1950s required less coercive direct action due to four interrelated factors. First, the Chinese were disorganized by state suppression of the 1940s, and had little confidence in the new state-sponsored union movement. Secondly, the fact that the colonial state-sponsored Indian trade union leaders were moderate anti-Communists (see Zaidi, 1975) ensured a compliant and responsible trade unionism. Thirdly, the fact that control of the trade union movement was passed to the Indians, who were smallest and least influential group, contributed to the movement's numerical and political weakness (see Jomo and Todd, 1994). Fourthly, the consolidation of ethnically-based political parties in the post-1957 independence period served to undermine the union movement's ability to develop symbiotic links with political parties without undermining the horizontal basis of trade union solidarity.

In the light of its political weakness, the labour movement's option of working with and through the multiethnic, but largely conservative, coalition of the 1970s Barisan National, dedicated to low-wage export-oriented industrialization, carried the possibility of incorporation. The counter-strategy of working with and through opposition parties has been equally problematic owing to the essentially ethnically predominant membership bases of opposition parties. The 'third way' of independent critical commentary has itself been problematic in a context where Malay labour constituted a minority, and control of the trade union movement was vested in Indians. Two reasons may explain this. First, the 1969 'race riots', precipitated by Chinese political gains in urban areas, put at centre stage a Malay nationalist discourse that emphasized the economic and cultural weakness of Malays in Malaysia. This resulted in the post-1970 affirmative action programmes, as embodied within the New Economic Policy (NEP), which sought to elevate the position of the Malays (Means, 1991). Consequently, trade-union issues of distribution have been seen as secondary, and at times dysfunctional, to the developmental process that was presented as a policy shift to enhance Malay opportunity as a whole, and intellectually articulated as a necessity for 'racial' peace in an ethnically segmented economy and multicultural society. Second, the size, structure and perception of UMNO as the most powerful representative and advocate of the Malay interest created an ambiguous boundary between it and trade unions. UMNO has an organizational structure that permeates to the root and branch of Malay society, and has 2.4 million members, out of a Malay population of approximately 12 million. The consequence is that

> When you have a labour dispute, often you have a situation where labour leaders go and appeal to the local UMNO leader to come and resolve the dispute or to influence the management. So you have a labour dispute being channelled into a political process, or a political institution, which strengthens it. ... UMNO is a very broad, massive organization – down to every village, every branch ... practically every work-site has UMNO representatives (Interview A, 1999).

While many Malay workers have seen UMNO, rather than trade unions, as the first channel for labour grievances, the fact that UMNO also represents the business interest has resulted in the exposure of its ability to represent the Malay rank and file

(Ibrahim, 1998). In the development decades, the state's accommodation of multinational, particularly anti-union, American corporations has further exposed the implications of state dependency on foreign direct investment. Nevertheless, the developmentalist dependent state has been able to utilize the notion of 'national interest' to undermine oppositional trade unionism. At workplace level, management has also sought advantage from the potential fractures to trade union solidarity on grounds of ethnic closure based on Malay identity, interest and cultural practices (Casparez, 1998; Smith 1994).

In these circumstances, trade union involvement with opposition political parties, particularly non-Malay parties, carried the potential accusation of ethnic political association and lack of commitment to the policy of Malay advancement and nation building. These factors have left the oppositional elements in the labour movement open to state suppression, vilification and possible accusation of being politically, and thus ethnically, partisan if they publicly challenge state policy at national or international levels. The Malaysian Labour movement's dilemma was summed up by C.V. Devan Naira, Secretary General of the Singapore National Trades Union Congress:

> The de-politicization of trade unions in Malaysia, wherever such politicization, exists is fundamental to the healthy growth of trade unionism in the region. If we condone trade unions which develop as branches of political parties, then we are all in for a very rough time. In a multi-party parliamentary system in a multiracial society as we have in Malaysia, this would mean that trade unions would develop not only along political party lines, but also along racial and communal lines. This would sound the death knell of democratic trade unionism in Malaysia and act as the harbinger of chaos and anarchy in the working class movement (Quoted in Zaidi, 1975).

Aware that trade unions cannot remain outside politics, the MTUC has produced a labour manifesto specifying the conditions on which the movement would endorse parliamentary candidates and particular political parties during elections. In this manner the movement has avoided being ideologically and/or ethnically tied to particular parties. Nevertheless, the 'pulling' integrative forces of a labour identity have been 'pushed' by individual activism and attachment to ethnically based political parties within the ruling coalition and in opposition.

The development decades, commencing in the 1970s but significantly accelerating in the 1980s and 1990s, have altered the ethnic composition of the workforce and business class and seen the ethnic re-configuration of the MTUC. For instance, in 1970 64 per cent of Malays were engaged in agriculture and five per cent in manufacturing, but by 1995 the comparable figures were 21 per cent and 25 per cent respectively. In absolute numbers, manufacturing provided employment for just over 73,000 Malays in 1970, but over one million in 1995. The comparable figure for services, which together with manufacturing accounted for 50 per cent of Malay employment in 1995, are 224,000 in 1970 but just over one million in 1995 (7th Malaysia Plan, 1996; Jomo and Todd, 1994). The labour movement is concomitantly reflecting this relative and absolute change through increasing Malay dominance of the union movement. This is reflected in the fact that over 70 per cent of trade union leaders and members, 60 per cent of the MTUC general council and 75 per cent of its executive are Malay (Interview B, 1999). Affirmative action-based development also saw increasing Malay business and the growth of Malay professionals and managers (Gomez and Jomo, 1997). Thus while NEP objectives have, to varying degrees, been achieved, this success has itself thrown up the potential for intra-Malay political manoeuvring in issues over the relative gains among the Malays themselves in a context that could be described as a dialectic of ethnic development.

While economic growth and concern over inter-ethnic economic distribution has served to submerge debate over intra-ethnic inequality, 'success' threatens to alter the landscape of Malay politics, not least by inserting labour and class issues into the political agenda. The potential threat to Malay solidarity from a united labour movement has not been lost on the ruling elites within the Mahathir government. While the government, rather than attempt incorporation, has excluded labour from the export-oriented developmentalist agenda through fragmentation and marginalization, this has been complemented by the 1980s' promotion of business-oriented in-house unionism and the discourse of 'Asian values' (Wadd, 1988; Jomo and Todd, 1994; Wadd and Jomo, 1994; Kuruvilla and Ponniah, 1995). Implicitly the MTUC and the labour movement have continued to be represented as secondary to the primary goals of economic and cultural advancement and protection of the Malay. Such a position has enabled the government publicly to attack and undermine those elements of the movement deemed to be oppositional. The government also attempted to fragment the labour movement by sponsoring the Malaysian Labour Organization (MLO) in 1988, in the context of the MTUC's increasing criticism of government policy and involvement with opposition parties. This has operated within the wider ideology of a common ethnic and national interest, and, in light of the changes in the composition of the workforce and economic advancement of the Malays, the state has pitted the interests of the Malaysian (increasingly Malay) worker against the 'protectionist' tendencies of 'Western ' trade unions to avoid granting concessions.

The state direction of an ethno-development strategy underpinned by affirmative action resulted in some political factions gaining from business interests while enabling politicians to distribute economic opportunities and thereby sponsor a Malay capital class. The scale and distribution of opportunities has, however, been uneven and those who have gained most are those closest to the incumbent UMNO 'dominant coalition'. Thus, while industrialization has expanded Malay waged labour, economic growth has enabled and created a Malay bourgeoisie and government sponsored rentier class (Gomez, 1991; Kua, 1996). The resulting ambiguous boundary between government, party and economic interests has created a new dynamic in Malaysia's political economy (Bowie, 1994) as *intra*-Malay *inter*-class economic inequality has grown. There have been growing visible divisions between the wealthy and the poor, public-sector professionals and businessmen and the politically included and excluded business class. This was reflected in public concern of the mid 1990s, largely from the urban Malay professional and middle classes (teachers, civil servants etc.) over political business, political fortunes amassed from share purchases and business links. This has been exacerbated by the increasing failure of politicians to obscure their business dealings (Jomo, 1989; Gomez and Jomo, 1997), as well as concerns over the growing significance of money in political

campaigning – the focus of discussion in the press as well as in
UMNO's general assembly. While these factors did little for regime
legitimacy they did not undermine it in the context of full
employment, a growing economy, increasing wages and enhanced
job opportunities for Malays in particular, and others in general.
The 'Asian economic crisis' coincided with increasing public
knowledge and Malay middle-class disquiet over the 'private'
sphere of Malaysian political business, and contributed to a fracture
in Malay politics. These factors, in the context of the economic
crisis, had the potential to draw the labour movement into political
debates without accusations of disloyalty, oppositionalism and
failure to credit the state with Malay advancement. It also provided
an opportunity for the labour movement to break out of the log
jam resulting from the policy of being 'non-aligned but at the same
time not non-committed, independent but not neutral' (S. Zaidi,
1973, in Suara Buroh, 1973), which was an outcome of a dated, but
intact, socio-political structure that contained within it the seeds of
subjugation of the labour agenda. The following sections evaluate
the scale and impact of the financial crisis and contextualize the
ensuing political ruptures and trade union responses within the pre-
crisis period, by focusing on the actions of 'key actors'.

METHODOLOGY

This paper is based on primary research conducted between 1999
and 2000. In-depth semi-structured interviews were conducted
with key trade union players, and frank, open and lengthy
interviews were obtained. The president, general secretary and
research officer of the MTUC were interviewed at length in 1999.
Between May and June 2000 email questionnaires were posted to
the General Secretary of the MTUC and President of one of the
most active and campaigning in-house unions in Malaysia.
Electronic communication via ICQ and email was undertaken
between 1999 and 2000 with the research officer, who had left his
position to campaign for the opposition and to found Malaysia's
first independent Internet newspaper. Further interviews were
conducted with the ex-research officer and the president of the in-
house union in June and July 2000; both of whom had close
involvement with the unfolding relationships between the trade
union movement, the new opposition and the incumbent political

leaderships. This was supplemented through further interviews with leaders of an opposition party and key academic analysts who are close to the opposition coalition.

FINANCIAL CRISIS, POLITICAL RUPTURES AND TRADE UNIONS

The short- and medium-term impact of the crisis has been variable (see Booth, this volume) and has left considerable uncertainties over the nature, efficacy and management of the globalized financial economy (see Chang, Palma and Whittaker, 1998). The debate among the academic economic community is divided. Those critical of the degree of uncontrolled deregulation have used the crisis to point to the inherent dangers in the unmitigated free flow of capital. In particular they have argued that the rapidity with which capital flows occur create herding instincts which may bear little resemblance to economic fundamentals. Their opponents have focused on the nature of nation-states and argued that institutional weakness and poor business practices underlie the response of the financial markets. These markets, acting as a disciplinary and re-allocative force, therefore ought not to be attributed with any inherent instability and irrationality (Nixon and Walters, 1999). In this sense Malaysia's move to create short-term stability, which gained support from economists such as Krugman and Stiglitz, while deemed risky at the time, has been in hindsight seen as the correct, if possibly badly managed (see Jomo, 1988) and unusual, policy response. For Malaysia there has been an early economic recovery with limited employment impact on Malaysian labour. Tables 1 and 2 show that GDP growth rates had recovered by 1999, while the impact on employment levels, which peaked in 1998, rapidly recovered after the first quarter of 1999.

Official unemployment figures are generally unreliable, and can mask as much as they reveal. For instance in the case of Malaysia there were inadequate criteria and mechanisms in place for monitoring and reporting staff reductions, and termination of fixed-term contracts and voluntary severance and voluntary turnover do not require to be reported. The figures also provide little information on levels of underemployment. While official figures show the numbers retrenched in 1998 as 83,865, of which almost 90 per cent were local workers (MTUC, 2000), it seems clear that

TABLE 1
MALAYSIAN GDP GROWTH RATES, 1994–99 (%)

1995	1996	1997	1998	1999
9.4	8.6	7.7	–7.5	5.4

Source: IMF, 1999; Government of Malaysia, Statistics Department

TABLE 2
MALAYSIAN UNEMPLOYMENT RATES, 1995–2000

1995	1996	1997	1998	1999	2000
2.8	2.6	2.6	4.9	3.0*	3.0**

* Final quarter figure, though crude average 3.6% owing largely to 1st quarter figure

** Estimate

Source: Government of Malaysia Department of Statistics; Ministry of Human Resources; MTUC.

unemployment among Malaysian citizens has not increased significantly, or for any length of time. Indeed, the impact has been less severe than expected by the government and labour movement, as indicated by the fact that early estimates of 500,000 unemployed, by December 1999, were downgraded to 130,000 (Interview B, 1999). The migrant workforce has borne the brunt of the impact.

Malaysia's economy was adversely affected but a number of interrelated reasons account for the limited recorded employment impact. Firstly, employers have been reluctant to dismiss permanent local workers, preferring instead to terminate fixed-term contracts, utilize temporary lay-offs and voluntary severance (Peetz and Todd, 2000). Secondly, Malaysia experienced a significant labour shortage in the growth years of the 1990s, and in the context of proximate tight labour market experience and an anticipation of a relatively quick upturn, employers may have retained staff. Thirdly, employers seem to have utilized flexibility strategies that fall short of redundancy. For instance the automobile industry moved from a three- to a one-shift operation and rotated three-month temporary lay-offs. High levels of overtime and variable pay, in which productivity bonuses can be as much as 40 per cent of final pay, as in Amalgamated Steel, provide much scope for adjustment of labour costs. This has been combined by the postponement of annual bonuses, which amount to between one-and-a-half and two months' salary per year (Interview B, 1999). Fourthly, such an approach may have been underpinned by Malaysia's relatively generous severance laws, which require ten days' pay for each year of service up to two years, and 20 days thereafter. This makes severance unattractive for employers (Peetz and Todd, 2000), but attractive to employees with long length of service and in industries with 'good' schemes, as is the case in the banking sector (Interview B, 1999). Finally, and most significantly, the estimated legal and illegal migrant labour force of 3 to 3.5 million (Human Rights Watch, 1998) provided significant numerical flexibility required for rapid adjustment (see Table 3). This has enabled Malaysia to buffer its citizens and to export the problem by sending the migrant workers back to some of the poorest or worst affected economies in Asia.

The migrant labour force bore the brunt of the Malaysian government's initial response to the unfolding of the crisis through its espoused policy of maintaining Malaysian employment at the expense of migrants. The sectoral concentration of migrants in industries such as construction, where migrants have been estimated to account for 80 per cent of the labour force (Interview B, 1999), plantations and other sectors, has provided national employment flexibility without significant political fallout. Local labour has

TABLE 3
SEMI-SKILLED AND UNSKILLED FOREIGN WORKERS, BY
NATIONALITY, PENINSULAR MALAYSIA, 1997-9*

Nationality	Total			Percentage		
	1997**	1998	1999	1997**	1998	1999
Indonesian	716,033	490,550	55,889	64.0	63.3	83.9
Bangladeshi	307,696	224,609	743	27.5	29.0	1.1
Filipino	24,882	14,828	222	2.2	1.9	0.3
Thai	21,438	7,222	437	1.9	0.9	0.7
Pakistani	18,052	8,905	2	1.6	1.1	0.0
Others	32,071	28,596	9,314	2.8	3.8	14.0
Total	1,120,172	774,810	66,607	100.0	100.0	100.0

* Figures at middle of September 1999
** Until November 1997.

Source: Immigration Department, obtained from MTUC, online at www.mtuc. org.my/statistics/

generally maintained employment although this may have been at the cost of downward flexibility in terms of pay and concomitant impact on purchasing power. However, the fact that job security has been largely maintained in conjunction with the relatively rapid recovery may have enhanced perceptions of regime competence.

POLITICAL RUPTURES PAST AND PRESENT

Malaysia's policy response was presented in the Western and Malaysian press as the outcome of Mahathir's reversal of the more orthodox, and responsible, prescriptions of Anwar Ibrahim, the Finance Minister and Deputy Prime Minister. Domestically this reversal was used to enhance the image of Mahathir as a politician who is able and successful in standing firm in the face of international adversity. The actions also allowed Mahathir to contain the tide that had swept President Suharto of Indonesia from power (see Hitchcock, this volume) and allowed Mahathir to act against Anwar Ibrahim's attempt to enhance his political power within UMNO. In so far as Malaysia escaped the dislocations of high unemployment – although a large proportion of the working population may have seen a significant reduction in their income and spending power – one source of a potential challenge from labour was also avoided. Future international analysis and memory of the Malaysian economic crisis will focus on the significance, or otherwise, of Malaysia's policy response. However, domestically the overriding memory, and continuing analysis, will be on the consequences and opportunity that the economic crisis afforded to the adversaries in addressing underlying and pre-existing tensions within Malaysia's political economy, and the impact of the formation of a new political party centred around Ibrahim. Not least of this analysis will be on the role and consequences of these events on labour.

The economic crisis coincided with, and accelerated underlying tensions that gave rise to a new and significant rupture at the centre of Malaysian politics, as factions seeking a widening of the distribution of economic patronage, in a context of the increasing importance of money in political campaigning, attempted to use the economic crisis to advance, or protect, their political positions (T. Gomez, personal communication). This was exemplified in the conflict between Anwar Ibrahim and Prime Minister Mahathir

Mohamed, which finally culminated in the former's dismissal and subsequent arrest and imprisonment. This set in motion a division within the United Malay Nasional Organisation (UMNO), led to the formation of a reform movement (*Reformasi*) and a new political party led by Anwar's wife, which drew upon Anwar's popular and grass-roots support. Such developments have the potential to fracture ethnic allegiances to the centre by creating intra-ethnic political competition. Indeed, a viable political discourse from which to mount an effective challenge for power would need to highlight difference as opposed to sameness, and thereby call into question the assumptions underlying notions of Malay ethnic and cultural unity and associated Malay political and economic advancement (Hua Wu Yin, 1983; Singh, 1988). This was not the first time UMNO was divided or labour drawn into the fractures. Competition over access to the resources of patronage, despite unequal distribution of Malay wealth, led to a split in the ruling Malay party UMNO with the formation of Semangat '46 by Tengku Razaleigh, ex-vice-president of UMNO, in 1987. Like the recent division this was publicly justified by the challengers on grounds that only some Malays benefited from the NEP and the most favoured were those close to the Prime Minister (Means, 1991; Milne and Mauzy, 1999). Razaleigh, the president of Semangat '46, in an attempt to broaden his support base and offer an alternative way to the 'autocratic and authoritarian' regime of the Barisan Nasional, ratified the MTUC labour manifesto for the 1990 election. The party promised to repeal oppressive labour legislation and give labour its 'due place under the Malaysian sun' (Surah Buroh, 1990). This challenge to UMNO was spearheaded by a coalition of opposition parties with which trade-union activists were attached, including the current president of the MTUC, who was a leading member of Semangat '46.

Union association with opposition parties and international campaigning over freedom of association issues in Malaysia's export-processing zones was not without cost. In the late 1980s to the mid-1990s, the MTUC came under increasing public government pressure, and trade union leaders such as Zainal Rampak, the president of the MTUC, were prosecuted and publicly attacked while the MTUC was bypassed in national forums in favour of the breakaway MLO, which was seen as an arm of the ruling Barisan Nasional. The opposition unions were accused of failing to credit the achievements of the Malay elite in advancing

the economic well-being of the Malay masses owing to their links
with political opponents. Leaders of the labour movement were
accused of being anti-nation, anti-democratic and, therefore, anti-
Malay (*New Straits Times*, various dates). International actions led
to accusations of tarnishing the image of the country abroad and
potentially jeopardising investment and thus employment levels
and workers' welfare. These sentiments were expressed in an
editorial which wrote:

> Pity workers whose trade union leaders no longer listen to
> their voices and pay no heed to their need for leadership.
> ... These are leaders ... who warble and yodel on
> international platforms to besmirch the government and
> paint a distorted picture of the welfare of the workers in
> this country. Critics, especially jaded trade union leaders
> who harbour hopes of an opportunity to become politicians
> ... turn a blind eye to the nation's achievement in
> protecting the labour force (*New Straits Times*, May 1993).

Rampak was a particular target due to his long-standing attachment
to the opposition, his presidency of the MTUC, his position as a
member of the general council of the ILO and his personification
as the trade-union voice of Malaysian workers. Personal criticism of
him has included labelling him a traitor to the nation, an accusation
that reportedly filtered down into his local community and affected
his children at school (Interview D, 2000). As an example, Deputy
Prime Minister Ghafar Baba proclaimed that:

> Destructive methods were being used by a small group of
> unionists, who also happened to be opposition party
> leaders ... who were not bothered about peace and
> harmony and who placed their own interest above the
> country's interest. ... We know that the workers form the
> majority of voters, and if they feel that we do not look
> after their welfare they would not have returned us (*New
> Straits Times*, September 1992).

Such a reaction has not only been about political claims over who
the guardians of the Malay interest are, but more significantly also
about the potential questions that the growth of Malay labour
raises over who is to define the Malay interest and what it should
constitute. In many respects UMNO, as the embodiment of the

Malay interest, has succeeded in undermining trade union action by incorporating the Malay workers into the nationalist project. The research officer of the MTUC paraphrased a typical Malay response in the following words: 'Why go on picket? Why are you picketing? You are damaging national harmony ... you are making us look bad to outsiders.' He concluded: 'The philosophy in Malaysia is that we have to cooperate, and be seen that we are cooperating for the good of the nation.' (Interview A, 1999)

Since the mid-1990s an internal challenge to political control was again mounted, this time by Anwar Ibrahim, the ex-deputy prime minister, in a bid to wrest control from the incumbent prime minister. However, unlike the earlier challenge, this was less explicit and more a battle of position within the structures of UMNO. Mahathir brought Anwar into government in the early 1980s largely in response to Anwar's popularity and widespread grass-roots Malay support. Since his entry to the government, Anwar developed a broad constituency forging links with, and being a friend to NGOs, the labour movement and other groups who lacked privileged access to the increasingly centralized and small network of dominant politicians and their business associates (T. Gomez, personal communication; Interviews A, C and D, 1999, 2000). Anwar also courted businessmen and raised funds to finance his political campaigns, but these businessmen are those that have been excluded from the first wave of patronage as a result of late entry (Gomez and Jomo, 1997). The growing importance of money for political campaigns threatened to marginalize those without access to funds (Milne and Mauzy, 1999); while the number of Malays using their contacts to gain monetary advantage grew, the most lucrative opportunities were reserved for those closest to Mahathir (Gomez and Jomo, 1997). These issues of power and resource distribution among factions were once again the terrain of intra-Malay conflict, although these were expressed in terms of *Korupsi Kronisma Nepotisma* (KKN or corruption, cronyism and nepotism). This intra-Malay competition has again created internal fragmentation and division and threatened 'in-group' solidarity, although initially the main threat was to the leadership of UMNO, rather than to UMNO as the institutionalized political form for the protection and advancement of the 'Malay world-view' (Ibrahim, 1998).

The ousting of Anwar Ibrahim led to the formation of an alternative party that drew much of its support from Anwar's UMNO followers and other reformers who had alternative affiliations in and out of the political party structure. Keadilan attempted to form a broad coalition of opposition parties with the aim of consolidating broad grass-roots support to unseat Mahathir and his close circle of political allies and businessmen. In response, Mahathir re-grouped his forces within UMNO and made much of ex- Semangat '46 members, who were re-incorporated into UMNO in October 1996 – a move thought by some to be aimed at countering the growing power of Anwar Ibrahim. Given Anwar's imprisonment, his expulsion from UMNO and weakening of his faction in UMNO, due to defections to Keadilan and realignments within UMNO, it is becoming increasingly unlikely that Anwar could return to UMNO's fold, in the near future at least. In the meantime Keadilan attempted to consolidate its position by considering a merger with the leftist Parti Rakyat Malaysia (PRM), and continues to attempt to form an alternative multiethnic coalition – the Barisan Alternative, which would include the reformist oppositional, and largely Chinese, Democratic Action Party (DAP). UMNO is concerned over the fact that it lost a substantial majority of the Malay vote to the opposition, and in particular, to PAS, the Islamic-based Malay opposition party. Despite the loss of the Malay vote, the ruling coalition has maintained power through the Chinese vote, which was possibly due to the representation of the Barisan Alternative as volatile and undisciplined in the Malaysian Press and thereby heightening fear of turmoil in the light of the violence against the Chinese in Indonesia.

MALAYSIAN LABOUR IN THE POLITICAL CRISIS

Since 1996 the state, and the prime minister, have appealed to the trade union movement to become a 'partner' in the private-sector-driven concept of 'Malaysia Incorporated' (*Star*, 30 July 1996). The condition that the unions accept a business orientation in the workplace and assist in attracting inward investment has been increasingly accepted by the peak union body, the MTUC. The state has continued to attack trade union leaders for tarnishing the country's image abroad (*Star*, 29 August 1996). The MTUC has been portrayed as less confrontational, although the personalization of conflicts between it and the state have changed. Both these factors have served to divide the labour movement in developing a common strategy to the political crisis.

Zainal Rampak had resigned his position from the oppositional Semangat '46 in 1994 and was being wooed into UMNO by Anwar Ibrahim, a friendship with whom dated from the early 1980s. In 1996, Rampak joined UMNO and his application was personally handled by Anwar Ibrahim, and passed by the latter to Mahathir Mohamed. Anwar Ibrahim also nominated Rampak for a senatorship, which while initially rejected by Mahathir was finally approved after Anwar's dismissal. The strategy of bringing Rampak closer to UMNO can be viewed in the context of Anwar's attempts to strengthen his position within UMNO and in the light of the changing ethnic composition of the working class, which has made it increasingly difficult for the state to bypass the Malaysian labour movement by asserting the primacy of ethnic restructuring. The state's recognition of this is reflected in the fact that after wooing Rampak into the UMNO fold, the minister of human resources advised the Malaysian Labour Organization (MLO) to dissolve itself and join the MTUC (Interviews A and B, 1999). This was prompted not only by the failure of the MLO to undermine the MTUC but by potential internal reconfiguration of the balance of forces within the MTUC itself. One of the respondents stated the merger between the MTUC and the MLO was

> again, very political. In the 1994 election Syed Shahir, a member of PRM, challenged Zainal [Rampak] for the first time. He lost by only four votes, so it was a close fight. The government suddenly realized that Zainal was losing ground in the MTUC, so basically they instructed the MLO to go back into the MTUC to strengthen Zainal's support, which was what happened. In the following election Zainal won by over 100 votes, which is roughly similar to the votes the MLO brought in by joining the MTUC (Interview A, 1999).

Since 1996/97, Rampak has been mobilizing his supporters and advocating that the labour movement adopt a strategy of the 'loyal opposition', within the ranks of the government, as the best means of extracting concessions. Indeed this strategy of working with the government is now being pursued by the president's advocacy of the Singapore model as one appropriate to Malaysia (Interviews D and E, 2000). Rampak himself recognizes the impact of the changing ethnic composition of the working class on trade union leaderships, arguing

> the bulk of the workers today are Malays, bumiputra-natives; in the early days of the labour movement there were not many Malay leaders. ... What is significant and quite encouraging [is] the situation has changed as far as Malay leadership and trade unions are concerned ... before it was an Indian majority, now it's a Malay majority. It's a very good sign – they know what they are looking for, they no longer have to rely on the government, they can rely on their own resources. ... There is a need for there to be Malay working-class leaders to make sure the balance is there ... the only people who can fight are the Malay leaders; of course, while *we* do that *we* don't forget about the other races (Interview C, 1999).

However, the extent to which political party affiliations and trade unionism can be reconciled is problematic, not least in the context of dependent development where the state is subservient to business interests. This is recognized by elements within the labour movement who have less of an attachment to UMNO. In the words of one respondent:

> Those that are strongly in UMNO manage to adopt a very dualistic approach. On the one hand they talk about Malays, the importance of joining UMNO and the Malay leadership in this country; on the other they talk about the rights of workers and workers' struggle, when in fact UMNO is the one who's actually being very anti-worker ... it's a very pro-business government (Interview A, 1999).

Rampak still feels betrayed by the challenge to his presidency, particularly in the light of his marginal 1994 victory, the loss of which would have been a severe blow after 40 years of commitment to the trade union movement (Interview C, 1999). The consequence of such a challenge has been that he has attempted to marginalize his opponents by filling the MTUC and union movement with the new and up-and-coming Malay trade unionists, which is also reconfiguring its ethnic profile. As one respondent reported,

> [the General Secretary] is the last remnant of Indian influence in the movement. ... In the last MTUC elections it was felt that the president wanted to push away all the Indians; [however] he needed [the general secretary] because he was able to bring a lot of the Indian delegates into Zainal's camp, but the Indians are feeling very much pushed out (Interview A, 1999).

The government is reinforcing the reconfiguration of the MTUC. Thus, in 1996, some two weeks after Prime Minister Mahathir expressed regret that the labour movement had not entered into the partnership implied in the notion of Malaysia Inc (*Star*, 30 July 1996), he offered to include union representatives in trade missions if the unions were to promote Malaysia. In the meantime, the Minister of Human Resources publicly identified and accused the Indian General Secretary of the MTUC of criticizing the government on international platforms. The public attack identified the General Secretary and his allies as critical opponents, in an attempt to identify the significance of personalities and ethnicities in government-trade union relations. According to the General Secretary, the human resources minister

> was trying to say that the MTUC is all right, the leaders are all right, except this one person ... [it] could be he wanted to try to create a kind of racial dissension. ... The government always likes to say the ethnic Indians are doing this, the ethnic Chinese are doing that, the Malays are all right. They always tried to create this kind of feeling. I think they were trying to separate us, and hoping that when the elections came the delegates would reject [me] (Interview B, 1999).

The change of media and government stance towards the MTUC has coincided with the political ruptures. These ruptures are significant to the labour movement, given the fact that the relationship between Anwar Ibrahim, Zainal Rampak and labour has been long-standing. For instance, Anwar was responsible for the withdrawal of criminal breach of trust charges against the MTUC president. He also assisted the MTUC president in projects relating to the education of labour while saving the Transport Workers Union (the president of which is Rampak) by arranging a bale-out and a low-interest loan. Some within the Malaysian labour movement question whether the MTUC is being coopted by the establishment in an attempt to re-orientate state strategy from opposition to incorporation to minimize the threat from labour as a result of the inherent dilemmas resulting from the development process. While Rampak professes friendship with Anwar and affirms his commitment to worker advancement, by ensuring that the MTUC officially remains distant from the political ruptures he has assisted Mahathir in neutralizing the labour movement's potential support of Anwar. Rampak argues that he joined UMNO the institution, not Anwar the man, and that the avenue for worker advancement is through the structures of UMNO rather than outside. However, such a strategy, rather than being collective, needs to be individually based. Thus Rampak revels in his position as senator and as a member of the National Economic Advisory Board, and his supporters believe that such positions can advance the labour agenda. In this sense the old strategy of the MTUC remaining out of politics but allowing individual involvement is being continued but with a justification based upon the possibility of achieving concessions. However, such a strategy does not appear to have been planned but possibly opportunistic. As Rampak says,

> it's not necessary [for the MTUC to attach itself to a political party], ... you can use a political party to strengthen your position. It's better ... if I can do it through the present government, why should we have to link with any political party? ... [However], Mahathir was very clever, he caught us before anybody snapped us. ... He has good intentions ... he's changed. He's been saying he appreciates the workers' contribution during the economic downturn, helping to make the economy recover unlike workers in Korea, Thailand and Indonesia (Interview C, 1999).

However, there are those who remain sceptical of Mahathir's strategy and fearful of possible trade union incorporation. The General Secretary for example argues that

> Mahathir planned to neutralize the labour movement prior to Anwar's dismissal. For instance, despite Mahathir's antagonism to labour, he called a MTUC

delegation to meet him personally, in August 1998, and out of the blue offered a minimum wage of 1200 Ringgits – we had asked for 600 ... A month later on September first he introduced currency controls. Then on September the second [he] announced the dismissal of the Deputy Prime Minister. It was quite clear to us that he had said this because he was getting his groundwork ready for the dismissal ... because for whatever reason Anwar Ibrahim had been a good friend of the MTUC. ... When the dismissal took place [Mahathir] of course knew there would be a lot of protests, and I think he wanted to be sure that the MTUC doesn't get into that protest (Interview B, 1999).

Indeed, the Prime Minister to date has rejected demands for a redundancy fund based on a nominal employer contribution, promised but not delivered on a national minimum wage and failed to ratify Core Labour Standards. As a result, the pro-government, pro-business press has been applauding the responsibility of Malaysian trade unions during the crisis. In the meantime the divisions within the labour movement are symbolized by the fact that (as at July 2000) a plaque that commemorates Anwar Ibrahim's opening of the new MTUC headquarters in Subang Jaya remains prominently displayed signifying the past and current link between Anwar Ibrahim and the MTUC. While the labour movement did not officially involve itself in the political ruptures, the MTUC General Council called on affiliates to wear white ribbons as a symbol of justice and freedom against the backdrop of protests over the detention of Anwar Ibrahim (MTUC, 1998).

Despite the support within the labour movement for Anwar Ibrahim, and what he has come to symbolize, the recent political ruptures led to a position where working-class issues were utilized less than in previous elections. Despite its long-standing policy, the MTUC did not issue the labour manifesto for the 1999 election, a result of behind-the-scenes mobilization by Rampak. As one trade unionist said, 'The outcome was orchestrated by Zainal Rampak. He mobilized his supporters to ... block the manifesto. More than 80 members were present, double than we normally have ... some who have never attended a meeting before' (email circular, MTUC, 1999). Another leader within the MTUC said 'this is the most shameful day in the 50-year history of the MTUC' (email circular, MTUC, 1999). While Rampak asserts the need to assist the government in times of economic crisis, he has made little public mention of the role of labour in the political turmoil. As a result some 17 unions independently issued a manifesto for the election, indicating division within the movement over the best tactics to advance the labour and political interest of Malaysian workers. Indeed, de facto political involvement is exemplified by the fact that in the summer of 1999, a number of trade unions and NGOs presented joint demands to the opposition front as a condition for endorsing their support. The result was the inclusion of a number provisions into the manifestos of opposition parties regarding the minimum wage, retrenchment funds as well as statements on fair distribution.

DISCUSSION AND CONCLUSION

Despite the changing context of labour politics in Malaysia's ethno-economy, the utilization of a potential labour movement split should the MTUC favour any particular coalition of parties has in effect assisted Mahathir in ensuring labour does not enter into the political arena over his split with Anwar. The MTUC president has utilized the historical precedent of individual political action despite, or because, of the changing context. Rampak and his supporters believe his entry into the government, which accords him 'greater respect when [he] meet[s] Ministers', enhances his potential to influence from within, and possibly extract concessions due to the leverage of the changing ethnic composition of the labour movement and workforce. The Prime Minister in the meantime is providing unprecedented access to Rampak in an attempt to keep him close to the centre lest he lead the labour movement into the opposition camp. Should the moderate stance provide returns, which it has not to date (MTUC, personal communication, 2000), Rampak would have advanced the labour interest after many years of government hostility, and contributed to sustaining the organizational unity of UMNO as a representative of the Malay interest. If labour cannot leverage concessions, the MTUC would have lost an opportunity fully to exploit the opportunity to directly influence the agenda of a multiethnic opposition coalition. This could have assisted in broadening the political discourse from one of ethnicity to one that incorporates issues of distribution, democracy and social justice. The President and his supporters have, at best, preferred to wait for more controlled and limited change within UMNO. They have possibly aligned themselves with the quiet but latent reformers and Anwar sympathizers within UMNO who believe that the breakaway strategy does not best serve the Malay interest. However, by so doing, and awaiting what are uncertain outcomes, these labour leaders have elevated UMNO above the labour interest. In the meantime, despite the past misgivings over Anwar's intentions for courting labour, he has become a symbol around which to mobilize. Indeed, one of the respondents reported cries of *Reformasi* (the opposition slogan) as an indication of labour resistance and opposition to injustice within one of the US-owned factories (Interview E, 2000). Anwar's increasing distance from UMNO could be regarded with optimism. If Anwar is to re-launch a political career, he needs, more than ever, to consolidate and deliver to his constituencies of support. In the meantime, the longer Anwar remains incarcerated the lower the likelihood of the issue being forgotten, and higher the likelihood of consolidating the loyal activists and support around him. The power of the symbolism of injustice also remains powerful in attempts to maintain, develop and extend mass support.

While issues of ethnicity have been an enduring phenomenon in Malaysian political and cultural discourse, this continues to impact upon the labour movement. Links between union leaders and the ruling and opposition political parties, together with the ethnic division of labour, have historically provided many opportunities for fragmentation and division and few for cross- and intra-ethnic labour solidarity. However economic development and the concomitant change in the ethnic composition of the Malaysian labour force are raising new issues of intra-ethnic difference. Recent perceptions of injustice and regime illegitimacy, which cut into the post-independence, post-NEP Malay 'consensus', have not been fully translated into cohesive political action, and this has occurred in a context where labour and labour issues are potentially less marginal than has been the case in the past. In this can be discerned the potential seeds of intra-ethnic differences over the best tactics for labour in the context of a Malay labour movement and labour force. These differences are unlikely to be overcome even if the incumbent UMNO leadership were to change its long-standing policy of labour exclusion. It is unclear if such a strategy could provide material concessions and avoid trade union incorporation, particularly in light of Malaysia's position as an export platform for multinational companies and the increasing representation of business and capital interests within UMNO.

For the moment, the Malaysian state has successfully contained the labour movement's official and active involvement in the Anwar Ibrahim issue and its potential ramifications for UMNO. The medium- to long-term prospects of an opposition coalition, united primarily by a desire to topple Prime Minister Mahathir Mohamed, remain uncertain, not least because of Malaysia's economic recovery. In this context, it is, arguably, fortunate that the labour movement's fundamental difficulty in resolving its dilemma of involvement in politics enabled it to avoid official identification with the opposition camp. The opposition however is still consolidating and reconfiguring. It is itself using the ethnic card in the publicity it has accorded to the importance of Chinese support in the BN victory at the last election. More significantly, it continues to represent the deep malaise and dissatisfaction among Malays, particularly over the treatment of Anwar Ibrahim. Should the opposition survive, the divisions within UMNO and between it and the new cross-ethnic, but largely, Malay opposition may result in the Malay vote being mobilized on Malay ethnic and other identities. This may be particularly the case if the proposed merger between Keadilan and the leftist PRM (Parti Rakyat Malaysia) goes ahead, as is likely. Such a situation, in the context of competition in an ethnically imbued political discourse would have difficulty in avoiding issues over the legitimate definition of the 'true spirit' of UMNO, the nature of Malaysian society and the issues of equitable returns to the Malay masses. Concession extraction and alliances could spring up between different factions within and across each of the parties, opening up the agenda of distributional struggle as the factions fight for the fractured Malay vote. Such a situation has the potential to lead Malaysia into a trajectory of economic dependency in a context of non-ethnic political pluralism. This situation, which was not the design of the major protagonists, can only bode well for Malaysian workers, and especially so if its representatives are outside and inside the ruling coalition. While the best that Malaysian labour can hope for, in the current climate, is incremental rather than transformational improvements, this situation is potentially a better one than the labour movement has been in for some time. Such a circumstance, however, is not one where labour organization is part of a social movement, and herein lies the felt lost opportunity for Malaysia's political activists and social reformers.

REFERENCES

Allen, S. (1994), 'Race, Ethnicity and Nationality: Some Questions of Identity', in H. Ashfer and M. Maynard (eds), *The Dynamics of Race and Gender: Some Feminist Interventions*. London: Taylor & Francis.

Bowie, Angela (1994), 'The Dynamics of Business-government Relations in Industrialising Malaysia', in A. MacIntyre (ed.), *Business and Government in Industrialising Malaysia*. Ithaca, NY: Cornell University Press.

Caspersz, Donella (1998), 'Globalization and Labour. A Case Study of EPZ Workers in Malaysia', *Economic and Industrial Democracy*, Vol.19, No.2, pp.253–286.

Chang, Ha-Joon, Gabriel Palma and D. Hugh Wittaker (1998), 'The Asian Crisis: Introduction', *Cambridge Journal of Economics*, Vol.22, pp.649–652.

Cheah Boon Kheng (1999), *From the End of Slavery to the ISA: Human Rights History in Malaysia*, keynote address to Second International Malaysian Studies Conference, 3 August 1999, University of Malaya, Kuala Lumpur. (Online at http://malaysiakini.com/pssm/conference/Cheah_Boon_Kheng_Keynote.htm)

Clegg, S., Ibarra-Colado, E., and Bueno-Rodriquez, L. (1999), *Global Management: Universal Theories and Local Realities*. London: Sage.

Deyo, Frederick (1989), 'Labour Systems, Production Structures and Export-manufacturing: The East Asian NICs', *South East Asian Journal of Social Science*, Vol.17, No.2, pp.8–24.

Fenton, Steve (1999), *Ethnicity: Racism, Class and Culture*. Basingstoke: MacMillan.

Giddens, Anthony (1984), *The Constitution of Society*. Cambridge: Polity Press.

Gomez, Terence (1991), *Money Politics in the Barisan Nasional*. Kuala Lumpur: Forum.

Gomez, Terence, and Jomo, K.S. (1997), *Malaysia's Political Economy: Politics Patronage and Profits*. Cambridge: Cambridge University Press.

Gomez, Terrence (1999), *Chinese Business in Malaysia: Accumulation, Accommodation and Ascendance*. Surrey: Curzon Press.

Hua Wu Yin (1983), *Class and Communalism in Malaysia*. London: Zed Books.

Human Rights Watch (1998), 'Bearing the Brunt of the Asian Economic Crisis: The Impact on Labour Rights and Migrant Workers in Asia', online at www.hrw.org/ reports98, November 1999.

Ibrahim, Zahadi (1998), *The Malay Labourer: By the Window of Capitalism*. Singapore: ISEAS.

International Monetary Fund (1999), *IMF Staff Country Report No.99/85*, Washington: IMF.

Interview A, Research Officer of MTUC, 14 July 1999, Subang Jaya, Malaysia.

Interview B, General Secretary of MTUC, 16 July 1999, Subang Jaya, Malaysia.

Interview C, President of MTUC, 20 July 1999, Subang Jaya, Malaysia.

Interview D, Trade Union Activist, 4 July 2000, Kuala Lumpur, Malaysia.

Interview E, Malaysiakini, 4 July 2000, Subang Jaya, Malaysia.

Jesudason, James (1989), *Ethnicity and the Economy – The State, Chinese Business and Multinationals in Malaysia*. Singapore: Oxford University Press.

Jesudason, James (1996), 'The Syncretic State and the Structuring of Oppositional Politics in Malaysia', in Garry Rodan (ed.), *Political Oppositions in Industrialising Asia*. London: Routledge.

Jenkins, R (1996), *Social Identity*. London: Routledge.

Jomo, K.S. (1989), *Beyond 1990: Considerations for a New National Strategy*. Kuala

Lumpur: Institute of Advanced Studies, University of Malaya.
Jomo, Sundaram, and Todd, Patricia (1994), *Trade Unions and the State in Peninsular Malaysia*. London: Routledge.
Kua, A. (1996), *Authoritarian Populism in Malaysia*. Basingstoke: Macmillan Press.
Kuruvilla, Surosh and Arudsothy, Ponniah (1995), 'Economic Development Strategy, Government Labour Policy and Firm Level Industrial Relations Practices in Malaysia', in A. Verma, T. Kochan and D. Lansbury (eds), *Employment Relations in The Growing Asian Economies*. London: Routledge.
Malaysia, 7th Malaysia Plan 1996–2000 (1996). Kuala Lumpur: Economic Planning Unit Statistics Department. Online at www.statistics.gov.my/english/keystats, accessed April 2000.
Ministry of Human Resources, online at wysisyg://118/http://www.jaring.my/ksm/key.htm, accessed April 2000.
Means, Gordon (1991), *Malaysian Politics: The Second Generation*. Singapore: Oxford University Press.
Mohapatara, Prabhu (1997), 'Asian Labour: Culture, Consciousness and Representation'. Amsterdam: CLARA Working Papers on Labour. Online at http://www.iisg.nl/~clara/clarawp.htm, accessed April 2000.
MTUC (1998), 'Call To Wear White Ribbon', Labour News, October.
MTUC, online at http://mtuc.org.my/statistics/, accessed April 2000.
Milne, R.S., and Diane K. Mauzy (1999), *Malaysian Politics under Mahathir*. London: Routledge.
New Straits Times, 8 May 1992; 'DPM: Don't Ape Foreign Unionists', 29 Sep. 1992; 'Partners in Unions', 15 Jan. 1993; 2 May 1993; 12 June 1997.
Nixon, Frederick, and Walters, Bernard (1999), 'The Asian Crisis: Causes and Consequences', *The Manchester School*, Vol.67, No.5, pp.496–523.
Peetz, David and Todd, Trish (2000), *Globalisation and Employment Relations in Malaysia*. Geneva: ILO (forthcoming).
Poole, Michael (1986), *Industrial Relations: Origins and Patterns of National Diversity*. London: Routledge & Kegan Paul.
Singh, Hari (1998), 'Tradition, UMNO and political succession in Malaysia', *Third World Quarterly*, Vol.19, No.2, pp.241–54.
Smith, Wendy (1994), 'A Japanese Factory in Malaysia: Ethnicity as a Management Ideology', in K.S. Jomo (ed.), *Japan and Malaysian Development*. London: Routledge.
Southall, Roger (ed.) (1988), *Trade Unions and the New Industrialisation of the Third World*. London: Zed Books.
Star, 'PM: Unions Can Help Make Malaysia Inc. Unbeatable', 30 July 1996; 29 Aug. 1996; 10 July 1993.
Surah Buroh (1990), Vol.34, No.2.
Valenzuela, Jaime (1992), 'Labour Movements and Political Systems: Some Variations', in M. Regini (ed.), *The Future of Labour Movements*. London: Sage.
Wadd, Peter (1988), 'The Japanisation of the Malaysian Trade Union Movement', in Southall, R. (ed.), *Trade Unions and the New Internationalisation of the Third World*. London: Zed Books.
Wadd, Peter, and Jomo, Sundaram (1994), 'In House Unions: Looking East for Industrial Relations', in Jomo, S. (ed.), *Japan and Malaysian Development*. Routledge: London.
Yun Hing Ai (1990), 'Capital Transformation and Labour Relations in Malaysia', *Labour and Industry*, Vol.3, No.1, pp.76–92.
Zaidi, S. (1975), *History of the MTUC*. Petaling Jaya: MTUC.

6

Tourism and Total Crisis in Indonesia: The Case of Bali

MICHAEL HITCHCOCK

A common theme within the literature of tourism is that political stability is a precondition for the prosperity of tourism. There is a widespread view among tourism analysts that international visitors are very concerned about their personal safety (Edgel, 1990: 119) and that 'tourism can only thrive under peaceful conditions' (Pizam and Mansfield, 1996: 2). Tourism is perceived as being particularly vulnerable to international threats such as terrorism (Richter and Waugh 1986: 238), though analysts recognize that it may be impossible to isolate tourists completely from the effects of international turbulence (Hall and O'Sullivan, 1996: 120). One of the most widely cited cases of the effect of international strife on leisure travel is that of the Gulf War in 1991. The downturn that accompanied the outbreak of hostilities had an impact not only on the area immediately surrounding the strife, but on international tourism generally. Indonesia, for example, was among those affected by the war, though it was located a great distance from the scene of conflict. Tourist arrivals in Indonesia tumbled in the first half of 1991 despite its designation as 'Visit Indonesia Year', part of an ASEAN-wide tourism promotion strategy (Hitchcock, King and Parnwell, 1993: 4).

In view of tourism's sensitivity, it is also widely held, particularly by tourism promotion boards, that the press has a particular role to play in helping alleviate the fears of travellers. In this respect the media is seen as being a major force in the creation of images of safety and political stability in destination regions (Hall and O'Sullivan, 1996: 107). Not only are obvious threats to tourism such as the press coverage of terrorism seen as a cause for alarm, but so is negative reporting in general. Following the onset of the Asian monetary crisis in 1997, for example, Thailand became increasingly alarmed about the future of its tourism industry in the wake of the poor publicity and sought to counter the flood of bad news by the positive promotion of the country as a cost-effective destination (Higham, 2000: 133). Thailand's use of tourism to simultaneously boost its image and offset its budgetary deficit at a time of crisis has been covered in the professional literature, though it certainly merits further investigation.

This contribution, however, concerns the impact of the 1997 Asian monetary crisis on the tourism industry of the Indonesian island of Bali. The Indonesian experience is especially noteworthy because, in addition to suffering a financial collapse, the country has undergone a political transformation. Among the countries affected by the crisis, Indonesia's experience was arguably the most acute, with a contraction in national income of between 10 per cent and 15 per cent in 1998 (Pincus and Rizal Ramli, 1998: 723). The monetary crisis that followed the flotation of the Thai Baht on 2 July 1997 eventually led to the toppling of President Suharto's 32-year-old regime, and Indonesia rapidly became engulfed in turmoil. The impact on the country's tourism industry was apparent from the outset as visitor arrivals of 5.04 million (5,036,000) for 1997 fell short of the projected figure of 5.3 million (*Travel and Tourism Intelligence*, 1998: 89; *Travel Asia*, 1998). The decline accelerated as the crisis continued unabated into 1998 and 1999.

What is interesting about Bali in this context is the number of articles that have appeared since the onset of the crisis stressing the island's safety. Many tourism analysts have noted that Bali has remained remarkably quiet and stable, and has continued to attract tourists (e.g. *Travel Asia*, 22 May 1998), and the island's image as an exotic haven seems to have been undented by the strife that has engulfed the rest of Indonesia. Explanations for why this should be the case are usually couched in cultural terms, namely that Bali's population is Hindu and peace-loving. If Bali really has succeeded in preserving its tourism industry at a time of great political upheaval, then this presents tourism researchers with a striking anomaly within the study of tourism. This essay thus charts the impact of the Asian crisis on Bali's tourism industry and investigates the claims concerning the island's security at a time of great political upheaval. In particular it asks whether or not cultural factors alone can account for the relative peacefulness of the Balinese as compared with other Indonesians.

There are good reasons for considering alternative explanations, not least the fact that tourism is used to manage Bali's relations with Jakarta. A theme running through Picard's exemplary work on tourism in Bali is the way this industry has enhanced the islanders' leverage over Jakarta (Picard, 1996). What remains unclear, however, is precisely how this influence has been achieved, and it is the intention here to revisit Picard's analysis within the context of the Asian crisis.

In particular, this essay argues that Bali, already something of an offshore haven for Jakarta before the crisis, has become a refuge for a variety of different constituencies since the fall of Suharto. Bali, with its good air links to the major Indonesian cities and numerous hotels, provided many Chinese with sanctuary at the height of the riots. In comparison with neighbouring Java, the island remained largely strife-free, and tourism and other export industries (e.g. handicrafts) kept the economy afloat. A closer examination of how Bali works as a haven also reveals much about how the interests of these constituencies are represented in the island.

THE ISLAND OF BALI

Bali lies due east of Java and is separated from its larger neighbour by a narrow strait. With a population of over 3 million and an area covering 5,632.86 square kilometres, Bali is densely populated. A mountain range running east to west divides the island, rising to a height of 3,142 metres on the volcano of Gunung Agung. The majority of the population resides in the south-central area, which slopes from the high mountain range to the southern coast. This fertile rice-growing region is cut through by many river valleys running north to south. The Wallace Line runs between Bali and Lombok, marking the boundary of the Asian and Australian ecological zones.

The Balinese language belongs to the Austronesian family, and the Balinese share cultural features with other Austronesian peoples in maritime South East Asia and Oceania. Bali, however, was strongly influenced by a neighbouring Austronesian people, the Javanese, who had incorporated elements of Hinduism and Buddhism into their belief system. The leading royal households of East Java and Bali established close links in the late tenth century following the marriage of the Balinese prince, Udayana, and an East

Javanese princess (Hobart, Ramseyer and Leeman, 1996: 27). In 1284 Bali was subjected to Singhasari rule from East Java, after which there was a period of renewed independence that ended in incorporation into the Hindu-Javanese kingdom of Majapahit (ibid.: 33). Towards the end of Majapahit rule (1515–28) Islam became the dominant faith in Java, but Bali remained steadfastly Hindu. According to legend, the refugees from Java who refused to convert to the new religion fled to Bali (ibid.: 38).

Since 1949 the islanders have been citizens of the Republic of Indonesia, though they may be divided on ethnic grounds into the Balinese themselves and Indonesians from elsewhere. The Balinese in turn can be broken down according to religion into the 'Bali Hindu', followers of the old religion, and converts to Islam, known as Bali Islam. The latter are few and Hindus comprise between 80 and 95 per cent of the population. In contrast, Indonesia's population is predominantly Muslim, and thus Bali is often described as a Hindu island in a sea of Muslims. Tourist brochures usually emphasize the religious affiliation of the Balinese, often describing the island as the 'land of a thousand temples'. Unusually in the hyperbolic world of tourism marketing, this is an understatement: the Bureau of Religious Affairs acknowledges the existence of 4,661 temples, excluding the minor ones. There is also a small Chinese minority in Bali, whose numbers were swelled by refugees from the anti-Chinese riots of May 1998. Indonesia's 7.2 million Chinese are mainly located in the major urban centres of Java, Sumatra and Sulawesi, but it remains unclear how many normally reside in Bali.

The idea that Bali is somehow qualitatively different from the rest of Indonesia, a separate state perhaps, is reinforced at airline terminals. Flights to Denpasar, Bali's capital city, for example, are often advertised as flights to 'Bali', whereas flights to other Indonesian cities are advertised under their respective names. Despite these illusions, Bali's affairs have been inexorably linked with those of its neighbours since the island's incorporation into the Dutch East Indies and eventual independence in 1949 as part of the successor state of Indonesia. Viewed from the perspective of Jakarta, Bali is but one of 26 provinces within the archipelago republic, albeit the only Indonesian province whose territory comprises a single main island (Picard, 1993: 92). Anomalous though Bali is, it is still not accorded special status by the

Indonesian authorities like the provinces of Jakarta, Aceh (Sumatra) and Yogyakarta (Java).

THE INTRODUCTION OF TOURISM

The introduction of tourism in Bali is closely associated with the expansion of the Dutch East Indies in the early twentieth century. The colonization of Bali, which had commenced in 1846, was completed by force of arms in 1906–8. The Dutch triumph, however, was overshadowed by the suicidal resistance of the court of Badung (today's Denpasar); accompanied by their families and retainers, the rulers marched on to the Dutch guns in a fight to the end, *puputan* (Hobart, Ramseyer and Leeman, 1996: 202). Dutch war reporters and press photographers accompanying the expedition force were at hand to witness these appalling events. Two other royal households offered the same kind of resistance, though not all courts chose to fight to the end.

The protests against colonial brutality were a source of embarrassment for the Dutch and they attempted to deflect criticism by sponsoring a new image based on the preservation of Balinese culture and the development of the island as a tourist destination (Picard, 1997: 185). This was also a realistic strategy because the island lacked lands suitable for colonial plantations and produced few export commodities (Boon, 1977). Following the introduction of a regular steam-packet service in 1924, the number of tourists began to rise, sparking off a mini tourist boom that continued into the 1930s despite the recession (Picard, 1996: 25–7). Western artists, musicologists and anthropologists who had taken up residence on the island were at hand to witness the rejuvenation of arts and performances that occurred partly in response to tourism.

Long before its incorporation into the Dutch East Indies, Bali had been viewed by Dutch orientalists as a 'living museum' of the Hindu-Javanese civilization that had been swept away by the rise of Islam (Picard, 1995: 47). Thus the Dutch not only encouraged tourism but also launched a policy, known as *Balisering* (Balinization), that was designed to salvage the island's precious heritage (Picard, 1995: 47). Not only was Balinese culture going to be presented to the outside world for appreciation, but the Balinese were to be taught how to be more authentically Balinese. The new measures were designed to protect Bali's precious heritage from the onslaught of modernization, but the images that were used to promote the island still dwelt on the more extreme or unusual aspects of its culture.

Bali continued to be seen as a meeting-place of the romantic South Seas and the mysterious Orient, but this began to change when resident Western artists and academics began to place emphasis on the island's artistic achievements. One of the most influential Europeans was the Russian-German artist Walter Spies, who had built a house and studio in the cool hills of Ubud (Hitchcock and Norris, 1995). Spies and his set offered in place their own vision of a vibrant folk culture, and a key element in this interpretation was *Dance and Drama in Bali* (1938) which Spies co-authored with the British dance critic Beryl de Zoete. Spies acted as an intermediary and a source of information on Balinese culture, and as his fame spread the rich and famous began to find their way to the artist's house in the hills. Charlie Chaplin, Noel Coward and Barbara Hutton were among those who sampled Spies's vision of aesthetic Bali at first hand.

CULTURAL PEAKS

Tourism declined in the wake of the Japanese invasion of 1942, and the independence struggles that followed World War II. Visitors began to rediscover Bali in the early days of the Indonesian republic, but became discouraged by the xenophobia of the Sukarno years. The rudimentary infrastructure and turmoil were also inhibiting factors. Seemingly oblivious to the problems, President Sukarno tried to turn Bali into a showpiece for state guests. Capitalizing on the island's fame, Sukarno inaugurated the construction of a luxury beach-side hotel and new international airport. The Bali Beach Hotel was completed in 1966 just as Indonesia closed its doors to foreigners in the wake of the massacres of suspected Communists that followed the alleged Communist coup of 30 September 1965. Tourists only started returning to Bali after the installation of Suharto and what became known as the 'New Order' regime. The launch of mass tourism may be linked to the opening of the Ngurah Rai International Airport in 1969 (Picard, 1995: 49).

The spectacle of thousands of holidaymakers queuing to visit the island enabled the new government to claim that it had earned the confidence and respect of the rest of the world. To a certain extent, the regime's methods were not unlike those of the Dutch earlier in the century; in both cases tourism was seen as an effective means of salvaging each regime's reputation (Picard, 1993: 95). It was also a pragmatic step in an economy blighted by strife.

In 'New Order' Indonesia the culture of Bali came to be seen as a resource, one of the 'cultural peaks' of the emergent national culture whose function was to facilitate the growth of tourism and foster national pride. The nation had been created in response to many centuries of European expansion, creating a kind of negatively defined consciousness. Indonesian nationalism was born out of the Herderian brand of nationalism in which the nation's founders are its people; they suffered under Dutch overlordship regardless of their ethnic or religious affiliation (Hubinger, 1992: 4). The government actively supported the development of many regional cultures that would subsequently contribute to the emerging national culture. Together these cultural peaks, *puncak-puncak dan sari-sari kebudayaan*, would lay the foundations of a rich national culture (Nugroho-Heinz, 1995: 16–17). Bali, in common with the other 26 Indonesian provinces, is expected to provide nuances of colour (*aneka warna*) to the national culture (Picard, 1993: 92). The point being that the province and not the ethnic group have become the source of culture; Bali is not a state within a state, but a 'regional culture' (*kebudayaan daerah*), an integral part of the cultural heritage of Indonesia. 'Cultural tourism' was inaugurated by the Balinese authorities in 1971 for their own purposes, and was adopted by the Indonesian authorities in 1979 as the country's principle tourism policy.

THE TOURISM BOOM

Bali was expected to take its place in the new national order, part of a set of many, but the end of the oil bonanza in 1983 forced the government to take a new look at its tourism policy. Bali was far too well known abroad, often better known than Indonesia itself, as government officials often cheerfully admitted, to be allowed to drift into obscurity. The cultural policy promoted by the Ministry of Foreign Affairs in 1983 was dubbed 'cultural diplomacy' (*Diplomasi Kebudayaan*) and was designed to appeal to potential visitors and boost 'cultural tourism'. Indonesian orchestras and performers travelled the world in the 1980s and early 1990s advertising Indonesia's cultural riches. According to Picard the aim was to utilize the nation's cultural riches to promote Indonesia abroad as a country of 'high culture'. In accordance with this policy, the Balinese dance troupes that were sent on tours were expected to serve as 'artistic missions' (*misi kesinian*) to develop international tourism and simultaneously promote Indonesia's cultural image'. As a recognized 'cultural peak', Bali is supposed to represent Balinese identity on one hand and Indonesian identity on the other, and thus Balinese culture is placed in a similar position with regard to both tourism and Indonesian nationhood (Picard, 1993: 94).

In material terms, Bali is one of the wealthiest Indonesian provinces, and this is due as much to its tourist industry as to its highly skilled farmers. The island's main products are textiles, handicrafts, rice, cloves, coffee, fruit, livestock and fish products. Tourism ranks second only to agriculture in terms of the island's economic priorities (Picard, 1995: 50). Among the main tourist attractions are the beach resorts of Sanur, Kuta, Nusa Dua, Jimbaran, Lovina and Candidasa, and the inland cultural tourism resort of Ubud. The sites frequented by tourists include the 'hall of justice' Kerta Gosa in Klungkung, the Sangeh 'monkey forest', the funerary monuments of Gunung Kawi, the Goa Gajah cave in Bedulu, as well as the temples of Tanah Lot, Taman Ayum in Mengwi, Goa Lawah, Uluwatu, Besakih, Batur, Kehen and Tirtha Empul in Tampaksiring. Since the late 1960s, when tourist arrivals numbered about 30,000 per annum, tourism rose to over one million visitors a year in the 1990s. The figures, however, are based on international arrivals and do not take into account domestic visitors (ibid.).

Tourism is also a vital source of employment in Bali and people have migrated to the resorts of south Bali not only from elsewhere in the island, but also from other parts of Indonesia (Cukier, 1996: 58). In 1990 the number of people employed in tourism in Bali was greater than any other sector with the exception of agriculture (ibid.: 62). It has been projected that by 2003 tourism will employ more people than agriculture (Wall, 1991).Tourism not only generates directly related employment, but also creates a great deal of indirect employment (Cukier, 1996: 63). By 1996 the Economist Intelligence Unit was predicting that Indonesia's visitor numbers would double to 11 million arrivals in the year 2005, a projection that is likely to be derailed by the disturbances of the late 1990s.

The introduction of infrastructure associated with tourism, such as roads and airports, has facilitated the growth of small factories, turning Bali into a major handicraft-exporting centre. Handicrafts move along the hub-and-spoke distribution systems of market economies and may involve quite different producers and retailers. Goods drawn from the length and breadth of the vast Indonesian archipelago may be purchased in Bali, often without any information whence they came. Entrepreneurs in south-central Bali, belonging to various ethnic groups including Balinese, may delegate production to client groups elsewhere in the island or further afield. The demand for high-quality Balinese-made goods, especially in interior design and fashion, has undoubtedly helped many Balinese businesses to flourish. The skill of Balinese craftsmen may be seen not only as reflection of the vitality of Balinese culture , but as a rich source of added value.

TOTAL CRISIS

A joke circulating in Bali in 1998 utilized the Indonesian love of acronyms and summed up the crisis and its impact upon Indonesia as follows: first there was *kriseco* (ecological crisis), then *krismon* (monetary crisis), this was followed by *krispol* (political crisis) and so now we have *kristal* (total crisis). The joke may have been funny in Bali because it was a way of coping with the constant stream of bad news and because the crisis did not appear to be as severe on the island as elsewhere in Indonesia. The news that Bali was safe (*aman*) also spread to other parts of Indonesia and was a popular conversational theme, though reasons for why the island was an exception were usually not offered.

In the early days of the crisis the Indonesian Tourism Promotion Board followed a strategy that was similar to Thailand's. A series of measures were introduced in order to resuscitate the industry and to win back visitors discouraged by the riots and political upheavals (Henderson, 1999: 300). The board launched a 'Let's Go Indonesia' campaign, but the initiative received marginal support from the Balinese authorities, who opted for a Balinese-focused approach (Hall, 2000: 164–5). In 1998 the Indonesian government closed down the Indonesian Tourism Promotion Board in Jakarta,

TABLE 1
NUMBER OF FOREIGN VISITORS

Year	Destination	
	Indonesia	Bali
1996	5,034,472	1,140,988
1997	5,184,486	1,230,316
1998	4,606,416	1,187,153

Source: Bali Tourism Statistics 1999: 1.

partly as a cost-cutting exercise, but also as an acknowledgement of the deteriorating security situation. Bali, however, continued to function as a tourism destination and, though total arrivals did dip in 1998, the industry was able to withstand the total crisis (see Table 1)

Staff at Singapore Airlines were quick to point out that it was safe to visit Bali, though Indonesia itself was risky. In Bali itself a common topic of conversation was the fact that there was hardly any trouble and that the island was at peace. Precisely why this should be the case and precisely who or what was protecting the island remained unclear. A popular view, almost a folk model, shared by Balinese tourism workers, tourists and representatives of the tourism industry, was that the Balinese were less prone to violence on account of their religious outlook. This was a perspective shared by Juliet Coombe writing in *TNT UK*, a popular travel magazine: 'One reason Bali remained a safe and peaceful destination is the locals' Hindu faith, which makes their outlook one of acceptance and patience' (*TNT UK*, 3 August 1998: 64).

Other analysts recognized the fact that political turbulence had spilled over to Bali, but emphasized the fact that the debates had been 'orderly' and 'confined to the campus area' (*Travel Asia*, 22 May 1998). In an article for *Telegraph Travel* Alex Spillius provided a more detailed analysis on the situation under the industry-friendly title of 'Bali: We're Safe'. He argued that, although there had been student demonstrations in Bali against corrupt politicians, the protests were peaceful and had ended when all 46 members of the legislature had agreed to resign. The fact that Bali should be treated differently from the rest of Indonesia was also mentioned in the article, and an industry spokesman Lothar Pehl of the Sheraton Nusa Indah was quoted: 'People should understand that there are a lot of direct flights to Bali. And consulates and embassies must differentiate between Bali and the rest of Indonesia' (Spillius, 1998: 2).

There may be some merit in the view that for cultural reasons Bali has avoided the strife that has blighted other Indonesian islands. It is also possible that the Balinese collective memory of the bloodshed that accompanied that last change of government in 1965 has acted as a restraining force. Unlike Java, which has sprawling cities and widespread urban poverty, Bali is a small and relatively prosperous island with a limited number of ports of entry. Security is also enhanced at the village level by a network of tightly-knit residential units (banjar) that have secular and visible responsibilities which include the regulation of interaction between village members (Hobart, Ramseyer and Leeman, 1996: 88).

A widely held fear among a large section of the Balinese population is that tourists would not come to their island if they perceived it as being unsafe. This preoccupation is apparent in official reports, in the local press and in informal conversation. Before the elections in June 1999, for example, which were widely expected to turn violent, there were roadside signs bearing the slogan 'Bali is safe: the tourists come' (Bali aman: turis datang). In order to test these viewpoints, however, it would be necessary to conduct the kind of attitude surveys that would possibly not be given clearance by the Indonesian authorities at the present time. All research applications have to be approved by the Indonesian Institute of Sciences (Lembaga Ilmu Pengetahuan Indonesia), an organization that is wary about granting permits to study religious affairs.

Bali's apparent peacefulness throughout this period of transition has reinforced the view that the island is not quite like the rest of Indonesia. Despite the lack of formal recognition, it would appear that the islanders have been able to secure a greater measure of autonomy in external affairs than many other Indonesian provinces, the 'Balinese' in this case being the island's indigenous social and political elites. By emphasizing Bali's separate identity and comparative security, spokesmen for the tourism industry have created what might be regarded as a virtuous and self-fulfilling circle. The island's successful tourism industry is closely linked to its peaceful image and it could be argued that it behoves both the Balinese and the Jakarta government to maintain the status quo. Explanations in the media for Bali's relative calm have been couched in cultural terms, namely that the islanders are by nature peace-loving. Explanations for Bali's comparative security may cite cultural factors such as religion, but these do not have to be accepted at face value.

The popularly held view that Bali was not involved in the crisis is ambiguous when one considers that the island is a stronghold of one of Indonesia's largest political parties, the Indonesian Democratic Party Struggle (*Partai Demokrasi Indonesia Perjuangan*, PDIP). In reality the Balinese are not detached from Jakarta and are very concerned about being represented in the relevant ministries, particularly tourism. At the same time there is a militant Hindu party (*Bali Merdeka*) agitating in favour of outright independence for the island.

Despite its real links to the political debate, Bali appeared to remain calm whereas neighbouring Java was convulsed by a series of disturbances, including ongoing student protest, grudge killings in the countryside and rising unemployment. Balinese leaders and public opinion agreed that Bali was peaceful (*aman*), which fitted in well with the touristic image of Bali that was established in the 1930s, though this was far from being the true state of affairs. In reality, there have been numerous violent incidents on the island since 1997, but the authorities have been careful not to spread the news abroad. This carefully nurtured image was, however, compromised by widespread reporting of the demonstrations in Denpasar that followed the rejection of the bid by Megawati Sukarnoputeri (the leader of the PDIP) for the presidency by the People's Consultative Assembly in October, 1999.

The Indonesian authorities appear to be condoning a contradictory policy of regarding Bali as an integral part of the nation for internal purposes, while allowing the island to promote itself as a separate entity in international circles. The Australians, New Zealanders and Japanese, however, who comprise the bulk of Bali's inbound tourists, are relatively well informed about Indonesian affairs and are unlikely to be taken in by these policies in the long term. The emergence of a 'Boycott Bali' campaign in New Zealand in 1999 in response to Indonesia's treatment of East Timor reflects the growing sophistication of consumers. By specifically targeting Bali in this context, the campaigners were drawing attention to Bali's status as an integral part of Indonesia. Continuing unrest in Ambon, combined with the negative publicity from East Timor, is likely to lead to a further reduction in visitor arrivals in 2000 in Indonesia as a whole (Prideaux, 1999: 287), though precisely how this will impact on Bali remains unclear.

CHINESE REFUGEES

The Chinese are not a homogeneous group and a distinction is made in the Malay-Indonesian world between the descendants of the earliest migrants, who are variously called 'Straits', *Peranakan* and *Baba* (*Nyonya*) Chinese, and more recent migrants. The former have adopted local languages and customs, often intermarrying into local families, but stopping short of adopting Islam. The latter are the descendants of nineteenth- and twentieth-century migrants, predominantly from the following South Chinese dialect groups: Cantonese, Chiu Chow, Hakka and Hokkein. On independence, the Indonesians inherited an economy that had been under Dutch control, with the Chinese occupying a subsidiary role as shopkeepers and traders, and acting as middlemen between foreign exporters and indigenous farmers (May, 1978: 71).

The Chinese rapidly consolidated their position in the new republic and by 1974, the daily newspaper *Nusantara* was able to report that 90 per cent of domestic capital was in Chinese hands (May, 1978: 392). A more recent estimate credits the Chinese with 70 per cent of the country's corporate assets, despite being only three per cent of the Indonesia's population (Gomez, 1999: 8). In particular, the Chinese are thought to control roughly three-quarters of the 140 big conglomerates that dominate the Indonesian private sector (*Economist*, 26 July 1997: 11). Businessmen critical of Indonesia's regulatory environment argue that the Suharto family operated in partnership with Chinese companies in squeezing out indigenous, *pribumi*, businesses (ibid.). It is widely acknowledged that the success of the Chinese is bitterly resented by the *pribumi*, population. The Chinese are subjected to bureaucratic harassment and are obliged to adopt Indonesian-sounding names, as well as being expected to carry identity cards to prove their right of abode. The riots that accompanied the downfall of President Suharto are reminiscent of the attacks on Chinese property that occurred towards the end of the Sukarno period in 1965 (May, 1978: 135).

A critical problem in post Suharto Indonesia is the integration of the Chinese. The capital and talent of the Chinese need to be harnessed if Indonesia is to prosper, but continuing discrimination undermines their confidence. The ethnic and religious intolerance that was unleashed during the overthrow of Suharto's regime has made investors wary (Pincus and Rizal, 1998: 732). Some analysts have argued the Indonesian crisis will be prolonged if economic hardship makes the Chinese minority an easy scapegoat (Godley, 1999: 53). The disproportionate economic power enjoyed by sections of the Chinese community under Suharto is an understandable source of discontent, but the violence directed against the community as a whole during the May 1998 riots has led to international condemnation. The attacks have been widely blamed on clandestine military operations manipulated by General Prabowo, but prominent Muslim intellectuals have also suggested that some kind of 'affirmative action' may be needed to redress the economic imbalance between the Chinese and *pribumi* (indigenous) populations.

The largest contingent of refugees in Bali appears to have come from Surabaya, though Chinese from other major centres such as Jakarta, Surakarta and Yogyakarta were also well represented. Estimates regarding the number of refugees from the anti-Chinese riots varied enormously from 10,000 to 100,000 depending on who was asked. By July 1999 approximately ten per cent of the population of Denpasar, a city of 400,000 inhabitants, was thought by academics at Udayana University to be Chinese.

Initially many Chinese businessmen simply wanted to find a safe haven for their families while they continued to manage their interests in Java by making use of Bali's efficient communications. But with their property rights still vulnerable in Javanese cities, many Chinese have decided to remain, perhaps indefinitely, on the island. Some have been attracted to the light-industrial centre of Gianyar, but many have chosen to remain in South Bali and invest in the industries associated with tourism. The influx of Chinese settlers and their attendant wealth into an already densely populated and highly urbanized part of Bali seems likely to put additional strains on the environment and infrastructure.

JAKARTA- AND FOREIGN-BASED CONGLOMERATES

The indigenous Balinese have retained a substantial stake in their tourism industry, particularly with regard to small-scale hotels, shops and restaurants. Many of the larger hotels and resort-style developments, however, have been developed with funding from Jakarta and abroad. This inward investment was also encouraged by senior Balinese politicians such as Ida Bagus Oka, who was governor of Bali from 1988 to 1998. The influx of external capital and know-how was not necessarily welcomed with open arms, and the governor was widely criticized during his term of office for selling off the island to 'foreign' interests.

There have also been persistent rumours that Jakarta-based conglomerates associated with the family of former president Suharto have huge investments in upmarket tourism in Bali. These stories appeared to be vindicated by the publication of the results of an investigation into Suharto's assets by the American magazine *Time* (24 May 1999). The publication alleges that over 30 years the Suharto family accumulated $2.2 billion in hotel and tourism assets, though their current holdings are much diminished. The family has allegedly worked hard behind the scenes to safeguard their investments, but given the use of holding companies to blur direct patterns of ownership these assets are difficult to link directly to the family. The Cliff Hotel, however, which is owned by Sigit, Suharto's eldest son, is 'one of several hotels in Bali that the Suhartos at least partly own' (Colmey and Liebhold, 1999: 38).

Time's research also lends credence to the assertion made by George J. Aditjondro (1995) that five-star hotels in Nusa Dua, Jimbaran and other locations have Suharto connections. These hotels were used to host national and international gatherings that have enhanced the prestige of Indonesia while simultaneously enriching the Suhartos. Not only do the Suhartos have investments in hotels, but they also are thought to own other industries linked to tourism. Sempati Airlines, for example, which is no longer in operation, seems to have been owned by a combination of the Indonesian army and Tommy Suharto.

Aditjondro goes further than other commentators in linking members of the Suharto family with specific conglomerates associated with resorts and other businesses in Bali – see Table 2.

TABLE 2
SUHARTO FAMILY LINKS WITH BALI BUSINESSES

Siti Hardiyanti Rukmana* (Citra Lamtoro Gung)	Nusa Dua Beach Hotel
Sigit Harjojudonto** (Arseto)	Bali Cliff Hotel, Ungaran
Bambang Trihatmojo*** (Bimantara)	Sheraton Nusa Indah Resort Bali Intercontinental Hotel, Jimbaran
Hutomo Mandalaputra Suharto**** (Humpuss)	Four Seasons Resort, Jimabaran
Ari Haryo Wibowo (Arha)	Liquor imports
Sudwikatmono	Nikko Royal Hotel, Sawanga
Sukamdani S. Gitosarjono (Sahid)	Sahid Bali Seaside Hotel
Probosutejo (Mercu Buana)	Inter Laser Travel Bureau

Notes:
*   Suharto's daughter ('Tutut'), born 1949
**   Suharto's first son, born 1951
***   Suharto's second son, born 1953
****   Suharto's third son ('Tommy'), born 1962

Sources: Adidjondro 1995; *Economist*, 26 July 1997.

The list is dramatic, but difficult to verify with certainty given the reasons outlined above by *Time's* researchers.

One of Bali's most controversial developments, the Bali Nirwana resort that overlooks the sacred temple of Tanah Lot, has also been linked to members of Suharto's family. *Contours* argues that the Indonesian owners of the resort, the Bakrie brothers, have prospered as result of their ties to Suharto's children and his half-brother, Sudwikatmono. The publication also mentions the involvement in Tanah Lot of a former Suharto minister, Tungy Ariwibowo, a business partner in Tommy Suharto's Sentul racing circuit (*Contours*, 1996: 2). The same publication also ties Tommy Suharto to the 650-hectare Pecatu Graha project and two Four

Seasons Regent hotels (ibid.). The situation appears to be further complicated by the involvement of a British-based company, Time Switch Investment Ltd, which is credited as having an 80 per cent stake in the hotel and golfing project by Tanah Lot (*Down to Earth*, 1994: 19). Both the military and the political party Golkar have allegedly strongly supported the Bakries' project (ibid.).

Adidjondro also links the Suharto family to another controversial project, the development of Turtle (Serangan) Island in South Bali. Bambang has allegedly been involved in this costly and as yet unfinished project that has angered environmentalists. By building over the island and linking it to the mainland, the developers have altered the direction of sea currents, which in turn has led to erosion and the destruction of wildlife habitats.

The conglomerates clearly have a vested interest in protecting their Balinese assets, but one should not lose sight of the fact that there is a substantial small and medium-sized tourism sector in Bali, much of it locally owned. Luxury enclaves such as Nusa Dua only have limited links to the domestic economy of Bali, but many of the facilities in Kuta, which caters to lower-budget mass tourists, particularly from Australia, are in Balinese hands (Bras and Dahles, 1999: 37). These businesses are as much at risk in a downturn in tourism as the larger concerns, and thus their owners have a stake in preserving the image of Bali as a peaceful destination. What should also not be overlooked is that some of the larger hotels are not owned by external investors, but by indigenous Balinese.

CONCLUSIONS

The fact that tourists have continued to visit Bali, albeit in reduced numbers, at a time of great political turbulence in Indonesia, is a remarkable phenomenon and one that raises questions about the relationship between travel and security. This unusual state of affairs has not been subjected to a great deal of serious scrutiny, and it has largely been left to the media to provide some kind of interpretation. Nearly all the commentators have opted to account for Bali's comparative peace and calm in cultural terms, namely the peace-loving and Hindu orientation of the islanders. What appears to have escaped the attention of these authors is that Bali's history has not been especially peaceful and that there have at times been periods of great bloodshed such as suicides of 1906–8 and the massacres of 1965. There have also been violent outbreaks since the onset of the Asian crisis, and though most have received little international media attention, the pro-Megawati riots of 1999 were televised widely. It is possible that other cultural factors, such as the cohesive structure of Balinese residential units (*banjar*), have helped to keep tensions in check, but this is at best a partial explanation.

Bali's comparative security at a time of great turmoil in Indonesia is less surprising when one considers that the island has become something of an offshore haven for Java. Various Jakarta conglomerates can be linked, albeit through complex business networks, to luxury hotels and other leisure enterprises in Bali and these have largely remained open for business since the onset of the crisis. Large numbers of Chinese sought sanctuary in Bali following the anti-Chinese riots that accompanied the crisis, and many have stayed on to pursue their business activities in the comparative security of Bali. The fact that the Balinese themselves also hold a considerable stake in the island's tourism industry doubtless also acted as an additional restraining force.

The policy of decoupling Bali from the rest of Indonesia for marketing purposes was working up until 1999, but was tarnished when a tourism boycott specifically targeted the island in the wake of the referendum on East Timor. It remains unclear, however, who was responsible for the media campaign, though some links can be drawn to the Jakarta-based conglomerates. Spokesmen for the industry have stressed the special character of Bali as compared with elsewhere in Indonesia, and it is significant that one of them, who was quoted in *Travel Telegraph,* was also employed by a hotel associated with Bambang's Bimantara group. Support for this approach to marketing Bali was not, however, confined to the conglomerates alone, and there appears to have been a much wider platform that included substantial numbers of influential islanders. Supporters included not only local owners of businesses associated with tourism and their numerous employees, but also significant numbers of what might be called opinion-leaders in other walks of life, notably politics, academia and the local press. The preoccupation with security is apparent in various interconnected ways: signs calling for restraint at roadsides, coverage in local newspapers, informal conversations with Balinese working in hospitality. The manner in which security has been managed throughout the crisis lends credence to Picard's view that so valuable is the perception of tourism that it can be used as a lever at the national level to secure benefits for the Balinese.

What emerges from this discussion is a picture of an island that is not as peaceful as it appears on the surface, but which is nonetheless able to manage a relatively stable tourism industry. The relative calm and peace of Bali, as compared with the rest of Indonesia, is attributable to various intersecting interlocutors: the all-important tourism, the vested interests of the Chinese and other powerful Indonesians investors. These outside interests are moreover closely interwoven into the island's economy via well-connected Balinese. These interest groups were also able to convince the media that Bali remained safe, despite the attention focused on Indonesia's troubles between 1997 and 1999. What should also not be overlooked is the powerful resonance of the name 'Bali' and its long established association with luxury and exotic travel. The prevailing view that security is vital to the success of tourism needs to be qualified in the light of this analysis, but it remains unclear whether or not any general conclusions can be inferred from this account, since Bali remains an island with many special characteristics.

ACKNOWLEDGEMENTS

The research on which this essay is based was made possible with grants from the British Council (Jakarta), the British Academy and the University of North London. I am also grateful to Professor I. Gusti Ngurah Bagus of Universitas Udayana, the Bali Human Ecology Study Group and two anonymous referees.

REFERENCES

Aditjondro, George J. (1995), 'Bali, Jakarta's Colony: the Domination of Jakarta-Based Conglomerates in Bali's Tourism Industry and its Disastrous Social and Ecological Impact', Working paper No.52, Murdoch Asia Research Centre (Sep./Oct.).

Bali Tourism Statistics (1999). Denpasar: Bali Government Tourism Office.

Boon, J.A. (1977), *The Anthropological Romance of Bali 1597–1972: Dynamic Perspectives in Marriage and Caste, Politics and Religion*. Cambridge: Cambridge University Press.

Bras, K., and Dahles, H. (1999), 'Massage Miss? Women Entreprenurs and Beach Tourism in Bali', in K. Bras and Dahles, H. (eds), *Tourism and Small Entrepreneurs: Development, National Policy, and Entrepreneurial Culture: Indonesian Cases*. New York: Cognizant Communications, pp.35–51.

Colmey, J., and Liebhold, D. (1999), 'All in the Family', *Time* (24 May), pp.36–9.

Contours, Supplement to, Vol.7, No.7 (Sep. 1996).

Cukier, J. (1996),' Tourism Employment in Bali: Trends and Implications', in R. Butler and T. Hinch (eds), *Tourism and Indigenous People*. London: International Thomson Business Press, pp.49–75.

De Zoete, B., and Spies, W. (1938), *Dance and Drama in Bali*. London: Faber and Faber.

Down to Earth, No.23 (April 1994).

The Economist, 26 July 1997.

Edgell, David L., *International Tourism Policy*, New York: Van Nostrand Reinhold, 1990.

Godley, M.R. (1999) 'The Chinese Southern Diaspora', *International Institute for Asian Studies Newsletter*, No.19 (June).

Gomez, T.G. (1999), *Chinese Business in Malaysia: Accumulation, Ascendance, Accommodation*. Richmond: Curzon.

Hall, C.M., and O'Sullivan, V. (1996), 'Tourism, Political Stability and Violence', in A. Pizam and Y. Mansfield (eds), *Tourism, Crime and International Security Issues*. Chichester: John Wiley, pp.105–21.

Hall, C.M. (2000),' Tourism in Indonesia: the End of the New Order', in C.M. Hall and S. Page (eds), *Tourism in South and South-East Asia*. Oxford: Butterworth/Heineman, pp.157–66.

Henderson, J.C. (1999), 'Southeast Asian Tourism and the Financial Crisis: Indonesia and Thailand Compared', *Current Issues in Tourism*, Vol.2, No.4, pp.294–303.

Higham, J. (2000), 'Thailand: Prospects for a Tourism-led Economic Recovery', in C.M. Hall and S. Page (eds), *Tourism in South and South-East Asia*. Oxford: Butterworth/Heineman, pp.129–143.

Hitchcock, M., King, V.T., and Parnwell, M.J.G. (1993), 'Introduction', in M. Hitchcock, V.T. King and M.J.G. Parnwell (eds), *Tourism in South East Asia*. London: Routledge.

Hitchcock, M., and Norris, L. (1995), *Bali: The Imaginary Museum*. Kuala Lumpur: Oxford University Press, pp.1–31.

Hobart, A., Ramseyer, U., and Leeman, A.(1996), *The Peoples of Bali*. Oxford, Blackwell.

Hubinger, V.(1992), 'The Creation of Indonesian National Identity', *Prague Occasional Papers in Ethnology* No.1, pp.1–35.

May, Brian (1978), *The Indonesian Tragedy*. London: Routledge & Kegan Paul.

Nugroho-Heins, Marleen Indro (1995), 'Regional Culture and National Identity: Javanese Influence on the Development of National Indonesian Culture', unpublished paper (EUROSEAS, Leiden).

Picard, Michel (1993), 'Cultural Tourism in Bali: National Integration and Regional Differentiation', in M. Hitchcock, V.T. King and M.J.G. Parnwell (eds), *Tourism in South East Asia*. London: Routledge, pp.71–98.

Picard, M. (1995), 'Cultural Heritage and Tourist Capital: Cultural Tourism in Bali', in M-F. Lanfant, J.B. Allcock and E.M. Bruner (eds), *International Tourism: Identity and Change*. London: Sage, pp.44–66.

Picard, M. (1996), *Bali: Cultural Tourism and Touristic Culture*. Singapore: Archipelago.

Picard, M. (1997), 'Cultural Tourism, Nation-Building, and Regional Culture: The Making of a Balinese Identity', in M. Picard. and R.E. Wood (eds), *Tourism, Ethnicity, and the State in Asian and Pacific Societies*. Honolulu, HI: University of Hawaii Press, pp.181–214.

Pincus, J., and Rizal Ramli (1998), 'Indonesia: from Showcase to Basket Case', *Cambridge Journal of Economics*, Vol.22, pp.723–34.

Pizam, A., and Mansfield, Y. (1996), 'Introduction', in A. Pizam and Y. Mansfield (eds), *Tourism, Crime and International Security Issues*. Chichester: John Wiley, pp.1–17.

Prideaux, B. (1999), 'Tourism Perspectives of the Asian Financial Crisis: Lessons for the Future', *Current Issues in Tourism*, Vol.2, No.4, pp.279–93.

Richter, L.K. and Waugh, W.L. (1986), ' Terrorism and Tourism as Logical Companions', *Tourism Management*, Vol.7, No.4, pp.230–8.

Richter, L.K. (1994), 'The Political Dimensions of Tourism', in B. Richie and C.R. Geoldener (eds), *Travel, Tourism and Hospitality Research*. Chicester: John Wiley.

Spillius, A. (1998), 'Bali: We're Safe', *Telegraph Travel* (*Daily Telegraph*, 13 June 1998).

Travel and Tourism Intelligence (1998), 'The Fall-out from the Asian Economic Crisis', *Travel and Tourism Analysts* No.6, pp.78–95.

Travel Asia, 22 May 1998.

TNT UK, 3 Aug. 1998.

Wall, G. (1991), *Bali Spatial Arrangement Plan: Preliminary Reactions*. Waterloo, Ontario: University of Waterloo.

7

The International Expansion of Thailand's Jasmine Group: Built on Shaky Ground?

PAVIDA PANANOND

The rapid growth of Thai telecommunication firms in the early 1990s was acclaimed as a sign of the country's increased level of economic development. The subsequent international expansion of these firms was received with even further awe and excitement. For some, these international investments were regarded as 'indications of the strength and readiness of the local giants in this tough business to take on international competitors' (*The Nation*, 25 December 1995). Since the economic crisis began in July 1997, however, Thai telecommunication firms have been among the hardest hit. This rapid rise and fall of international investment in Thai telecommunications firms raises a variety of questions, including: how they managed to grow so rapidly both at home and abroad; where do their competitive advantages lie vis-à-vis international competitors; why have some already given up their brief exposure of international expansion; and what lessons can be learned from their experience. This contribution presents some reflections on the above questions. Utilizing the third-world multinational enterprises literature, in-depth case study methodology is employed to chart how Thailand's Jasmine group grew from a domestic telecommunications firm into a regional player. It is argued that the Jasmine group's competitive advantages in the domestic market are based mainly on its vast networks of connections rather than its technological or managerial expertise. The prevalent short-term and opportunity-driven attitude was translated into an internationalization strategy, which aimed mainly at reaping new opportunities in the regional market. Such opportunistic moves may have been sustained in a growing market. The limitations of such a strategy, however, were exposed in the time of contraction.

HOW FIRMS FROM DEVELOPING COUNTRIES
EXPAND ABROAD

Using Dunning's eclectic paradigm, the main difference between multinational enterprises (MNEs) from developing countries and those from developed economies is argued to lie in the nature of ownership-specific (O) advantages of developing-country MNEs. In general, scholars agree that ownership advantages of MNEs from developed countries are derived from advanced proprietary technology, superior management skills or a larger capital base. Views on the nature of ownership advantages of MNEs from developing countries differ, and there are two schools of thoughts on the subject. The first group considers MNEs from developing countries as low-cost alternatives to traditional MNEs from developed countries. Ownership advantages of MNEs from developing countries are argued to lie in their lower production costs and lower prices, which can only be exploited in other developing countries with a similar or poorer economic status (see Wells, 1977, 1981,1983; Lecraw, 1977,1981; Kumar, 1982; and Lall, 1983a,1983b).

The second and more contemporary approach attributes developing-country MNEs to more sophisticated O advantages (see, for example, Cantwell and Tolentino, 1990; Tolentino, 1993; Lecraw, 1993; van Hoesel, 1997; Dunning et al., 1997; Yeung, 1998), and focuses particularly on the capability of developing-country MNEs to catch up with their developed-country counterparts through the process of technology accumulation. Proponents suggest that developing-country MNEs begin their technology accumulation process from learning simple manufacturing techniques, then innovating on incremental improvements to manufacturing processes and on minor product designs, and eventually introducing new products to the market (Hobday, 1995; van Hoesel, 1997). This view was strongly advocated in explaining the development of technology-intensive industries in developing countries (see Hobday, 1990). In his research on the development of the telecommunications industry in Brazil, Hobday (1990) stresses the role of both the state and the private sector in the process of accumulating telecommunications technology through the gradual learning from the low end of the production process.

Despite valuable insights, the literature on third-world MNEs is not without limitations. For instance, most studies concentrate on the industry rather than firm behaviour, with a heavy bias toward manufacturing (Yeung, 1994: 305). The theory development is derived from four East Asian newly industrialized countries (Hong Kong, Taiwan, South Korea and Singapore). Although some similarities with other developing countries may prevail, 'the East Asian model' is not representative of all developing countries (see, for example, Perkins, 1994; Jomo *et al.*, 1997; Petri, 1997). Finally, and most importantly, the tendency to compare MNEs from developing countries to their developed-country counterparts often leads to misleading stereotypes. For instance, while MNEs from developed economies are portrayed as large, capital- and technology-intensive, innovation-driven and vertically, horizontally and globally integrated; those from developing countries are believed to be small, labour-intensive, low in technological capability and limited to regional investments (Yeung, 1994: 301). Although the emphasis has recently shifted to the capability of these MNEs to accumulate technology, the implication of the international expansion of third-world MNEs remains rather deterministic. Only through a low-cost strategy or an incremental learning process can multinationals from developing countries emerge. Such interpretation is far too limited to capture the complexity and the diversity of the emergence of developing-country MNEs.

The above limitations result partly from the comparative approach adopted by most studies on developing-country MNEs. The primary drawback of the comparative approach is that it explains only what makes one group *different* from another (Limlingan, 1986). Because the purpose of the comparative approach is to highlight static differences between groups, explanations on how each group has reached its current position are often ignored. Much ink has been spilled on how developing-country MNEs differ from their competitors from advanced economies, but little is known about how they function in their own context and how their domestic development may influence their behaviour in international markets.

Some insights can be drawn from the literature on late industri-alization. The timing of a country's entry into industrialization has been discussed as one of the most important factors affecting domestic firms' strategy (Amsden, 1989,1995; Amsden and Hikino, 1993,1994; van Hoesel, 1997; Kock and Guillén, 1998). Whereas firms from early-industrialized countries benefit from technology inventions and innovations, firms from late-industrializing countries[1] have to rely mainly on borrowing and improving on the already available technologies. Without proprietary technology in new products and processes, firms from developing countries are likely to depend on an additional set of generic skills that are not product- or process-specific and that can be transferred to various unrelated functions or industries (Amsden and Hikino, 1994; Kock and Guillén, 1998).

According to Kock and Guillén (1998), one of the most significant skills for developing-country firms is the 'contact capability', the ability to utilize different types of contacts as competitive resources. Because markets in developing countries are often characterized by imperfections in market information and access, the ability to overcome these imperfections through the use of contacts and connections becomes the most important competitive strategy of domestic firms in their initial development. In her study of the evolution of South East Asian business, Lim (1996) argues that the main competitive advantage of South East Asian firms is derived from their vast network of connections. The rapid growth of the pre-crisis period had favoured and rewarded opportunistic, risk-taking and entrepreneurial activities which were based on connections and relationships (Lim, 1996: 53).

Prior to the economic crisis, South East Asian firms' reliance on connections was regarded as a distinctive cultural phenomenon, resulting from the hierarchy-based society and informal interpersonal trust. Proponents supported the view that cultural differences in Asia could influence the way local firms behave and that personal networking was appropriate given their environmental context (see, for example, Redding, 1990 and 1995; Hamilton and Biggart, 1988; Biggart and Hamilton, 1990; Orru et al., 1991). Post-crisis critiques, however, argue that the connections-based way of doing business was one of the major causes of the economic crisis. From the praise that 'Asian networks' had contributed to the 'Asian miracle'; the world is now inundated with comments on how 'Asian cronyism'[2] brought about the 'Asian debacle'.

It cannot be denied that personal networking could result in reckless investments or even outright corruption. However, to blame all that went wrong in Asia on sins of crony capitalism is far too simplistic an explanation. As Johnson (1998: 655) stated, 'crony capitalism was not the intent but a by-product of the structural characteristics of the Asian-type economies'. This is not to deny that Asian firms' heavy reliance on personal networks plays no role in their present decline, but to say that *ex post* analyses should also take into consideration specific characteristics of the phenomenon they are scrutinizing. Given all the relevant literature discussed above, this contribution attempts to explain the mechanism that drove the domestic and international growth of a Thai telecommunications firm and to understand how such mechanism became vulnerable in the recent economic context.[3]

INDUSTRY BACKGROUND

The telecommunications industry in Thailand had been a public monopoly until some forms of liberalization were introduced in the late 1980s. Currently, three government agencies are responsible for telecommunications services: the Post and Telegraph Department (PTD); the Telephone Organization of Thailand (TOT); and the Communications Authority of Thailand (CAT). All three agencies report to the Ministry of Transport and Communications (MTC). While the TOT has monopoly control over domestic telephone services and international long-distance services to Laos and Malaysia, the CAT controls the country's postal services as well as all international telecommunications services. The PTD is responsible for radio-based and satellite-based services (Srisakdi, 1994).

The recent development of telecommunications technology has led to an integration of various services in the industry. For instance, satellite technology can be used for mobile phone as well as other data transmission methods. As a result, the authorities and functions of the three government agencies, which were previously separated, have increasingly overlapped. Apart from overlapping functions, the lack of cooperation among relevant agencies, strong political interference, poor management and limited investment contributed to the underdevelopment of telecommunications infrastructure in Thailand (*Business in Thailand*, November 1989: 28).[4]

Rapid economic expansion after 1985 increased the demand level for basic telephone services. Given the resource limitation of the Thai government, privatization of state enterprises was seen as the only way to meet the government's target of ten telephones per 100 people by the end of 1996 (Piché *et al.*, 1997: 63). However, because the direct method of selling public assets to the private sector was strongly opposed, and the laws prevent the private sector from owning telecommunications facilities, the Thai government turned to other forms of private sector participation such as concession-based agreements or turnkey projects (Kraiyudht, 1993: 289–90). The government introduced the build-transfer-operate (BTO) system to enable it to benefit from the private capital and expertise without giving up ownership in the telecommunications networks. Under these BTO concessions, the awarded companies build the telecommunications networks, transfer ownership to either TOT or CAT, and then operate the networks on a revenue- or profit-sharing basis (Harrington, 1995: 94). The introduction of the BTO system has led to the rapid emergence of several local telecommunications firms since the early 1990s. Before discussing the domestic development and international expansion of the Jasmine group, a brief introduction to the four most influential domestic telecom groups is presented to provide the context of domestic competition.

Major Players: The Big Four

In the Thai telecommunications industry, the strongest and most influential domestic firms are fixed-line and mobile network operators. Equipment manufacturers play a relatively restricted role compared to service providers. An oligopoly of four to five network carriers plays the most important role in the industry (Natthapong, 1996: 41). The so-called 'Big Four' are the four major government concessionaires: two fixed-line carriers with geographically based fixed-line concessions (TelecomAsia and TT&T) and two mobile phone carriers in direct competition with each other (Shin Corp and Ucom) (*Corporate Thailand*, September 1996).

TelecomAsia (TA) holds a 25-year concession to install and operate 2.6 million telephone lines in the Greater Bangkok areas (a concession of 2 million lines was awarded in 1991, and an additional 600,000 lines in September 1995). TA is the first private-sector company allowed to provide local telephone services, an area long monopolized by the TOT. As part of the

Charoen Pokphand (CP) group, TA benefits from CP's assets including political connections and financial resources. With no previous experience in telecommunications, the way in which TA won its concession from the TOT remains one of the most controversial stories of Thailand's privatization history (see Sakkarin, 2000).

Thai Telephone & Telecommunications (TT&T) is a consortium led by Jasmine International and the Loxley group. TT&T won the contract to install and operate one million phone lines in the provinces outside Bangkok in 1992, and an additional 500,000 lines in 1995. Details of the consortium will be discussed further in the following section.

The third major player is the Shinawatra group. The group changed its name to Shin Corp in 1999, allegedly to separate the group's identity from its founder's political activities (*The Nation*, 22 June 1999).[5] The group's key subsidiary, Advance Info Service (AIS), was granted a 25-year concession from the TOT to operate a cellular telephone service in 1990 (Tisco, 1998). The group's other telecommunications activities include satellite communication services and paging services.

The last among the Big Four is the United Communication Industry (Ucom) group. Ucom's flagship company, Total Access Communication (TAC), is in direct competition with Shin Corp in mobile telephony. TAC was awarded a 27-year concession to provide mobile telephone service from the CAT in 1990 (Tisco, 1998). The group also holds two other concessions to operate paging and trunked radio services. AIS and TAC are the two largest mobile phone companies, controlling more than 90 per cent of the market among themselves (Tisco, 1998).

With the exception of TA, the other three have had some experience in activities related to the telecommunications industry. While Ucom started off as telecommunications equipment distributors for foreign multinationals, Shin Corp began as a computer system integrator and later expanded into telecommunications. Jasmine International, the largest shareholder in TT&T, began as a turnkey engineering consultant for the TOT. The four groups altogether hold most of the concessions awarded by TOT and CAT. The following section details the growth and development of the Jasmine group.

THE JASMINE GROUP: GROWTH AND DEVELOPMENT[6]

The Jasmine group had a modest beginning in 1982 as an engineering consultancy with an initial registered capital of Bt1 million. Within less than two decades, the group has expanded rapidly and become one of the largest telecommunications firms in Thailand. Before its latest consolidation in 1999, the group comprised 16 subsidiaries and associated companies with a registered share capital of Bt3,336 million (US$ 90 million)[7] and a total revenue of approximately Bt7 billion (US$ 190 million). At its peak in 1996, the group employed 1,853 employees, consisting of 24 per cent engineers, 26 per cent technicians and 50 per cent administrative staff. The group was involved in five lines of business: telecommunications operation; service and distribution; manufacturing; international investment; and energy. However, activities in manufacturing and energy have been dropped since 1997. This section discusses Jasmine's growth in three major phases: turnkey engineering (1982–92); telecommunications services (1992–97); and international expansion (1994–97). This division is based on the group's most outstanding activity during each period.

Turnkey Engineering (1982–92)

The beginning of the Jasmine group dates back to 1982 when Adisai Bodharamik founded Jasmine International (JI) as an engineering consultancy. Prior to starting the company, Adisai had worked at the TOT from 1962 to 1978 (*Who is Who in Business*, July 1995). During its early years, JI focused mainly on turnkey engineering activities, which involved system design, equipment selection and installation, system implementation and testing as well as maintenance services. Its main customers were state agencies, particularly the TOT.

It was only in the late 1980s that Jasmine expanded into telecommunications. The industry attracted much interest from the private sector as the government introduced privatization through the contract-based system. Two major concessions obtained from the TOT in 1988 and 1991 marked the group's beginning as a telecommunications service provider. The first one was a 15-year concession to install and provide satellite communication networks and the second was a 20-year concession to build and operate a submarine fibre-optic network in the Gulf of Thailand. Jasmine set up two wholly owned subsidiaries (Acumen and Jasmine Submarine Telecommunications, JSTC) for these tasks.

Although the group's operations in the first decade were predominantly characterized by its specialization in turnkey engineering activities, Jasmine began to expand into telecommunications as new opportunities emerged in the late 1980s. Following a golden period of rapid growth and expansion in a wide variety of telecom activities, the group expanded its domestic and international operations between 1992 and 1997.

Telecommunications Services (1992–97)

The group's low-profile operations in the first decade changed tremendously after 1992, when the consortium led by the group won the one-million-phone-line concession from the TOT. Jasmine was a major shareholder in Thai Telephone & Telecommunications (TT&T), one of the two concessionaires of TOT's infamous three-million-line project. Other shareholders included Nippon Telegraph and Telephone of Japan, the Loxley group and Italian-Thai Development.[8] TT&T was awarded the concession to install and operate 1.5 million telephone lines in Thailand's provincial areas. The concession was to last 25 years, with an exclusive five-year protection period.

With more areas of telecommunications services opening up in the 1990s, the Jasmine group diversified into a variety of value-added services such as paging and data communications. New companies were also set up to provide related services to the group's existing subsidiaries. When TT&T began its installation work, the group had various subsidiaries supplying equipment or providing necessary services to TT&T.

Like other telecommunications firms, the Jasmine group turned to the stock market as a major source of capital. The group was able to list both its holding company, Jasmine International, and TT&T in 1994. Despite the public listing, the largest shareholder remains the founder's family. Adisai Bodharamik alone had held more than 65 per cent of registered shares until he transferred 25 per cent of his holding to his only son in 1996. Altogether, the Bodharamik family hold a total of 68 per cent of the equity.

The second decade of the Jasmine group was characterized by extensive diversifications in both telecom-related and non-telecom industries. Jasmine's interests in non-telecom industries emerged in the second half of the 1990s and included investment in the energy sector, real estate and a brief flirtation with commercial banking. Apart from domestic expansion, the group also began its investment abroad during this period. The next section looks at the group's international expansion in more detail.

International Expansion (1994–97)

During the period of rapid expansion (1994–97), the Jasmine group began to explore opportunities abroad. In 1994 the group set up Jasmine International Overseas (JO) as its international investment arm, handling all the overseas activities of the group. The first international expansion came in 1994, when the group acquired 49.75 per cent of PT Mobilkom Telekomindo of Indonesia. Mobilkom has been granted the build-own-operate licence from the Indonesian government to operate a national trunked mobile radio network.

Between 1994 and 1997 the three main international projects were: the Asia Cellular Satellite System (ACeS) project; JT Mobiles in India; and Island Country Telecommunications in the Philippines. ACeS was to provide satellite mobile telephone services across the Asian region. The project was initially a three-partner joint venture among Jasmine, Pasifik Satelit Nusantara (PSN) of Indonesia and Philippine Long Distance Telephone (PLDT). For its project in India, Jasmine was part of a consortium that included three local companies as well as Telia of Sweden. Jasmine also held a 40 per cent stake in United Telecommunications, an equipment manufacturer that was one of the three Indian firms in the consortium. JT Mobiles has been awarded licences to build and operate cellular telephone services in Andhra Pradesh and Karnataka. Service began in 1997 and the company expects to break even in 2000. The third project was a 19 per cent investment in Island Country Telecommunications, a joint venture between Jasmine, the Italthai group and Guoco Holdings of the Philippines. In addition, Jasmine held a small equity (2.36 per cent) in Digital Telecommunications (Digitel), a land-line telephone operator in the island of Luzon.

Besides these actual investments, the Jasmine group also announced its participation in two other projects in Vietnam and Nepal. In Vietnam, the group held a 21.5 per cent interest in

TABLE 1
JASMINE GROUP'S INTERNATIONAL INVESTMENTS

Company	Country	Year	Equity (%)	Project Value (US$mil)	Type of Activity	Partners	1999 Status
PT Mobilkom Telekomindo	Indonesia	1994	49.75	10 (regist. cap)	Trunked mobile radio network	PT Mobilkom Telekomindo; Goldman Sachs (5%)	Cancelled
PT Asia Cellular Satellite (ACeS)	Asia	1995	33.33	750	Satellite phone network	PT Pasifik Satelit Nusantara (PSN); Philippine Long Distance Telephone (PLDT)	Retain only 9.9%, the rest sold to PSN, PLDT, and Lockheed Martin
Nam Theun2	Laos	1995	10	1,500	Hydroelectric power	Phatra Thanakit; Ital-Thai; Transfield (Australia); Electricite de France	Cancelled
JT Mobiles	India	1995	13	17	Cellular telephone	Telia (26%); TOT (10%); Sanmar Electronics;United Telecoms	Jasmine's stake on sale
United Telecom	India	1995	40	n.a.	Equipment manufacture	United Telecoms	
Island Country Telecommunications	Philippines	1996	19	10.8	Paging services	Ital-Thai; Guoco Holdings (Philippines)	
Digitel	Philippines	1996	2.36	250 (regist cap)	Fixed line operator	JG Summit (Philippines); Cable&Wireless (28%)	All sold to Ing Baring (Phil.) and Merrill Lynch
MC Management	Nepal	1996	70	3-4	Paging services	n.a.	
NewTel	Vietnam	1996	21.54	20 (regist cap)	Equipment	Sigel (VN); Goldman Sachs; Ital-Thai; One Holding; CKDS Thailand; Nikko Securities	

Source: Jasmine annual reports, 1996, 1997; 56-1 forms, 1996, 1997; Stock Exchange of Thailand; various publications

Newtel, a manufacturing joint venture led by Ital-Thai Development (*The Nation*, 18 July 1995). The investment in Vietnam had yet to take place when the economic crisis broke out in 1997, and has since been put on hold. Similarly, the group's investment in Nepal has been suspended. Jasmine had announced earlier that it acquired a 70 per cent equity in MC Management, a company that was awarded licences from the Nepalese government to operate radio paging services.

Like Thailand, other countries in the region have been embarking on the process of privatization or liberalization of the telecom industry. Jasmine joined other regional telecom firms (for example, Singapore Telecom, Hong Kong Telecom and Telstra of Australia) to venture into regional markets. During 1994–7, Jasmine increased its international exposure by entering Indonesia and the Philippines as well as India.[9] Details of Jasmine's international activities are summarized in Table 1.

BUILDING UP OWNERSHIP ADVANTAGES AT HOME

As mentioned earlier, the literature suggests that ownership (O)advantages of MNEs from developing countries can be derived from their lower costs or their capability in improving their technological skills through learning. Hobday (1990) argued that the O advantages of telecom firms from developing countries were accumulated through an incremental learning process, which started from manufacturing equipment and gradually progressed to operating telecom systems. Once technological capabilities in operating and managing small systems are achieved, developing-country telecom firms can then proceed to more technologically complex systems.

The rapid development of the Jasmine group, however, does not quite fit the above explanation. Although the group's emergence was built on a certain level of technological know-how in the telecommunications industry, a closer look at the group's experience showed that its O advantages in the domestic market resulted not so much from its technological skills, but more from what Kock and Guilléén (1998) called 'contact capabilities', the abilities in using contacts and connections to bring about favourable results.

With regard to Jasmine's levels of technological skills, let us first consider which type of technology is fundamental to the group's growth. Natthapong (1996: 49–50) argued that there are two kinds of technology involved in the telecommunications industry. The first is the technology embedded in telecommunications equipment and hardware, and the second is that of managing and operating telecommunications systems. According to him, there are few telecommunications firms in the world that 'own' the former type of technology, due to the high cost of research and development required in the development process. Most telecommunications system operators, regardless of their country of origin, are dependent on telecommunications equipment bought from various suppliers. Natthapong therefore argued that not 'owning' technology in equipment and networks was not a critical weakness for Thai firms as long as they could freely source equipment and networks from any supplier.

It is therefore the second type of technology that matters more to Thai telecommunications carriers. The experiential knowledge of operating and managing telecommunications systems cannot be purchased in a package and has to be accumulated through the process of learning by doing. Western telecommunications firms certainly possess more skills and knowledge than Thai firms thanks to their longer experience. However, Natthapong argued that Thai telecommunications firms should be able to compensate for their lack of experience through their better understanding of the local market and its institutional environment.

A similar view was expressed by a senior Jasmine executive, who explained that most telecommunications operators in both developed and developing countries were equally dependent on suppliers' hardware technology (interview, 6 January 1999). According to him, the competitive edge of Thai telecommunications service providers was built on know-how in operating and managing telecommunications systems, rather than on manufacturing technology. For this reason, the Jasmine group chose to procure almost all of its hardware and equipment from foreign suppliers. The group did engage in some manufacturing of basic telephone cables and wires, although the amount and significance of equipment supplied by its manufacturing subsidiaries were negligible.

With regard to management and know-how, Jasmine benefited from its own learning as well as from the expertise of other foreign multinationals. Technological skills were acquired from foreign experts through both equity partnership and contract-based ties. Foreign technology partners could provide skills in operating specific telecommunications systems and networks, though they were less capable of instructing Jasmine on issues specific to the Thai market, especially consumer behaviour. A senior executive stressed the group's ability to reduce the costs of imported technology by replacing some parts with cheaper inputs from other sources. He claimed that the group's knowledge of the available technology enabled it to choose equipment from different suppliers and to design an optimum system with lower costs (interview, 15 December 1998). Such ability is considered valuable for telecom firms in developing countries, which generally lack the necessary knowledge and experience to plan and specify the necessary equipment (Inkelbrecht, 1995: 199).

The assertion that Jasmine's engineers mastered skills in system design and equipment selection was, however, opposed by an expatriate telecommunications expert who had had long experience working with Thai telecom firms.[10] He explained that, in the process of bidding for the supply of equipment for telecom infrastructure projects in Thailand, system design, equipment selection, project costing and installation procedures were carried out not by Jasmine's (or other Thai telecom firms') engineers but by suppliers' technical teams. According to him, the role of Jasmine's engineers was to understand all the procedures mentioned previously, approve them or suggest additional changes. Once selected, the supplier would send in a team responsible for executing the project, while Thai engineers worked alongside for training purposes. In general, the training's main objective was to enable Thai engineers to take over the running of the network after two to three years. He therefore suggested that Thai engineers, once trained, would have the general working knowledge of the network. He strongly disagreed, however, that Thai telecom firms could claim that they were well equipped with the skills required in system design and equipment selection.

Whether or not Jasmine has achieved such a level of engineering skill remains debatable. On the contrary, it is rather obvious that Jasmine's skills in managing and marketing its networks can still be improved. A close look at its operations shows that Jasmine has been largely relying on operations in semi-protected markets, where entry is granted through concessionary rights and where competitors are scarce. Moreover, the group's revenue structure (see Table 2) and details of key customers for each subsidiary (see Table 3) show that the better-performing subsidiaries are the 'cash-cow' projects, those with government concessions, and those which benefit directly from the 'cash-cows'. As shown in Table 2, the two top earners that have contributed largely to the consolidated group's financial status are Acumen and Jasmine Submarine Telecommunications (JSTC), two key concessionaire of the TOT. Moreover, TOT is the only customer for these two subsidiaries and is expected to pay a fixed sum of revenue to them over the concession period. This explains why, despite the financial difficulty resulting from the currency devaluation in 1997, these two subsidiaries remain the best performers of all the group's subsidiaries. In 1997, Acumen and JSTC together contributed more than 40 per cent of the group's consolidated revenue (see Table 2). Apart from these two, other subsidiaries with satisfactory performances are spin-offs whose main objective is to serve associated companies within the group. Table 3 shows how Jasmine's several subsidiaries benefited from serving TT&T, the group-led consortium that has been awarded a concession to provide telephone services in provincial areas. For example, Siam Teltech derived 93 per cent of its total revenue in 1997 from TT&T alone. The amount of revenues received from associated companies in 1996 was as high as 56 per cent (Jasmine International Annual Report 1997).

Without these guaranteed conditions, the performance of Jasmine's other subsidiaries is not quite as impressive. For example, Jasmine Smart Shop, the group's retail arm, has been accumulating losses since its beginning (see Table 2). TT&T, despite its concession, has been plagued with management conflicts among shareholders as well as serious revenue miscalculations. The conflict at TT&T concerned other shareholders who were not happy at the extent to which the Jasmine group dominated and profited from TT&T (*The Nation*, 28 May 1996). The concession that TT&T holds translated into business opportunities for its various shareholders, although Jasmine was the one which benefited most from the consortium. The conflict resulted in a string of resignations from TT&T executives representing other shareholders. On top of these conflicts, TT&T also suffered from a severe loss resulting from its obligation to pay TOT a 43.1 per

TABLE 2
REVENUE AND PROFIT CONTRIBUTION OF KEY SUBSIDIARIES (PERCENTAGE)

Key Subsidiaries	1994		1995		1996		1997	
	Revenue	Profit	Revenue	Profit	Revenue	Profit	Revenue	Profit
Jasmine International	n.a.	n.a.	n.a.	n.a.	6.9	(0.74)	12.2	(37.8)
Jasmine Telecom Systems	-	-	0.7	0.4	31.2	39.28	20.98	(0.6)
TJP Engineering	10.8	7.2	31.6	7.9	21.85	11.51	9.96	0.8
Siam Teltech Computer	21.8	19	12.2	5	9.8	6.97	11.5	0.44
Jasmine Smart Shop	0.6	(1.3)	3.5	(0.5)	3.1	(2.01)	4.8	(0.66)
Acumen	12	8.3	11.5	8.2	8.6	13.20	17.7	1.32
Jasmine Submarine Telecommunication	38	40.8	27.9	22	17.01	32.1	21.89	13.29
Jasmine International Overseas	-	-	4	4.7	1.7	(10.56)	0.99	(24.29)
TT&T	n.a.	n.a.	n.a.	n.a.	n.a.	9.19	n.a	(51.9)
Others	16.8	26	8.6	47.7		1.06		(0.55)

Source: Jasmine annual reports, 1996, 1997; 56-1 forms, 1996, 1997.

TABLE 3
JASMINE GROUP'S MAJOR CUSTOMERS (1997)

Subsidiaries	Major Customers	(%) of Revenue Contribution
Acumen		
– ISBN	TT&T in the top-ten	4
– TDMA	Telephone Org of Thailand (TOT)	100
Jasmine Submarine Telecommunication	TOT	100
Siam Teltech	TT&T	93.36
TJP Engineering	TT&T	57.15
	Ital-Thai Development	24.76
	TOT	6.21
Radiophone	TT&T	9.14
	TelecomAsia (TA)*	6.22
	TOT	3.08
	TJP Engineering	1.4
Ericsson Thai Network	Ericsson (Thailand)	92.23
Jasmine Submarine	TT&T	58.51
	TOT	20.02
	Jasmine Submarine	3.3

*   TA is part of the CP group, which holds 60% in Radiophone.
** Ericsson Thai Network Products was set up mainly to supply the installation
    work of the 1.5m telephone line project of TT&T. The installation was sub-
    contracted to Ericsson.

Source: 56-1 form, 1997.

cent share of revenue. This rate was based on an over-estimation of
TT&T's revenue per line. Unable to achieve the estimated income,
TT&T struggled intensely to meet its contract with the government
(*The Nation*, 21 July 1997).

   These problems suggest that managerial capabilities are not yet
the group's strongest qualities. In addition, the group's
technological capabilities remain debatable. Despite the
technology-intensive nature of the telecom industry, little attention
has been given to activities such as R&D or market research. Staff
training in operation and maintenance is the most that the group
has invested in R&D-related areas. Yet, the group has grown

rapidly and become one of the four most influential players in the industry.

Contacts and Connections as Ownership Advantages

It may be unfair to claim that Jasmine's domestic growth is based entirely on the group's vast connections, but to deny it at all is unrealistic given the highly politicized nature of the industry. Adisai himself admitted in an interview that 'a person who has many friends can do well in business and that is a difference between Thailand and Western societies. Because our society relies considerably on links to a group, it can be seen as using contacts to get things done, and I think it is necessary' (quoted in *Bangkok Post*, 7 July 1997). The experience of the Jasmine group reveals that the group has benefited from at least three types of connections. First, amicable relationships with relevant state agencies are invaluable. It is widely known that the Jasmine group enjoys exceptionally close ties with the TOT, thanks to Adisai's previous career at the agency. The group is the TOT's largest contractor, holding five major concessions, not to mention joint investment in two other projects.[11] Adisai's connections within the state agency are considered one of the group's strongest advantages (interviews, 1 December 1998, 6 January 1999; *Far Eastern Economic Review*, 1 September 1994: 66). His colleagues who remained at the agency have risen to several powerful positions. One of those is Sumet Tantivejkul, who once held the chairmanship of the TOT's board of directors (*Phujadkarn Rai Deun*, September 1997). Sumet was reported to be very close with the Jasmine group and had sat as a director on the group's board before taking up the TOT's board chairmanship (*Phujadkarn Rai Deun*, September 1997; *The Nation*, 3 October 1997). For those TOT executives who no longer wanted to stay at the agency, the Jasmine group provided a launch pad for their new careers in the private sector. Several ex-TOT department heads have joined the group in various high-ranking positions including President and CEO of Jasmine International Overseas, the group's arm for international investment (*Business Day*, 22 January 1996; *Phujadkarn Rai Deun*, September 1997).

Links with state agencies alone are not enough; political connections are also crucial in this industry. The Jasmine group is widely known to be a major financial supporter of the Chat Pattana party (CPP), one of the main political parties in Thailand. Adisai's close ties with the party became even more evident when he was named the party's deputy leader and executive member in late 1999 (*Bangkok Post*, 13 December 1999). The group's support for the CPP resulted from Adisai's close ties with the CPP's former leader, Chatichai Choonhawan. Their close relationship bore fruit when the latter became prime minister during 1988–91. The two most profitable concessions Jasmine won in its early development were awarded by the Chatichai government. Close connections between Adisai and the CPP were said to be 'strongly helpful' in winning the two concessions (interview, 1 December 1998; *Phujadkarn Rai Deun*, September 1997).[12]

Because of the rapid proliferation of opportunities in telecommunications markets of developing countries, access to finance became an important success factor for firms in those countries (Inkelbrecht, 1995: 196). Jasmine's financial linkages were so well established that the group president once claimed that the company was 'well supported by financial institutions' (*The Nation*, 9 May 1995). This assertion is well grounded given the group's close relationships with the Loxley group and Phatra Thanakit. Both are part of the Lamsam family empire, which is centred around the Thai Farmers Bank, Thailand's third largest bank. A senior executive admits that the group's links with the Loxley group have helped improve its creditworthiness among foreign financial institutions. In addition, government concessions can be used as collateral for most financial institutions. The same executive even claimed that different financial institutions 'came knocking on my door offering loans' (interview, 15 December 1998). The statement is no exaggeration as the group's debt-to-equity ratio rose from 0.38 in 1994 to 5.96 in 1997, while its equity remained unchanged (Jasmine International, 1997).

INTERNATIONAL EXPANSION

The literature on the international expansion of firms is based on two main assumptions: first, that the nature of the process is incremental, reflecting the learning-by-doing mechanism; and second, that internationalizing firms possess some kinds of ownership advantages that can be transferred to overseas markets. The incremental nature of the internationalization process is reflected in both the sequence of markets entered as well as the organizational form selected in each market.

The international expansion of the Jasmine group, however, poses challenges on the above assumptions. This study argues that the group's international expansion reflects an opportunistic attempt to reap new market opportunities that were rapidly opening up, rather than the accumulation of technological or managerial capabilities. Rapid international expansion of telecommunications firms can be explained as an attempt to seize first-mover advantages (Sakar *et al.*, 1999), although Jasmine's arbitrary choices of international projects show the group's lack of a clear international strategy. The group's opportunistic approach to its international expansion was clearly echoed by most executives interviewed; as one remarked:

> We did not have any particular strategy in terms of selecting countries nor areas of telecom services [e.g. mobile, fixed-line, paging, etc.]. We were contacted either by local investors or foreign multinationals, or sometimes by our financial advisor. Decisions were based mainly on each project's opportunity and profitability (interview, 6 January 1999).

The quest for new opportunities is evident in Jasmine's market selection as well as in its choices of project. The group had announced its investment in a variety of projects in several Asian developing countries almost all at the same time. Within the period of three years, the group invested in a trunked radio network in Indonesia, a regional satellite mobile telephone network, a paging service in the Philippines and mobile telephony in India, not to mention its failed attempt in a hydroelectric power plant in Laos (see Table 1 for details).

The apparent differences among these projects make it necessary for the group to include other partners who can provide relevant technology and local knowledge. This is the main reason why the group chose joint ventures as the main entry strategy for all its overseas investment (interview, 6 January 1999). In all its international projects, Jasmine sought reliable local partners who could contribute local knowledge or local connections. These local partners are domestic telecom carriers, which, in most cases, have been granted concessions or licences for their operation. In some circumstances, Western telecom firms are sought to join the consortium as shareholder and technology provider.

In common with Thailand, the telecom industry in other Asian developing countries is equally politicized. Finding a well-connected local partner in each market can benefit the project in the same way that Jasmine's connections in Thailand had done for its domestic growth. The group's contact capabilities at home appear to have been translated into its understanding of how political manoeuvring is handled in other developing countries. With such understanding, Jasmine has been fairly competent in finding local partners with the 'right' contacts to compensate for their lack of connections. For example, the group's ACeS project was started as a joint venture among three 'well-connected' regional telecom carriers. Besides Jasmine, the project comprised Philippine Long Distance Telephone (PLDT) and PT Pasifik Satelit Nusantara of Indonesia (PSN). PLDT is the largest telephone carrier in the Philippines, holding more than 90 per cent of the market. The company was controlled by a local family, the Cojuangcos, which is one of the most influential families in the country. PLDT's previous leader was a close associate of Ferdinand Marcos, and its current president, Antonio Cojungco, is a nephew of another ex-president, Corazon Aquino. PLDT had held the monopoly of the telecom industry for 64 years before ex-president Fidel Ramos broke its control in 1993 (*Far Eastern Economic Review*, 6 May 1993). The political connections of the Indonesian partner are no less impressive. Among its shareholders are the state-owned domestic telephone monopoly and another company controlled by Suharto's son, Bambang Trihatmodjo (*Far Eastern Economic Review*, 18 May 1995).

Jasmine's reliance on local partners for local knowledge, and on foreign multinationals for necessary technology, raises the question of what then is Jasmine's contribution in its international investment projects. When asked what role the group played in its overseas projects, Jasmine executives stressed its contribution in engineering activities as well as project financing (interviews, 15 December 1998; 6 January 1999). Jasmine also claimed that its skills in system designing, equipment selecting and installing have been beneficial to its overseas joint ventures. From its experience in Thailand, Jasmine can share with its developing-country partners its skills in controlling project costs through system design and equipment selection. It also reported that the use of Thai engineers is less costly than hiring their Western counterparts with the same qualifications (interview, 6 January 1999). However, this could be simply a convenient answer as the group's level of technological skills has been strongly questioned, as discussed earlier.

Although Jasmine wants to stress its technological role in these overseas projects, it appears that the most important contribution from the group is its ability to share the financial burden. Because of the rapid proliferation of telecom projects in developing countries, the ability to find project financing becomes an important success factor for new telecom projects (Inkelbrecht, 1995). With more and more activities, traditional sources of finance such as equipment suppliers or development banks are finding themselves spread thinly among various projects. Major equipment suppliers become less committed to give as much financial support as they have in the past (*FEER*, 5 October 1995). Besides, not all Western telecom firms are interested in uncertain projects in developing countries (interview, 6 January 1999). Thailand's financial liberalization in the early 1990s allowed domestic firms to seek loans from a variety of domestic and international financial institutions. Different liberalization schemes, along with the Thai firms' longer experience in telecommunications, as compared with those in India or the Philippines, made it possible for them to obtain relatively cheaper loans (interview, 6 January 1999). On top of that, Jasmine's connections with different financial institutions enable the group to seek loans from various sources. One executive remarked:

> Not everyone knows everything. Between shareholders, we can form a consortium with all necessary resources. Jasmine's contribution is mainly to share the financial burden, as well as to provide some of our engineering expertise. In these developing-country markets, it is important to get there early (interview, 6 January 1999).

The opportunistic undertaking of international investment has cost the group dearly. Jasmine's heavy dependence on debt financing for both its domestic and international projects was severely felt when the devaluation of the baht in 1997 almost doubled the amount of foreign currency loans. Financial crisis aside, the group also suffered from several miscalculations of opportunities in its international investment. For example, the group's investment in India could not meet its expected revenue target. Most companies, Jasmine included, overestimated the potential and the profitability of the Indian market. These telecom projects required a huge investment but its return is much slower than expected (*The Nation*, 8 January 1997; *Asia Week*, 27 November 1998). In addition, the fact that all Jasmine's international projects are still in their developmental period and have yet to generate much financial returns worsens the group's financial liabilities. Given all these problems, Jasmine decided that the group's international projects be sacrificed to save its domestic situation. The group's attitude toward international projects has changed from a positive confidence to despair in a matter of a few years. In an interview with a local newspaper, one board director stated that 'Jasmine believes it can survive by simply selling the stakes in overseas companies' (*The Nation*, 22 January 1999).

The first one sold was the group's 2.36 per cent stake in Digitel, a land-line phone operator in the main Philippine island of Luzon. Jasmine's equity was sold to ING Baring (Philippines) and Merrill Lynch (Philippines) in February 1998. Soon after, the group's stake in the much-promoted Asia Cellular Satellite (ACeS) was largely reduced from 33.33 per cent to a mere 9.9 per cent. The group's shares were sold to Lockheed Martin, and the project's two other shareholders in 1999 (Jasmine International, 1999). In addition, the group wanted to dispose of its shares in JT Mobiles, the cellular phone operator in India (*The Nation*, 22 January 1999). Meanwhile, the group is trying to pull out from its energy-related investment in Laos. In sum, the group's only international strategy by 1999 was to get out of all international projects.

CONCLUSION

This study unveils important factors behind the domestic and international growth of a leading Thai telecommunications firm, the Jasmine group. It shows that an industry located in a growing market, with low competition due to high entry barriers and strong political interference can develop quickly. The firm's survival, however, was based on various connections and contacts at the expense of necessary technological or managerial skills. The experience of the Jasmine group shows that its growth both at home and abroad has been based mainly on its ability to take advantage of its vast networks and connections. In fact, these 'contact capabilities' should not simply be dismissed as cronyism, the downside of business expansion in Asia. Contacts may even be a significant part of the game, given the nature of the telecommunications industry in developing countries. Without these contacts, Jasmine may not have been there in the first place. Jasmine's rapid international expansion is also understandable as first movers do enjoy numerous advantages, such as setting standard process or establishing physical networks.

However, this is neither an excuse for relying solely on the group's networks of contacts, nor for doing nothing to improve on other skills. Various concessions and other protections that the group enjoys partly contributed to its relaxed attitude. In addition, with all the new opportunities opening up in the region, it might be too tempting to sit back without thinking through the implications. Frenzy flows of capital, which entered Thailand after its financial liberalization in the early 1990s, facilitated the financing of Thai firms' international projects. All these external factors may have influenced the group's chosen path. Nonetheless, the bottom line is that Jasmine has relied too much on its contact capabilities while not investing enough in developing other kinds of advantages that can be sustained in the long run. The recent economic crisis has given the group a valuable and expensive lesson, as succinctly put by one executive: 'All we have done in the past was trying to grow from the top of a tree. Now we know that a tree needs strong roots before it can grow' (interview, 15 December 1998).

ACKNOWLEDGEMENTS

My sincere thanks go to the participants of the Association of South-East Asian Studies UK seminar on 'Asian Management in Crisis' in June 1999, Dennis Mugwanya, Mhinder Bhopal, Mike Hitchcock and the two *Asia Pacific Business Review* referees who have provided numerous constructive comments. The financial support from the Faculty of Commerce and Accountancy, Thammasat University is highly appreciated. Lastly, this study would not be complete without the participation of all informants.

NOTES

1. Late-industrializing countries refer to those that industrialized in the twentieth century, especially after World War II (Amsden 1989, 1995). All developing countries fall under this late industrialization category.
2. This essay follows Yoshihara (1988)'s definition and takes cronyism as the practice whereby private-sector businessmen benefit enormously from their connection with the state.

3. Due to the weakness of statistics on Thai outward direct investment, the case-study methodology is preferred over the quantitative analysis. The Jasmine group was chosen because it was one of the most aggressively internationalizing Thai firms. The case study is based on information based on various sources, including interviews, annual reports, academic theses, and reports submitted to the Stock Exchange of Thailand.

4. The telecommunications bottleneck worsened in the late 1980s. Compared to other developing countries with a similar level of per capita income, the number of telephones per 100 persons in Thailand in 1987 was much lower. While Thailand had 1.67 telephones per 100 persons, Chile, Malaysia and Turkey had 4.64, 6.85, and 7.66 telephones respectively (Sakkarin, 2000: 12).

5. Shin Corp's founder, Thaksin Shinawatra, became prominent on the Thai political scene in the mid-1990s. He now leads the Thai Rak Thai (TRT) party, a new political party founded in 1997, and became Thailand's Prime Minister in January 2001.

6. Unless stated otherwise, the information in this part was drawn from the Jasmine group's annual reports and its additional reports submitted to the Stock Exchange of Thailand (56-1 forms).

7. The average exchange rate in 1999 ranged between Bt36 and Bt38 to US$1.

8. The Loxley group is controlled by the Lamsam family. Despite its variety of business, the Lamsam family is most well-known for its banking and finance activities. The family's interest in banking is represented by the Thai Farmers Bank, the country's third largest bank. TT&T's other major partner, Italian-Thai Development, is also a family-controlled conglomerate most well-known for its activities in infrastructure construction.

9. Jasmine's international projects discussed here have been identified in the company documents. However, there were reports on other projects that were not confirmed in both the company's sources and interviews. First, Jasmine International was reported to hold 15 per cent in a consortium which had won a US$900 million contract to renovate two airports in the Philippines. Two other partners were Ital-Thai (25 per cent) and Chinese Imagine Dragon (60 per cent) (*Bangkok Post*, 15 July 1995). The second project linking the Jasmine group with investment in the Philippines was another joint investment with the Ital-Thai group in a major residential-commercial real estate project in Manila Bay (*The Nation*, 13 October 1995).

10. Dennis Mugwanya, director of R & D at an AT&T subsidiary in Thailand (1992-94) and expatriate director of R & D at a Thai telecommunications company (1995–7), personal communication.

11. The two projects are: Mobile Communications Services (MCS) and JT Mobile in India. MCS, a 70:30 joint venture between Jasmine and the TOT, was established in 1997 to provide marketing services for TOT's own mobile telephone networks. The TOT had a 10 per cent equity investment in JT Mobile. However, the state agency withdrew its participation after the 1997 economic crisis (*Bangkok Post*, 27 January 1998).

12. Adisai was early associated with the CPP but switched camp to join the Thai Rak Thai party for the January 2001 election.

REFERENCES

Amsden, Alice H. (1989), *Asia's Next Giant: South Korea and Late Industrialisation*. Oxford and New York: Oxford University Press.

Amsden, Alice H. and Takashi, Hikino (1993), 'Borrowing Technology or Innovating: An Exploration of the Two Paths to Industrial Development' in R. Thompson (ed.), *Learning and Technological Change*. New York: St. Martin's Press.

Amsden, Alice H. and Takashi, Hikino (1994), 'Project Execution Capability, Organizational Know-how and Conglomerate Corporate Growth in Late Industrialization', *Industrial and Corporate Change*, Vol.3, No.1, pp.111–47.

Amsden, Alice H. (1995), 'Like the Rest: South-East Asia's "Late" Industrialization', *Journal of International Development*, Vol.7, No.5, pp.791–9.

Asia Week, 27 November 1998.

Bangkok Post, various issues.

Bangkok Post Mid-Year Review, 30 June 1991.

Biggart, Nicole Woolsey, and Gary G. Hamilton (1990), 'Explaining Asian Business Success: Theory No.4', *Business and Economic Review*, No.5, pp.13–15.

Business Day, various issues.

Business in Thailand, various issues.

Cantwell, John, and Tolentino, Paz E.E. (1990), *Technological Accumulation and Third World Multinationals*. Discussion Papers in International Investment and Business, No.139. Reading: University of Reading.

Corporate Thailand [in Thai], various issues.

Dunning, John H., van Hoesel, Roger, and Rajneesh Narula (1997), *Third World Multinationals Revisited: New Developments and Theoretical Implications*. Discussion Papers in International Investment and Management, Series B. Reading: University of Reading.

Economist Intelligence Unit (1999), *Thailand: Country Profile*. London: Economist Intelligence Unit.

Far Eastern Economic Review, various issues.

Hamilton, Gary G., and Biggart, Nicole Woolsey (1988), 'Market, Culture, and Authority: A Comparative Analysis of Management and Organisation in the Far East', *American Journal of Sociology*, Vol.94, Supplement, pp.S52–94.

Harrington, Andrew (1995), 'Companies and Capital in Asia-Pacific Telecommunications' in J. Ure (ed.), *Telecommunications in Asia: Policy, Planning and Development*. Hong Kong: Hong Kong University Press.

Hobday, Michael (1990), *Telecommunications in Developing Countries: The Challenge from Brazil*. London: Routledge.

Hobday, Mike (1995), 'East Asian Latecomer Firms: Learning the Technology of Electronics', *World Development*, Vol.23, No.7, pp.1171–93.

Hoesel, Roger van (1997), *Beyond Export-Led Growth: The Emergence of New Multinational Enterprises from Korea and Taiwan*. Rotterdam: Erasmus University.

Inkelbrecht, Nick (1995), 'Asia: The Supplier's Dilemma' in J. Ure (ed.), *Telecommunications in Asia: Policy, Planning and Development*. Hong Kong: Hong Kong University Press.

Jasmine International (1997), 56-1 Form [Additional Report Submitted to the Stock Exchange of Thailand, Bangkok].

Jasmine International (1999), Report submitted to the Stock Exchange of Thailand, 6 January and 23 February 1999.

Jasmine International Annual Report, various years.

Johnson, Chalmers (1998), 'Economic Crisis in East Asia: The Clash of Capitalisms', *Cambridge Journal of Economics*, Vol.22, No.11, pp.653–61.

Jomo, K.S., *et al.* (1997), *Southeast Asia's Misunderstood Miracle: Industrial Policy and Economic Development in Thailand, Malaysia and Indonesia*. Boulder, CO: Westview Press

Kock, Carl, and Guillen, Mauro F. (1998), 'Strategy and Structure in Developing Countries: Business Groups as an Evolutionary Response to Opportunities for Unrelated Diversification'. Paper given to Academy of International Business Conference, Vienna, November 1998.

Kraiyudht, Dhiratayakinant (1993), 'Public Enterprises' in P.G. Warr (ed.), *The Thai Economy in Transition*. Cambridge: Cambridge University Press.

Kumar, Krishna (1982), 'Third World Multinationals: A Growing Force in International Relations', *International Studies Quarterly*, Vol.26, pp. 397–424.

Lall, Sanjaya (1983a), 'The Rise of Multinationals from the Third World', *Third World Quarterly*, Vol.5, No.3, pp.618–26.

Lall, Sanjaya (1983b), *The New Multinationals: The Spread of Third World Enterprises*. New York: John Wiley.

Lecraw, Donald (1977), 'Direct Investment by Firms from Less Developed Countries', *Oxford Economic Papers*, Vol.29, No.3, pp.442–57.

Lecraw, Donald J. (1981), 'Internationalization of Firms from LDCs: Evidence from the ASEAN Region' in K. Kumar and M.G. McLeod (eds), *Multinationals from Developing Countries*. Lexington, MA: D.C. Heath.

Lecraw, Donald (1989), 'Third World Multinationals in the Service Industries' in P. Enderwick (ed.), *Multinational Service Firms*. London: Routledge.

Lecraw, Donald (1993), 'Outward Direct Investment by Indonesian Firms: Motivations and Effects', *Journal of International Business Studies*, Third Quarter, pp.589–600.

Lim, Linda Y.C. (1996), 'The Evolution of Southeast Asian Business Systems', *Journal of Asian Business*, Vol.12, No.1, pp.51–74.

Limlingan, Victor S. (1986), *The Overseas Chinese in ASEAN: Business Strategies and Management Practices*. Manila: Vita Development Corporation.

The Nation, various issues.

Natthapong, Thongpakdi (1996), *Kwam Toklong Tuapai Waduay Karnka Borikarn lae Utsahakam Torakomanakom khong Thai* [General Agreement on Trade in Services (GATS) and theThai Telecommunication Industry, in Thai]. Bangkok: Thailand Research and Development Institute.

Orru, Marco, Biggart, Nicole Woolsey, and Hamilton, Gary G. (1991), 'Organizational Isomorphism in East Asia' in W.W. Powell and P.J. DiMaggio (eds), *The New Institutionalism in Organizational Analysis*. Chicago, IL: University of Chicago Press.

Perkins, Dwight (1994), 'There are at Least Three Models of East Asian Development', *World Development*, Vol.22, No.4, pp. 655–61.

Petrazzini, Ben A. (1995), *The Political Economy of Telecommunications Reform in Developing Countries: Privatization and Liberalization in Comparative Perspective*. London: Praeger.

Petri, Peter A. (1997), 'Common Foundations of East Asian Success' in D.M. Leipziger (ed.), *Lessons from East Asia*. Ann Arbor, MI: University of Michigan Press.

Phujadkarn Rai Deun [Manager Monthly, in Thai], various issues.

Piché, Maureen D., Park, Ben, and Carlson, Roger (1997), 'NYNEX's Experiences in Thailand with TelecomAsia: An Example of Foreign Cooperation in the Opening Up and Expansion of the Telecommunications Sector in Asia' in D.J. Ryan (ed.), *Privatization and Competition in Telecommunications: International Development*. London: Praeger.

Redding, Gordon (1990), *The Spirit of Chinese Capitalism*. New York: Walter de Gruyter.

Redding, Gordon (1995), 'Overseas Chinese Networks: Understanding the Enigma', *Long Range Planning*, Vol.28, No.1, pp.61–9.

Sakar, M.B., Cavusgil, S. Tamer, and Aulakh, Preet S.(1999), 'International Expansion of Telecommunications Carriers: The Influence of Market Structure, Network Characteristics and Entry Imperfection', *Journal of International Business Studies*, Vol.30, No.2, pp. 361–82.

Sakkarin, Niyomsilpa (2000), *The Political Economy of Telecommunications Reforms in Thailand*. London: Pinter.

Srisakdi, Charmonman (1994), 'Thailand' in E. Noam, S. Komatsuzaki and D.A. Conn (eds), *Telecommunications in the Pacific Basin: An Evolutionary Approach*. New York and Oxford: Oxford University Press.

Tisco (1998), *Privatization: Opportunities Pending (Telecommunication Sector)*. Bangkok: Tisco.

Tolentino, Paz E.E. (1993), *Technological Innovation and Third World Multinationals*. London: Routledge.

Ure, John, and Vivorakij, Araya(1997), 'Privatization of Telecom in Asia' in D.J. Ryan (ed.), *Privatization and Competition in Telecommunications: International Development*. London: Praeger.

Wells, Louis T. (1977), 'The Internationalisation of Firms from Developing Countries' in T. Agmon and C.P. Kindleberger (eds), *Multinationals from Small Countries*. Cambridge, MA: MIT Press.

Wells, Louis T. (1981), 'Foreign Investors from the Third World' in K. Kumar and M.G. McLeod (eds), *Multinationals from Developing Countries*. Lexington, MA: D.C. Heath.

Wells, Louis T. (1983), *Third World Multinationals: The Rise of Foreign Investment from Developing Countries*. Cambridge, MA: MIT Press.

Who is Who in Business [in Thai], July 1995, pp.82–95.

Yeung, Henry Wai-Chung (1994), 'Third World Multinationals Revisited: A Research Critique and Future Agenda', *Third World Quarterly*, Vol.15, No.2, pp. 297–317.

Yeung, Henry Wai-chung (1998), *Transnational Corporations and Business Networks*. London: Routledge.

Yoshihara, Kunio (1988), *The Rise of Ersatz Capitalism in South-East Asia*. Oxford: Oxford University Press.

8

Downsizing the Thai Subsidiary Corporation: A Case Analysis

TIM G. ANDREWS

In the wake of the Asian economic meltdown, Thai businesses habituated to seemingly inexorable sales and profit growth were suddenly faced with the prospect of shrinking purchasing power, rising production costs and excessive staffing levels (*Bangkok Post*, 1998; Bardacke, 1998). As the crisis deepened and corporate productivity levels continued to deteriorate, the domestic subsidiaries of formerly indulgent Western 'parents' were placed under an increasingly critical microscope from corporate headquarters, a development that was to result in the local imposition of a stream of organizational restructuring programmes. But in spite of the apparently sound strategic objectives of these measures, the vast majority suffered from resistance and dilution at the stage of implementation, causing productivity decline and poor performance (InfoThai, 1998; Nivatpumin and Sivasomboon, 1997).

This contribution aims to develop existing research into the impact of indigenous business culture on the fortunes of these Western corporate restructuring programmes during the initial stages of the Thai economic crisis. More precisely, it seeks to add richness to our understanding of how the key *cultural* dimensions can determine the acceptance or resistance of change among local management and staff. Drawing on the author's years of experience at the Thai subsidiary of a European oil marketer, the intention is to provide the reader with an in-depth analysis of how the Western-corporate and Thai-societal elements of the subsidiary's culture can fragment and conflict while in the throes of an externally-imposed programme of organizational restructuring. In contrast to the majority of statistically-based cross-national analyses, this paper adds to the field a rare internal Thai case study founded on qualitative, in-depth participant observation which takes advantage of the author's largely unhindered access to the internal workings of the organization.[1]

This contribution is organized as follows: sections two and three review and develop the relevant literature on organizational downsizing (with special reference to Thailand) and organizational culture as the 'driving engine' of both change initiation and subsequent resistance. Section four provides an overview of the empirical context to our case study and the methodology employed. An overview of the culturally-based Thai 'reaction' to the downsizing programmes precedes section six which relates the relevant future implications for both management theorists and practitioners seeking to understand the Thai business arena. Section seven summarizes the key findings drawn from the study and elicits some tentative conclusions.

ORGANIZATIONAL DOWNSIZING

Depicted as the most prevalent business dilemma of recent years, the preoccupation of Western companies with organizational downsizing in the past two decades is held to be an occidental reaction both to lower growth and to the changing international business setting. Viewed as a 'correction' or 'antidote' to the over-expansion of firms with no concurrent increase in value, this oft-cited euphemism for 'layoffs' has become the favoured strategy of many companies attempting to reduce unsustainable cost-structures and ensure high productivity levels. (Morden, 1997; Labib and Appelbaum, 1993).

A recent empirical survey into downsized US firms concluded that repeated layoffs tend to produce lower profits and declining worker productivity. This, in turn, prompted a re-examination of the importance of the methods employed by corporations in implementing their downsizing strategies. Nonetheless, the literature suggests that the practice does not appear to be dissipating, with a reported 60 per cent of companies planning to continue downsizing over the next few years. The recent spate of economic crises in both East and West indicates that worldwide competition has not only intensified but that continuing and even more painful restructuring may lie ahead (Mishra and Spreitzer, 1998; Cameron, Freeman and Mishra, 1991).

Downsizing in Thailand

Most of this sparse body of literature stems from the prosperous, almost carefree attitude that reigned before the recent economic recession became deeper and more serious than anyone had anticipated. Prior economic conditions in Thailand had been so strong that the concept of laying off staff seemed a remote and alien prospect, something that 'only happened in the West'.

The traditional Thai antipathy to downsizing – particularly by Western-parented companies – is reflected in a labour law which makes layoffs difficult and potentially costly. The nature of social relationships in Thai culture is such that the need for externally imposed change programmes is invariably construed as a 'loss of face' by senior local executives accustomed to the traditional top-down management system. The potential for conflict involved in the displacement of individuals through concepts such as downsizing and 'restructuring' runs counter to the Thai notion, grounded in a stable, continuous agrarian history, of the need to preserve societal harmony. Thai-run corporations thus tend to stress incremental as opposed to radical change and opt for early retirement – or 'lateral displacement' – as the preferred method for reducing staff headcount. (Mead, 1998; Kind, 1997; Lawler *et al.*, 1997; Nivatpumin and Sivasompoon, 1997; Lawler and Atmivanandana, 1995).

The successful implementation of Western 'delayering' systems in socially hierarchical Thailand should begin with a careful consideration of Thai societal culture. Companies must therefore focus their attentions beyond the conventional preoccupation with restructuring the hierarchy and devote their time to the more subtle, demanding task of changing individual practices, attitudes and values (e.g. Hallinger, 1998; Holmes and Tantongtavy, 1995).

ORGANIZATIONAL CULTURE

The growing disenchantment with theories that portray efficiency as the driving force behind decision-making have led modern institutional theory to emphasize the *cultural* aspects of an organization's structure and heritage (Brown, 1995; Schein, 1985). Although the literature concerning these matters offers no settled definitions, the term organizational or corporate culture usually refers to the informal aspects of an organization which impact upon its behaviour or methods of working (as opposed to the 'formal structure' which refers to the organizational hierarchy). The fundamental distinction to be made within the Western-parented Thai subsidiary is between the influences of this *corporate* (or organizational) culture on the one hand and *societal* (usually national) culture on the other (Abell, 1996; Smith, 1998).

Corporate Culture

Corporate culture, particularly where selection, socialization and other such internal practices are rigorous, is held to overcome or minimize the influence of national identity by design. In essence, being a truly global organization implies having a *universal* corporate culture where *all* members of the organization – regardless of nationality – hold similar views and beliefs that guide their behaviours when transacting business (Neal, 1998). Adherents to the power of corporate culture view it as the 'hidden adhesive' holding geographically dispersed units together (Ralston *et al.*, 1997; Schneider and Barsoux, 1997).

National Culture

As business becomes increasingly global, the transferability of management theory and practice across national borders has become a widely debated topic, particularly in the wake of Hofstede's empirical studies – discussed ad nauseam in the international business literature – which have set the agenda for a strong culturalist analysis of management practice (Hofstede, 1980). Subsequent studies have concurred in the view that managerial attitudes and beliefs, and consequently the pattern of decision-making, are shaped by national culture (Neal, 1998; Schneider and Barsoux, 1997; Erramilli, 1996).

Increasingly, researchers and practitioners have concluded that the *exportability* of management theories and practices is also determined by the comparability of cultural values between the exporting and importing nation. Fundamental differences, manifest in the thought, behaviour and actions of employees worldwide are believed to increase conflict potential between overseas headquarters and subsidiaries by encouraging communication breakdown and resistance to parent-company directives (Hennart and Larimo, 1998; Lubatkin *et al.*, 1997; Bigoness and Blakeley, 1996).

In this context it is necessary to explore what is referred to as the 'Thai national culture', seeking to capture and define the elusive 'Thai-ness' of a locally-embedded organization, and the implications this may hold for the Western corporation seeking to implement a programme of change.

The Societal Environment: Thai Business Culture

Home to an established constitutional monarchy and a relatively stable, democratic political system, 'wildly capitalistic' free-market Thailand would appear to be the ideal candidate for the successful reception of Western management practice. Beneath the surface, however, the Thai kingdom has been able to retain its language, culture and tradition almost entirely intact. Ethnically much less diverse than most of its neighbours, Thailand boasts the distinction of being the only South East Asian country never to have been colonized by the forces of 'Western imperialism' throughout a national history spanning over 800 years.

As an offshoot from traditional Asian environmental culture, the literature on Asian *business* culture has traditionally focused on Japanese and, more recently, Chinese management styles. Much of the sparse and fragmented literature surrounding Thai managerial culture – which underpins traditional business relations with the West – tends to be centred on the superficial conventions of social discourse aimed primarily at the short-term corporate expatriate (e.g. Cooper, 1993).

More substantially, a limited number of studies have sought to frame Thai managerial values within the confines of the Hofstede criteria, apparently demonstrating that Thai culture expresses relatively high needs to 'avoid uncertainty', a high level of 'societal collectivism' and 'high power distance.' The majority of such research focuses primarily on the latter two elements, the 'power distance' factor held to be reflected in the highly centralized, autocratic decision-making process.

In the context of the workplace, Thai culture tends to emphasize the harmony of the group over the needs of the individual, with the typical senior manager taking a greater degree of responsibility for the personal lives of his constituents than his Western counterpart. Individuals define their identity by their relationships to others through group membership and strive for a sense of belonging. It is thus this strength of patronage and family loyalties rather than bureaucratic norms that determine relationships between company members. In such an environment information is gathered predominantly through informal channels and personal relationships – and then interpreted through intense, face-to-face discussion and debate in the belief that multiple perspectives and extensive information sharing are necessary to comprehend external ambiguity (Hallinger, 1998; Lawler *et al.*, 1997; Infothai, 1998; Holmes and Tangtongtavy, 1995).

Thai Subsidiary Corporations: The Cultural 'Hybrids'

Cultures often go unnoticed – until we try to implement a new strategy or programme which is incompatible with the central norms and values of the organization. Then the hidden power of culture tends to emerge, particularly when the implemented programme is incompatible with existing business practices (Birkinshaw and Hood, 1998; Smith, 1998).

As the Thai subsidiary of a UK multinational, the 'culture' inherent in the case study presented in this contribution is a blend of the Western home office culture on the one hand and the Thai societal culture on the other. In assessing the relative strength or balance between these twin dynamic elements in the organization's culture, scholars responsible for the small but growing body of literature differ widely. At one extreme authors such as Burack believe that corporate values are 'deeply ingrained', giving rise to patterns of uniformity in behavioural patterns among organizational units regardless of geographic, functional or business boundaries. Schein suggests that corporate values could be as influential as national culture and recent 'convergence' proponents cast doubt on the relevance of Hofstede's national dimensions as an outmoded concept in a world of global markets and transnational corporations (Barkema and Vermeulen, 1997; Schneider and Barsoux, 1997; Erramilli, 1996).

Towards the opposite end of the spectrum authors such as Hofstede (1991) and Laurent (1986) doubt whether corporate culture can ever seriously modify more deeply ingrained national culture values. As Smith (1998) points out, corporate culture is based in the visible practices of an organization and may be walked away from, modified or consciously changed. Real changes in national culture, on the other hand, may take generations. In the words of Schneider and Barsoux (1997), 'the tip can melt but below the surface the reach of (national) culture remains profound.' Ultimately the single foreign subsidiary will always express a relative point on a cultural continuum represented by the 'corporate way' at one end and the 'societal way' at the other. Although, conceptually, there has never been a systematic attempt made to disentangle these constituent elements, it is held that in the context of a highly sensitive Western programme of organizational downsizing imposed in economically-beleaguered Thailand this may now be possible. With traditional business values and norms increasingly under threat from home office demands for change, one would expect the existing mix of cultural elements to fragment – thereby providing the ideal opportunity to examine Western corporate and Thai societal values in internecine conflict.

EMPIRICAL BACKGROUND: THE CASE OF SAC (THAILAND) CO. LTD

Overview

A successful marketer of premium-grade motor lubricants, the SAC group comprises a world team of some 10,000 people supplying products through 80 subsidiaries and a further 50 agents. SAC corporate philosophy turns upon the 'lubricant' metaphor, used to denote the reduction of friction, of 'keeping things running smoothly', both internally and for their customers. With its focus on the premium end of the market, SAC has traditionally competed on product differentiation as 'the route to competitive advantage'.

Core values build on the 'premium specialist' tag to embrace 'technology-leadership' and 'high performance'.

SAC 's stated goal is to be a 'multi-local multinational', which they claim means bringing in the best of their 'international expertise' while 'making sure it is absolutely right for the local people'. SAC lubricants are well established in East Asia – formerly the 'jewel' in the corporate fold – with business units in China, Malaysia, Singapore, Vietnam and Indonesia, as well as Thailand. In spite of the recent economic turmoil, the region remains a 'key plank' of the company's forward corporate strategy, evidenced by the relocation of SAC regional headquarters from the UK to Hong Kong at the end of 1998 in order to better 'live, breathe and feel the markets on a day-to-day basis'.

Initial growth levels at SAC Thailand prompted head office to upgrade the Thai unit into a fully-fledged corporate subsidiary, a move previously only attempted in the former British colonies of Hong Kong and Singapore. The Thai unit began operations as an agency some 30 years ago before sustained levels of growth led to the formation of a wholly-owned SAC subsidiary in 1976. Expanding concurrently with the rapid rise of the Thai economy from the mid-1980s, the company enjoyed strong sales and profitability growth to the extent that by the early 1990s the Thai unit had risen from nowhere to number four in the global corporate fold. Credited with developing the Thai unit from its inception, the long-serving and widely respected British CEO was left relatively unquestioned by corporate headquarters as to his distinctive 'laissez-faire' management style.

Cultural Make-Up

As with any subsidiary corporation, in its formative years the organizational culture of this Thai division was primarily shaped by the 'corporate element', with a high percentage of expatriate workers on hand to formulate the norms and values of the corporate home office. This approximates to the miniature replica system aspired to by ambitious Western corporations in their quest for a seamless global organization. During the years that follow, however, such companies have come to expect a progressive and potentially costly influx of influence from the surrounding – in this case 'Thai' – environment to 'seep in', enhanced by the gradual transfer of technology skills and the repatriation of Western executives (see also Prahalad and Doz, 1981).

In the case of SAC (Thailand) Ltd the organization became steadily more 'indigenous' in flavour as day-to-day power was gradually invested by the CEO in the six Thai directors who together comprised the unit's 'executive committee'. Taking pride in the fact that 90 per cent of its top managers in the company were Thai, the SAC quota of 'foreigners' was kept by the chief at far less than the permitted maximum (either by SAC corporate or Thai authorities) of 15 per cent. A major thrust of the locally-inspired business practice philosophy at SAC Thailand was therefore that this 'Thai' division responsible for the 'Thai' market must be managed the 'Thai way'.

Data Collection

From the outset it was decided that a quantitatively-based study would be inappropriate for researching the downsizing of a Thai-based case study organization. In the Eastern social context it simply cannot be assumed that managers will respond in the same way as their Western counterparts. Along with Adler *et al.* (1989), it is held that the *qualitative* method in the form of a case study design is the only suitable methodology for conducting business research in South East Asia. The most significant advantage of case research lies in multiple sources of data that can be used for analysis, although it also allowed the author to employ and develop personal connections (or *guanxi* in Mandarin) with the senior managers at SAC's Thai subsidiary.

As a former employee of the company in question, the author relied heavily upon both participant and direct observation of both the programme of downsizing itself and the subsequent local reaction to the implementation methods employed between November 1997 and November 1998. Systematic semi-structured and unstructured interviews were conducted in a mix of English and Thai with three 'senior' managers from all six functional departments, with a focus on marketing and sales (where the majority of the change measures had been imposed). Observation and informal discussions were then used to gauge the opinions of the junior managers and their staff. Verbal questioning sessions across the company were held with a number of externally appointed 'advisers/consultants' drafted into the Thai unit by corporate home office in order to calibrate the reliability of some of the internal viewpoints. Finally, intra-corporate reports, memorandums and communiqués were also collected and examined.

Economic Meltdown: 1997–98

Almost without exception the literature cited above pertains to the period prior to the onslaught of economic and financial meltdown in South East Asia. The devaluation of the Thai baht in July 1997 precipitated the region's worst economic crisis in four decades, wreaking havoc on corporate-sector balance sheets Motor lubricant consumption, traditionally a reflection of economic activity, shrank by some 15 per cent for 1997 and nearly double that figure in the following year, intensifying the already fierce competition among lubricant marketing firms. Most of the oil marketing companies hardly made any profit in the first year of crisis and many were running at a loss and heavily in debt by year-end 1998. 'Survival' appears to be the current industry watch-word as companies have continued to struggle with tightening marketing margins, investment commitments and rising operating costs (Bardacke, 1998; Siamwalla and Sobchokchai, 1998; Stiglitz, 1998).

The traditional brand loyalty shown towards the likes of Shell, Mobil and Caltex eroded rapidly through 1998, with traders placing greater emphasis on getting maximum volume returns. As the recession wore on, price effectively surpassed brand as a deciding factor in product choice among hard-hit motorists. A flood of cheaper mineral brands found their way onto the Thai market as the low-cost, often illegal local distributors have been the only suppliers to have increased their volume sales.

The switch to Thai local produce was also exacerbated by the unprecedented wave of culturally-insular, anti-Western xenophobia stirred in the local media. Foreign – particularly Western – producers along with the IMF-controlled 'programme of economic recovery' were stigmatized as the twin destroyers of the Thai economy. Even the King began to berate the tendency of some Western businesses to 'gold-dig' the country in its 'hour of need' (Bardacke, 1998; Santimatanedol, 1999).

SAC Pre-Crisis: 1996–97

Towards the end of 1996, almost as a reflection of the wider Thai economy, the 'boom' period at SAC appeared to be nearing its end. Against the backdrop of shrinking local purchasing power, the company appeared to have become internally unbalanced, evidenced by its progressively unsustainable staffing levels, recruitment having doubled from 1993 to 1996. Efficiency levels were deemed to have become sub-optimal, reflected by the gradual decline in levels of profitability growth. Beyond the concern with the unit balance sheet, home office had also begun to show signs of impatience with underlying local business practices and norms. As the year progressed the Thai senior management was confronted with an influx of strategic advisers drafted in to assess the situation from corporate headquarters.

Information garnered from these new corporate arrivals sheds some light on the externally-perceived influence of indigenous cultural practice upon the Thai subsidiary's day-to-day business methodology. To begin with, concern was expressed at the 'despotic' power of the six departmental directors, referred to as the 'Thai barons'. These functional heads appeared to have consolidated their positions by their relationship with their intensely loyal subordinates, among whom they were perceived as providing direction, control and support. Corporate advisers claimed to be 'staggered' at the breadth and depth of nepotism within each department, even among the administrative staff, chauffeurs and maids. However, as an indication of the strength of the informal, relations-based structure in Thai business culture the literature tends to support this state of affairs as being fairly typical. In a society where secrecy and appeal to the loyalty of the group form the crux of commercial activity, there appears to be little room for Western notions of the 'professional manager' (Smith, 1998).

As the Thai market began to slow further, SAC corporate began to criticize the unit's internal structure as being 'over-manned' and 'ponderous' – giving rise to 'lengthy, rambling meetings', 'slow processing routines' and 'excessive monitoring'. The flexibility once regarded as being ideal for the local environment were now being viewed as a hindrance to the installation of international business codes of conduct, particularly in the light of Thailand's failure over five years to acquire ISO 9000 – the only unit in the region without the award. From the perspective of the newly employed Quality and Environmental Executive there appeared to be an astounding lack of any written records or procedures, widespread duplication of tasks and an ambiguous, conflicting set of job descriptions. Within the marketing sphere the company's promotion campaigns were deemed to be 'haphazard' in design and implementation, with little or no evidence of planning, feedback or performance measurement.

SAC Post-Crisis: 1997–98

The full effects of the economic downturn took several months to filter through to the corporate sector. For the vast majority of SAC staff, July 1997 was remembered chiefly as the month in which the long-serving British CEO retired and was replaced with the corporate-selected Western newcomer, David Lloyd. However, within a few months the new chief was to display a style of management perceived by Thai employees as being diametrically opposed to 'traditional' methods. Depicted as a 'hands-on' financially-oriented strategist, Lloyd was in many respects the apotheosis of the 'SAC corporate manager', held to typify the Western home office culture and mentality. Lloyd's new programme of 'internal cost management' began with a notice announcing a reduction of the traditional annual bonus and a cancellation of the New Year staff party. By year-end Lloyd had retracted nearly all of the jealously guarded perquisites enjoyed by the directors and had reduced the size of the management committee with little apparent regard for the ensuing loss of face, status and position.

Among SAC respondents these events were expressions of this 'new style' of doing business and strongly resented. The previous incumbent, perceived as a 'well-loved' and 'kindly' figure was fond of the directional style known as 'management by walking around', content to play the role of avuncular figurehead with trust in his team of directors to run their own departments. With seemingly ever-increasing profits, SAC headquarters had traditionally allowed a considerable amount of autonomy at their Thai unit, content to agree with the CEO's philosophy that local affairs were best run the 'Thai-way'.

Lloyd, by contrast, had years of experience of managing SAC units in other parts of Asia, Europe and even South America, with a track record of turning around loss-making ventures into highly profitable 'cash cows'. SAC corporate representatives later admitted that the nature and severity of the economic crisis had caused them to substitute Lloyd over a – presumably – more 'placid' colleague who they had originally earmarked for the task of directing SAC Thailand. Part of Lloyd's mandate was to initiate deeper change at the business-process level as a move towards trying to bring the Thai unit 'back into line' with SAC corporate business practice. In this context Lloyd's stated refusal to alter 'his' agenda for the sake of preserving Thai working methods seems understandable.

Incensed by the length of meetings and endless face-to face discussions, Lloyd swiftly enforced the 'corporate' method of transparent internal communication by electronic mail with meetings being kept to a one-to-one basis and convened as rarely as possible. This locally perceived 'darkroom' management style jarred with the Thai managers, however, who considered e-communication as being inappropriate for the local business environment. The traditional method employed by the SAC directors was to keep all information stored mentally among two or three close confidants with as little written evidence in circulation as possible – claimed, again, as the 'Thai way' of doing business. On a broader level Lloyd's changes were increasingly resented by the Thai staff as 'dictatorial', 'arrogant' and 'aggressive' – with Lloyd himself perceived as the archetypal Western expatriate with neither the time nor inclination to listen to his local subordinates.

'PROJECT DELTA': THE SAC SEPARATION PROGRAMME

Although under considerable pressure to re-align their employee needs, SAC corporate HQ were initially very wary of announcing a programme of layoffs for fear that they might be liable to lawsuits or other such discriminatory measures by the local Labour and Social Welfare Ministry (having just passed legislation designed to protect Thai employees from the perceived 'slash and burn' tradition of Western companies). At the local level the management committee reiterated the traditional Thai antipathy towards layoffs and stressed their commitment to achieving any job losses by means such as natural turnover, redeployment and a reduction in the use of temporary staff. Management committee representatives felt at the time that such measures would be enough to achieve the savings needed to be made while at the same time 'saving face' for all concerned.

However, as the situation deteriorated corporate headquarters felt they could only press ahead with redundancies in order to survive. Following a number of joint enquiries initiated by the key Western players, the path for downsizing was effectively cleared with the Thai authorities as of October 1997. Apparently oblivious to these developments, the Thai management at SAC began to warn staff of the gravity of the trading environment and the changes that may come 'as a last resort'. A human resources handout was distributed among staff to provide an overview of the company situation with an outline of why certain changes *might* be needed and what they *might* mean for company staff. As of the following January respondents claimed that open invitations were being made to staff to 'register their interest in taking voluntary redundancy'. Again, this was apparently being done with the tacit though non-committal approval of the CEO.

In this context the 'sea-change' in implementation methodology three months later came as an almost complete surprise to the Thai directors. Following the traditional week-long *Songkran* water-festival holiday in mid-April, staff returned to the office on Monday 19 April 1998 to find an announcement pinned to the company noticeboards. This announcement, outlining a 'programme of separation' for SAC staff, would prove to be the document which entailed the termination of employment for almost a fifth of the company's employees. In substance this 'programme' – with its relatively generous redundancy package – was to focus almost exclusively on administrative staff, factory workers and part-timers. At this juncture the only comment to be issued from Lloyd's office was that such measures were 'necessary' at the structural level due to the severity of the economic crisis, and as opposed to any desire or whim on the part of corporate HQ.

Among the vast majority of Thai employees, by contrast, the announcement was viewed as a flagrant breach of traditional commercial practice. The announcement had been made with little or no consultation with the management committee, no face-to-face debates to gauge the reaction of staff and no apparent warning. Decisions on such matters were traditionally taken on consensus, with notions of 'loyalty' and 'commitment' seen as the all-important qualities for staff and senior management alike. But in this case a predominantly young set of employees – with no experience of economic recession – were informed of the existence of a 'layoff list' which they were to consult within 48 hours of the appearance of the notice. Each head of department was to act as a 'keeper'. i.e. as the channel through which an individual was to learn of his fate within the company.

The second part of the announcement dealt with certain other structural changes, notably the removal of administration from HR over to Finance, as well as the division of sales and marketing into two separate units (a move that would effectively demote the existing sales and marketing director). Finally, in mid-1998 a regional policy was enacted to re-assess staffing needs by means of a 'performance-appraisal' grading garnered from a company-wide input/output process matrix. On this basis a handful of individual 'casualties' were to be determined annually by the departmental heads with an emphasis on the more costly middle-management positions.

REACTIONS TO THE PROGRAMME: SAC AND 'THAI VALUES'

The imposition of a Western-oriented programme of downsizing – with its concurrent threat to Thai business norms – appears to have led to the fragmentation of the corporate and societal elements of the SAC (Thailand) organizational culture. The key issue to determine here is whether or not the corporate downsizing measures implemented by Lloyd were congruent with local business culture values. Although it was generally acknowledged among local staff that change in some form of downsizing was inevitable, it was the *manner* in which the separation programme was imposed that served as the catalyst for concern.

To begin with, Lloyd's decision to announce the changes by way of a notice was perceived as being confrontational and at odds with 'the ways things were done' in Thailand. Local management claimed unanimously that 'cultural factors' and 'human resource limitations' meant that any organizational delayering programme should have been phased in incrementally. In the word's of SAC Thailand's marketing manager, 'they can't just use a foreign model here and chop, chop, chop. Like head office we are also looking for the minimum costs per unit but for us this does not automatically mean we must cut headcount. There are other methods – many other ways.'

One particular criticism of the 'layoff list' made by the Thai managers concerned the perceived callousness of the targeted 'deadwood' staff. Both marketing and operations departments had long-serving middle-aged managers holding senior administration posts who, although having served the company for more than 30 years each, were apparently considered as expendable by Lloyd due to their age and perceived lack of IT literacy. So far as local management was concerned, the loss of such staff was considered wholly unsuitable to a culture where the qualities of age and seniority – as opposed to performance and knowledge – remained paramount.

Appealing to local 'paternalistic' responsibilities at a depth beyond Western business norms, the concept of 'performance' in the occidental sense was rejected on the grounds of irrelevancy – 'performance appraisal' in the Western sense of the term was deemed inappropriate for a Thai sales department. Management pointed instead to the targeted employees' 'loyalty' and 'integrity of character' as being of far more import. The Thai concept of 'kreng jai' – whereby an individual seeks to avoid potentially traumatic or discomforting situations even where his or her own interests may be compromised – and 'bunkhun' – the psychological bond formed from reciprocated favours over time – were also alluded to as factors in the debate. These Thai cultural idiosyncrasies were deemed as having a marked effect on the local boss-subordinate relationship beyond what any Western-oriented set of values could either ever comprehend or seriously impose. In this context the apparent unwillingness among many members of the 'layoff list' to actually leave the company premises begins to seem logical, despite expressions to the contrary from resident Western expatriates. Certainly the remaining departmental heads implicitly approved the return of redundant former staff on an almost daily basis to converse and dine with their ex-colleagues and employers – often doubling, of course, as friends and family (see also Holmes and Tangtongtavy, 1995; Cooper, 1993).

More generally, the perceived corporate strategy of focusing entirely on financial returns as the means for mobilizing change was vociferously disputed. Lloyd's stated desire to 'straighten out the business first' before 'worrying about the people' was held as a culturally-flawed methodology in the Thai business environment. One notable comment from the marketing director summarizes this felling when he states that 'if you give Thais the message that you come only for profit and forget about relationships, this will give you many big difficulties with business, especially in the long-term'. In a sense, this strengthening of the threatened 'Thai element' in the culture of the organization was compounded by the wider rise of local nationalism in the local media, as Western investors and the IMF were targeted for the extent of the crisis. SAC local staff assumed and feared that the intent of Lloyd's separation programme was to destroy this existing culture, to undermine its coherency and dissolve cherished Thai national identities, values and assumptions.

From a narrower perspective, the fact that none of the five Western employees had been selected to join the separation programme was particularly resented, notwithstanding the fact that all five positions were viewed from HQ as representing indispensable, technical roles. The assumption made among the Thai staff was that the Westerners had all been informed of the plans to downsize, each of them safely in the knowledge that they would be secure under the direction of 'one of their own' (i.e. Lloyd). The broad feeling was that these 'foreigners' – including Lloyd – were simply passing through the Thai unit in order to boost their international careers at the expense of a local business which they were now seeking to dismantle.

In this climate a series of anonymous and threatening letters began to circulate across the company premises, damning and threatening in their description of the arrogant 'Western imports'.

Among middle and senior-ranking Thai staff the frequency of interaction at the *informal* level began to demonstrate a subtle but pervasive polarization of the workforce along national lines. The growing perception among local staff was that they were being held ransom to a Western conspiracy designed to 'destroy' their cherished style of working which, until very recently, had been the target only for unreserved praise and admiration.

IMPLICATIONS FOR MANAGEMENT AND FURTHER RESEARCH

Implications for Management

It would appear from this study that the *Thai* cultural element of SAC was the key determinant of whether or not Western-oriented change was accepted. This was in contrast to how Lloyd – and by default SAC corporate – had ascertained the situation prior to implementing their downsizing programme. The Thai national culture, inherent in the unit's managerial norms and values, became the major impediment to change acceptance, exacerbated by the nature of the economic crisis and the retreat into nationalist sentiment. The organizational culture of SAC (Thailand) Ltd thus expresses a point firmly to the Thai national extreme of the 'corporate-societal' continuum.

While SAC were correct in their perception of the need to rationalize and reorganize their Thai subsidiary, they were flawed in their implementation methodology, failing to account for the strength and resilience of the informal unit structure predominated by Thai values and processes. The corporate objective of imposing a 'blanket' programme of organizational restructuring across its South East Asian units is a needlessly high-risk strategy founded on assumptions that are both misguided and naive. Thai business norms express qualitatively distinct ideas of what constitutes appropriate management practice and Western management would do well to assume the same for other foreign subsidiaries – both in Asia and beyond – before attempting to push ahead a policy perceived as a cultural threat. The failure of SAC even to try and see – yet alone understand – this issue was to result in an extended period of dysfunctional working practices, disharmonious relations and poor performance that continued to suppress profitability throughout rest of 1998.

On a broader level, the idea that one can transcend geographical cultural differences through the imposition of a 'top down' corporate culture should be treated with caution. Against the assumption that holds that all institutions are driven by the same desire for short-term bottom-line efficiency – regardless of societal context – corporate headquarters should avoid seeking to extrapolate uniform values across cultures to save resources. In general terms the case of SAC (Thailand) Ltd appears to highlight the need for an international 'patchwork' structure of change programmes, attuning corporate sales and marketing processes to the needs of individual market cultures (see also Neal, 1998; Gomez-Meija and Palich, 1997; Hofstede, 1991).

Recommendations for Management

From a practical perspective, SAC might consider the appointment of a number of Thai corporate 'diplomats' to facilitate the acceptance of corporate change. Operating at the cross-functional interface they could facilitate the business-culture congruency of any future corporate change package. Implementation agreements reached between both headquarters-subsidiary and internal departments would allow some flexibility in interpretation to encourage the rapid emergence of optimal working solutions attained through a greater degree of consensus.

Secondly, the chance of a smooth transition to new organizational designs in Thailand would be enhanced by paying close attention to the selection of an *appropriate* country manager attempting to implement change in an *appropriate* manner (i.e. via a more conciliatory approach in the case above). The country manager in Thailand plays a particularly crucial role and should be able to function in both the culture of the local environment and that of the corporate home office. Any organizational culture based in Thailand will be more opaque to the Western recruit than to the native Thai and the ideal Western CEO would pay close attention to the sensitivities of the local management. The failure by Lloyd at SAC Thailand to pursue such notions is borne out by his premature and unexpected departure at the end of 1998 – just 15 months into his five-year tenure at the helm. In order to mollify local management a more 'moderate' replacement was installed in the form of a half-British, half-Chinese marketing executive with more than a decade of experience with SAC units in Eastern Asia.

Implications for Future Research

The cultural ramifications of implementing a Western-oriented programme of downsizing in Thailand is still under-researched, and the issues suggested in this article are relatively novel. However, it would be presumptuous to assume a wider environmental applicability for this single case study and the results we have presented must therefore be used with caution. Nonetheless, this case study of SAC (Thailand) Ltd can be viewed as a rich and detailed database for further case studies, comparative studies and surveys of a more quantitative nature. It is also anticipated that these observations – made in the Thai environmental context of a UK multinational enterprise – may provide insights for corporate strategists operating in other transition and developing economies, particularly those of South East Asia.

CONCLUSIONS

Textually, we have sought to add richness to our current understanding of how the business values of a developing ASEAN economy can impact upon the imposition of Western-sponsored programme of organizational change. From this detailed empirical analysis of one revelatory Thai subsidiary corporation we have demonstrated how a culturally incongruent implementation methodology can engender a myriad of informally-based disputes with regard to local management practices and values. Face, status, seniority, *kreng jai*, *bunkhun* and the host of other norms unique to Thai business culture were shown to exert a powerful influence upon a controversial programme which was perceived as a threat to the existing structural network The resilience of traditional managerial values from this case appears to bode ill for simplistic Western notions of the 'seamless' global corporate culture.

NOTE

1. Corporate and individual identities are protected in this study by the use of pseudonyms.

REFERENCES

Abell, P. (1996), 'A Model of the Informal Structure (Culture) of Organizations: Help, Trust, Rivalry and Team Spirit', *Rationality and Society*, pp.433–52.

Adler, N., *et al.* (1989), 'In Search of Appropriate Research Methodology: From Outside the People's Republic of China Looking In', *Journal of International Business Studies*, Vol.28, No.1, pp.61–74.

Bangkok Post (1998), *Foreign Investment: The World in Thailand*. Bangkok: Post Publications.

Bardacke, T. (1998), 'Asia's Great Depression', *Financial Times*, 1 July.

Barkema, H.G., and Vermeulen, F. (1997), 'What Differences in the Cultural Backgrounds of Partners are Detrimental for International Joint Ventures?', *Journal of International Business Studies*, Vol.28, pp.845–65.

Bigoness, William J., and Blakely, Gerald L. (1996), 'A Cross-National Study of Managerial Values', *Journal of International Business Studies*, Vol.27, No.4, pp.739–53.

Birkinshaw, J., and Hood, N. (1998), 'Multinational Subsidiary Evolution: Capability and Charter Change in Foreign Owned Subsidiary Companies', *Academy of Management Review*, Vol.23, pp.773–96.

Brown, A.D. (1995), *Organisational Culture*. London: Pitman

Cameron, K.S., Freeman, S.J., and Mishra, A.K. (1993), 'Organizational Downsizing' in G. Huber and W. Glick (eds), *Organizational Change and Redesign: Ideas and Insights for Improving Performance*. New York: Oxford University Press, pp.19–65.

Cooper, R. (1993), *Thais Mean Business*. Singapore: Times Books International.

Erramilli, M.K. (1996), 'Nationality and Subsidiary Ownership Patterns in Multinational Corporations', *Journal of International Business Studies*, Vol.27, No.2, pp.225–49.

Gomez-Meija, L.R., and Palich, L.E. (1997), 'Cultural Diversity and the Performance of Multinational Firms', *Journal of International Business Studies*, Vol.28, No.2, pp.309–36.

Hallinger, P. (1998), 'A Challenge for Don Quixote: Reengineering Higher Education in Thailand' in *International Conference on Reengineering the Thai University*. Chiang Mai: Centre for Leadership and Development.

Hennart, J.F., and Larimo, J. (1998), 'The Impact of Culture on the Strategy of Multinational Enterprises: Does National Origin Affect Ownership Decisions?', *Journal of International Business Studies*, Vol.29, pp.515–39.

Hofstede, G. (1991), *Cultures and Organisations: Software of the Mind*. London: McGraw Hill.

Hofstede, G. (1980), *Culture's Consequences: International Differences in Work-Related Values*. Beverly Hills, CA: Sage.

Holmes, H., and Tangtongtavy, S. (1995), *Working with the Thais*. Bangkok: White Lotus.

Infothai Co. (1998), 'The Thai Attitude to Work'. *Infothai CM*, 18 June.

Kind, S. (1997), 'Please Hammer Don't Hurt Me', *Bangkok Post*, 18 Sep.

Labib, N., and Appelbaum, S.H. (1993). 'Strategic Downsizing: a Human Resources Perspective,' *Human Resource Planning*, Vol.16, pp.69–94.

Laurent, A. (1986), 'The Cross-Cultural Puzzle of International Human Resource Management', *HR Management*, Vol.25, pp.91–102.

Lawler, J.J., Siengthai, S., and Atmiyanandana, V. (1997), 'HRM in Thailand: Eroding Traditions', *Asia Pacific Business Review*, Vol.3, No.4, pp.170–196.

Lawler, J.L. (1996), 'Diversity Issues in South-East Asia: The Case of Thailand.' *International Journal of Manpower* Vol.17, pp.152–68.

Lawler, J.J., and Atmiyanandana, V. (1995), 'HRM Management in Thailand' in Larry F. Moore and P. Devereaux Jennings (eds), *Human Resource Management on the Pacific Rim: Institutions, Practices and Attitudes*. Berlin: de Gruyter, pp.294–318.

Lubatkin, M.H., Ndiaye, M., and Vengroff, R (1997), 'The Nature of Managerial Work in Developing Countries: A Limited Test of the Universalist Hypothesis', *Journal of International Business Studies*, Vol.28, No.4, pp.711–35.

Mead, R. (1998), *International Management*. Oxford: Blackwell.

Mishra, A.K., and Spreitzer, G.M. (1998), 'Explaining How Survivors Respond to Downsizing: The Roles of Trust, Empowerment, Justice and Work Redesign', *Academy of Management Review*, Vol.23, pp.567–89

Morden, T. (1997), 'A Strategic Evaluation of Reengineering, Restructuring, Delayering and Downsizing Policies as Flawed Paradigm', *Management Decision*, Vol.35, pp.240–340.

Neal, M. (1998), *The Culture Factor: Cross-National Management and the Foreign Venture*. London: Macmillan.

Nivatpumin, C., and Sivasomboon, B. (1997), 'Corporate Focus: Making Layoffs the Last Resort', *Bangkok Post*, 5 June.

Pralahad, C.K., and Doz, Y.L. (1987), *The Multinational Mission: Balancing Local Demands and Globalization*. New York: Free Press.

Ralston, D.A., Holt, D.H., Terpstra, R.H., and Kai-Cheng Yu (1997), 'The Impact of National Culture and Economic Ideology on Managerial Work Values: A Study of the United States, Russia, Japan and China', *Journal of International Business Studies*, Vol.28, No.1, pp.177–207.

Santimatanedol, A. (1999), 'Prawasee Fires Anti-Western Broadside: Occidental Thinking Leads to Disaster', *Bangkok Post*, 12 Jan.

Schein, E.H. (1985), *Organizational Culture and Leadership*. San Francisco, CA: Jossey-Bass.

Schneider, S.C., and Barsoux, J. (1997), *Managing Across Cultures*. London: Prentice Hall.

Siamwalla, A., and Sobchokchai, O. (1998), 'Responding to the Thai Economic Crisis'. Thailand Development Research Institute Conference, 22 May. Bangkok: UNDP.

Smith, M. (1998), 'Culture and Organisational Change', *Management Accounting*, No.76, pp.60–4.

Stiglitz, J. (1998), 'Lessons of the Asia Crisis', *Financial Times*, 3 Dec.

9

Conclusion:
ASEAN Economic and Institutional
Development in Perspective

MHINDER BHOPAL and MICHAEL HITCHCOCK

Over the last three decades discussion of the changing nature of the global economy could not neglect consideration of the growth of the Asia Pacific region. The interaction of export-oriented growth, increased foreign trade and East Asian movement into new and labour-intensive technologies and industries produced a rate of economic expansion which eclipsed that of the rest of the world. Many believed that we were witnessing new global trends (Kennedy, 1988; Dickens, 1992). The 1997 crisis has spawned a more critical approach to the East Asian miracle and put into perspective, if not undermined, some previous accounts purporting to explain the high rates of growth.

Economic Growth: Extent and Implications

The swift and ongoing pace of development of seven Asia Pacific countries, collectively known sometimes as the 'Seven Dragons', brought about a major reappraisal of development studies. The dragons comprised Hong Kong, Indonesia, Malaysia, Singapore, Taiwan, Thailand and South Korea, and up until the Asian Crisis all had been growing very rapidly. This is indicated by the fact that East Asian GDP growth rates averaged 7.5 per cent between 1965 and 1980 and 7.9 per cent between 1980 and 1989 (World Bank, 1991). This continued into the 1990s with growth rates of 7.1 per cent in 1990 and 6.1 per cent in 1997 (World Bank, 2001). Since the 1960s this collection of countries had grown faster than any other regional group worldwide (see Freeman, 1998), though Indonesia's entry into the club was delayed by the turmoil of the end of the Sukarno period (1965–67). It took time for the significance of this rapid transformation to be appreciated, though as early as the 1970s, the term 'Four Tigers' was being applied to four members of the group – Singapore, South Korea, Hong Kong and Taiwan – in recognition of their consistently high growth. This occurred during a time of increasing concern over the de-industrialization of North America and Europe and concomitant increases in unemployment (Dickens, 1992). In particular, the explosion of the Japanese onto the world stage, initially as a manufacturing and latterly as a financial power, gave rise to increasing concern over the changing balance of economic and political power.

States and Markets

Explanations of East Asian growth have drawn from one of three positions. Firstly, according to the prevailing orthodoxy of the time, East Asian growth was attributed to adoption of market-oriented policies and open-door policies regarding foreign trade and inward investment. As it became clear, however, that these states were not following the prescribed path, a modified version of the Western developmental model was proposed. These states were merely preparing the groundwork for economic transition by using government investment to establish the right kinds of conditions for entrepreneurial activity by providing certain socially necessary services such as basic education. Finally, there emerged analysts who began to doubt that government intervention in the Asian tigers was aimed at ensuring market conformity and came to regard the efforts of these governments as market-leading. It was argued that these Asian states were employing selected policies to direct investment towards aims that conformed with their own national priorities. This approach, though often varying considerably between the various countries concerned, came to be regarded as a kind of 'state capitalism', in which the government was primarily concerned with intervening to promote the interests of the business sector (see Chowdhury and Islam, 1993).

   While some of the above approaches utilized analysis of Asian growth to advance explanations for, and even defences of, particular systems, others tried to identify broad lessons that would help them to advocate reform of their own business and political systems. But as in all discourse this was not neutral or uncontested. Politicians and academics from the neo-liberal camp emphasized the significance of markets, market-oriented institutions, low levels of public expenditure, societal and organizational integration and entrepreneurship as the engines of Asian growth to serve their own political projects. Such projects were related to the competition over the efficacy of different capitalist systems, as indicated from President Reagan's comments in 1985 when he declared that 'America's economic success ... can be repeated a hundred times in a hundred nations. Many countries in East Asia and the Pacific have few resources other than the enterprise of their people. But through free markets, they've soared ahead of centralized economies' (quoted in Bello and Rosenfeld, 1992: 7). Other projects related to utilizing the threat of, and growth in, Asia to justify domestic policies and reconfigure the psychological contracts which had arisen from the post-World War Two European experiments in social democracy. This was particularly the case in Thatcherite Britain, where Japanese inward investment was utilized as a strategy to discipline labour and 'modernize' management practice (Elger and Smith, 1994). This strategy was continued by Chris Patten, the last governor of Hong Kong, who was singing the praises of the Asian model until shortly before the Asian financial collapse.

On the other side of the discourse, social democrats attempted to undermine the utilization of Asian models to serve neo-liberal ends. They emphasized the cultural and structural basis of East Asian growth and the role of the state in directing and managing it while mediating the potentially maleficent effects of uncontrolled markets. Thus, the Asian models of South Korea and Japan were embraced in order to advance arguments for the significance (and therefore need) for investments in education, training and state support and long-term financing of industry. In particular, attention was focused on what was seen as the dysfunctional aspects of the market and the benefits of relational and network-based contracting (Dore, 1994; Chowdhury and Islam, 1993).

THE MODEL CRISIS

The above had the effect of shifting interest in Asia from the periphery to centre stage in many disciplines, including management, organization studies, politics and economics. While some of these studies concentrated on comparative and international analysis, they were accompanied by an increasing interest in the form and substance of Asian societies.

As a result many accounts have utilized a multidisciplinary

analysis focusing on economy, society and culture (see Kao *et al.*, 1999; Chowdhury and Islam, 1993). Some academic analysts went as far as arguing that state-directed instrumental developmentalism combined with Asian family values and communitarianism contributed to a virtuous cycle of growth and social order. Meanwhile, some Asian political elites attempted to construct, and leverage, cultural resources to reinforce consensus, acquiescence and harmony (see Preston, 1998) in attempts to address the perceived potential negative consequences of rapid industrialization. Both these elements of ASEAN (Association of South East Asian Nations) management have been the subject of debate and contestation.

Economic neo-liberals argued that East Asian economic growth was a vindication of the significance of markets, market-oriented institutions, low levels of public expenditure and well-integrated societies and organizations. On the other hand interventionist-minded analysts pointed to the significance of the state in mediating the potential worst effects of uncontrolled markets, and its role in directing investment into industry, education and training. In this sense the East Asia model was either an explicit or implicit resource in various debates surrounding the desirable relationship between states, firms and markets for economic growth. In this context, it is not surprising that the crisis has been utilized as an empirical demonstration of the dangers of government and political involvement in business and the ensuing dysfunctional impact on resource allocation, which market-based mechanisms supposedly avoid. These debates regarding the nature and role of states, firms and markets has not, therefore, abated in the wake of the crisis, but rather the crisis has been utilized in attempts to vindicate the need for market supremacy and transparency.

GLOBAL DISCOURSE AND LOCAL REALITIES

Economic Debates

As Booth points out in this collection, three years after the crisis there are important differences of opinion as to its causes, and this reflects differences between and within different schools of thought. Booth considers, and refutes, grand explanations and in particular rejects the view espoused by many analysts critical of unregulated globalization, namely, that the crisis can be attributed to unmanaged financial liberalization and foreign speculation. She makes a persuasive case that the most plausible explanations are those that see the crisis as home-grown. While there is no single cause of the crisis, there were many differences in the financial structures and economic arrangements of Indonesia, Thailand and Malaysia. In the light of this, a more satisfactory appreciation of the causes of the economic meltdown requires analysis derived from local knowledge of the respective economic and socio-political circumstances. This locally sensitive view of the cause of the crisis may also help explain different consequences and differential recovery. Nonetheless, the fact that these economies were all affected at the same time does indicate that there were some common factors at play.

In the context of inadequately regulated financial environments, private sector, rather than government, borrowing was a problem for Malaysia, Thailand and Indonesia. The main reason for capital flight was widespread change in the perception of risk; this was affected by the interpenetration of political and business interests in the context of growing economies and consequent enhanced business opportunities. Growing middle-class perceptions of corruption and self-serving behaviour in the context of an increasing belief in the declining ability of the government technocracy to manage economic shocks contributed to domestic capital flight, and merely indicated the pre-existing lack of belief in the ability of the respective regimes to manage the crisis. While many political analysts have alluded to the limited prospects of organized middle-class political opposition (Aspinall, 1996; Jesudason, 1996), what is interesting is that perceptions of corruption that undermine public confidence in economic management can give rise to a 'flight to safety' among increasingly wealthy, and savings-oriented, South East Asian middle classes. The ensuing financial crisis certainly opened up political spaces, although in some countries, for instance Malaysia, government action saved an economic meltdown and possibly enabled the regime to weather, at least to date, the subsequent political storm – a position which contrasts markedly with Indonesia. This would indicate that emphasis on international speculation, however accurate, needs to be supplemented with analysis of domestic financial behaviour in the context of perceptions of the nature of the emerging political economy.

Culture, Identity and Politics

The crisis raised increasing demands for transparency and utilization of stringent market criteria for the allocation of credit and contracts. However, this market-oriented approach has yet to become widespread, and most reports indicate that the pace of reform has been uneven and has slowed in the post-crisis period. The idea of infrastructural reform, which threatens established interests, has been most vociferously resisted by Prime Minister Mahathir in Malaysia, who has utilized notions of race and nationalism in his advocacy of locally sensitive and locally-driven solutions. The issue of transparency and the utilization of Western business practices however is not a debate restricted to the macro level, and indeed the discourse of identity also provides a potential resource at the local level. Andrews' account here of the local response to multinational downsizing in the context of the economic crisis does precisely this. While social and cultural identity in the context of growth can give rise to feelings of enhanced group worth, Andrews shows that in the context of decline the cultural discourse can equally be utilized to represent externally imposed change as inappropriate, short-term and culturally inappropriate. In this sense issues of Asian identity, supported by the local media and governments, can give rise to resources for micro resistance. This potentially feeds into, and draws from, wider debates about the power of Western capital and institutions to impose Western solutions that undermine national expectations as to what the appropriate political, social and cultural policy response might be. This does not imply any fundamental clash of civilizations but possibly a situational use of identity to resist unwelcome change.

Given the heavy penetration of multinational corporations in South East Asia and its location in the global economy, interesting issues arise regarding how host country or host region identities can be, or have been, galvanized to resist what are represented as Western-imposed solutions. This has implications not only for the micro-management of firms, but also for the zone of manoeuvre for macro adjustments at the level of the nation-state. In the case of the latter, particular adjustments may be demanded, recommended or prescribed by international institutions, experts and commentators who seek to define the appropriate policy response informed by the dominant prevailing discourse. Such prescriptions may have political support in affected nations, especially among those who feel they have been excluded from the major benefits of growth in what are seen as structures of mutual, but differential, benefit within the ruling elite. This indicates that while Asian economies can be market-oriented, the domestic socio-political context cannot be ignored in determining whether, how and to what degree particular prescriptions are enacted and represented as legitimate to the population. Furthermore, given the prevalence of political factions, clashes over normative behavioural and managerial responses to critical events have the possibility of exacerbating internal political conflict. In the ensuing political competition, and feelings of nationalism and group closure, there is the potential that events such as the Asian Crisis rather than undermining the Asian model may serve to consolidate the sentiments that have been expressed in the rhetoric over Asian-Western discourse as exemplified by the 'Asian values' debate. Importantly, however the actors who utilize this agenda may not be those claiming to pursue economic development, as indicated by the electoral gains of Islamic parties in post-crisis Malaysia and Indonesia.

Sustainability of South East Asian Business

The growth of East Asia has not only been based on foreign multinational-driven export orientation, but has equally been underpinned by the growth of domestic firms. While most of these companies emanated from Japan, South Korea and Taiwan, the 1980s and 1990s saw an increase in the growth of multinationals from the second-tier newly industrializing economies (NIEs). In many senses this growth precipitated anticipation of the growth of developing-world multinationals. Panond's analysis of the Thai telecommunications sector shows that their growth has been the result of government direction and support. She concludes that without embedded technological capability, expansion based on connections and finance provide an unstable foundation for sustainable competitive advantage. This draws attention to the limited capacity of indigenous companies within the second-tier NIEs to emulate the success of those in the first. While such firms may be able to operate in peripheral markets under particular conditions, their hold is tenuous, raising issues over the durability and sustainability of such companies, and indeed of the ability of the second-tier countries to attain the same position as others such as South Korea (Rowley and Bae, 1998).

What emerges from Hitchcock's discussion in this collection is that the effects of the Asian crisis were highly variable and that there was a flight of finance and personnel into areas within the region that were perceived to be comparatively stable. Bali may not have been peaceful as it appeared on the surface, but was nonetheless able to maintain a relatively stable tourism industry. Bali's relative security, as compared with the rest of Indonesia, is attributable to various interconnected factors: the all-important tourism, the vested interests of the Chinese and other powerful Indonesians elites. The Jakarta-based conglomerates were closely linked into the island's economy via well-connected Balinese with political influence. Representatives of Bali's tourism industry were also able to partially convince the media that Bali remained safe, despite the attention focused on Indonesia's strife between 1997 and 1999. Despite the onset of democratization in Indonesia, the locally-owned conglomerates proved to be tenacious in Bali and were shielded from the full brunt of the recession. The idea that certain places with special characteristics like Bali can act as havens in financial storms, even if imperfectly, requires further investigation.

The picture is somewhat different, however, when one looks at what happened to the majority of indigenous companies when the crisis struck. The weaknesses of many of the local businesses were rapidly exposed as the crisis worsened and it is clear that indigenous companies growing with political connections and elite involvement can yield large short-term returns, but are vulnerable to large losses. In the event of a downtown, the issue is whether or not they can contract sufficiently without incurring substantial losses. This highlights what has been an ongoing debate in the region, namely that when substantial losses are incurred by private but politically connected businesses, who should be liable to bear the cost? Furthermore, in the context of retraction and consolidation in home markets, do the most efficient firms survive or the politically well-connected? If the latter prevail, then the structures of political business and associated issues of nepotism, cronyism and corruption, which have plagued Indonesian and Malaysian corporate structures, will remain largely intact. These questions raise fundamental issues concerning the nature and form of qualitative and quantitative change in the character of business systems in South East Asia. Indeed, despite significant prescriptions over the necessity for qualitative change in the institutional structure of business in many of the affected countries, Asia's rapid recovery seems to have placed the political business issue into 'cold storage'. In this context it should not surprise us if future stagnation or shock is attributed by internal and external critics to lack of real reform in the structure of East Asian corporate sector. While the economic crisis may be past its worst, such analysis is suggestive of future economic and political flashpoints.

Limits of Reform

A commonplace assumption about the crisis was that it would lead to the reform and re-structuring of many South East Asian business and management practices. The contributions in this volume are inconclusive with regard to this contention, and it is perhaps still too early to arrive at a clear assessment of the impact of the crisis. While it is possible to observe the short-term ramifications of the crisis from the standpoints of politics and economics, it is much harder to evaluate the longer-term social and cultural implications. As Hitchcock shows, the legacy of the Suharto era, namely the complex network of political and business allegiances, lingers on long after the collapse of the regime that spawned this system. In view of the complex web of holding companies that are designed to obscure direct patterns of ownership, the reform of this state of affairs is an uphill struggle. Patronage remains an enduring feature of post-Suharto Indonesia partly because of the slow pace of political reform and partly because of cultural factors. At a time of uncertainty, patronage, for all its faults, provides a sense of security and seems likely to remain a characteristic of South East Asian styles of management. When viewed from a South East Asian standpoint, markets and Western styles of management are not seen as rational and objective, and may be perceived as culturally loaded.

New Technologies, New Possibilities?

The Asian Crisis also raised issues about the ability of Asian states to stifle dissent, withhold information and camouflage political business. The fact that the crisis occurred at the time when the Internet was becoming a medium of communication, which respected no national boundary, means that its use, for political purposes, indicates a possible new trajectory for political discourse within and about the region. Thus while on the one hand technology is seen as enhancing business opportunity and attracting inward investment, on the other it calls for greater transparency, accountability and, moreover, gives rise to the use of the very same technology for oppositional commentary. In particular, by reducing the financial and potentially oppressive cost of opposition and critical scrutiny, the Internet has served to open up the nature of political economy to oppositional (re)presentation, surveillance and commentary. Political business in South East Asia may be characterized by state oppression and individual powerlessness and a political elite which places emphasis on harmony, integration and Asian social values. However central and state control over the structures of mediation is being undermined by the new developments in the infrastructures of communication as exemplified by the Internet. These developments have the potential to contribute to the creation of a new context of political openness in which the debates over economic management, social policy, justice and fairness find avenues for expression. The Internet makes political differences more transparent, and provides the potential for exposure of what otherwise has been submerged and hidden in the structures of mutually beneficial networks.

Political authoritarianism has for long been associated with the region, and the crisis saw the unravelling of many old structures of authoritarian control as political factions that existed prior to the crisis utilized the new threats and opportunities to advance their respective positions. This democratic opening and political competition provides the potential prospects for a more interest-group-based politics, and not least to gain from this could be labour, given its centrality in the export-based growth of the region. However, whether this happens is dependent upon the degree to which the crisis, as an event, has set in motion medium-to long-term change in political structures and practices, and this still remains to be seen.

CONCLUSION

Many of the contributions in this volume have argued that the roots of the crisis are political and institutional as well as economic. This points to the need to explore the relationship between regulatory failure and corruption and collusion, as well as the possibilities of reform. If reform requires an underpinning legal structure to provide ballast, this would require a change of political will or a change of regime. Both would need to reconfigure institutional structures to support a developmental model where political vested interest control would give way to a democracy whose management would be guided by technocrats and checked by lawyers. However, such change ignores the impact of institutional sedimentation and the great social disruption that such change would entail. While this points to the need for locally driven transactional (as opposed to transformational) change, differing time-frames of legal and economic reform raise important issues over the domestic sustainability of institutional restructuring and modification as short-term economic pressures recede.

Unlike some of the reporting in the mass media and some academic commentary, what is clear is that analysis of the causes and consequences of the Asian crisis needs to be multi-faceted and multidisciplinary. The authors concur that the crisis has induced change and created new opportunities, but remain uncertain, uncommitted and unconvinced about the possibility for fundamental change, given the continuing importance of vested interests in nationally-specific configurations. However we cannot be entirely conclusive and need to draw attention to the ongoing micro impact arising out of the crisis, which needs to be sensitive to the diversity of the region and with a sensitive appreciation of the significance of the local in interpreting global trends.

The crisis that is the subject of this volume is widely referred to as the 'Asian Crisis' and a recurring theme in these contributions is that this is something of a misnomer. The crisis neither affected all the Asian nations nor was linked to Asian states alone. Many Asian countries remained largely unscathed, whereas some major non-Asian economies, namely Russia and Brazil, experienced a serious downturn. The start and causes of the crisis can, however, be pinpointed accurately to South East Asia and it is widely agreed that the onset first became apparent in Thailand, from where it spread to neighbouring countries before becoming a global phenomenon. Even within this context the ramifications of the crisis were uneven, with Singapore and Brunei proving to be quite resilient while their neighbours, all-important trading partners, went into decline. The countries that were affected worst at the outset – Thailand, Malaysia and Indonesia – though different from one another in terms of political systems, share a common feature, namely membership of ASEAN. They are moreover among the largest economies of the ASEAN block and are markedly more prosperous and market-oriented than the newer members, who are drawn largely from the former Communist block. Their relative openness, combined with their status of developing countries, may have rendered them more vulnerable to market pressure. In contrast, Singapore, though also an ASEAN member, is regarded as a fully developed economy and is thus better placed to weather economic storms. Despite these internal differences, it might be better to re-name the crisis the 'ASEAN Crisis' to locate it, at least in its onset, in its regional context.

REFERENCES

Aspinall, Edward (1996), 'The Broadening Base of Political Opposition' in G. Rodan (ed.), *Political Oppositions in Industrializing Asia*. London: Routledge.
Bello, W., and Rosenfeld, S. (1992), *Dragons in Distress: Asia's Miracle Economies in Crisis*. London: Penguin.
Chen, Min (1995), *Asian Management Systems: Chinese, Japanese and Korean Styles of Business*. London: Routledge.
Chowdhury, A., and Islam, I. (1993), *The Newly Industrialising Economies of East Asia*. London: Routledge.
Dickens, Peter (1992), *Global Shift: The Internationalization of Economic Activity*, 2nd ed. London: Paul Chapman.
Dore, R. (1994), 'Japanese Capitalism, Anglo-Saxon Capitalism' in N. Campbell and F. Burton (eds), *Japanese Multinationals: Strategies and Management in the Global Kaisha*. London: Routledge.
Elger, T., and Smith, C. (1994), 'Global Japanisation? Convergence and Competition in the Organization of the Labour Process' in T. Elger and C. Smith (eds), *Global Japanization: The Transnational Transformation of the Labour Process*. London: Routledge.
Evans, Peter (1995), *Embedded Autonomy: States and Industrial Transformation*. Chichester: Princeton University Press.
Freeman, C. (1998), 'The East Asian Crisis, Technical Change and the World Economy', *Review of International Political Economy*, Vol.5, No.3 (Autumn), pp.393–409.
Jesudason, James (1996), 'The Syncretic State and the Structuring of Oppositional Politics in Malaysia' in G. Rodan (ed.), *Political Oppositions in Industrializing Asia*. London: Routledge.
Kao, H., Durganand, S., and Wilpert, B. (1999), *Management and Cultural Values: the Indigenization of Organizations in Asia*. London: Routledge.
Kennedy, Paul M. (1989), *The Rise and Fall of the Great Powers: Economic Change and Military Conflict*. London: Fontana.
Preston, P. (1998), *Pacific Asia in The Global System*. Oxford: Blackwell.
Rowley, C., and Bae, J. (eds) (1998), *Korean Business: Internal and External Industrialization*. London: Frank Cass.
World Bank (1991), *World Development Report*. New York: Oxford University Press.
World Bank (2001) East Asia and Pacific, accessed at www.worldbank.org/data/ countrydata/ littledata/9.pdf

Notes on Contributors

Mhinder Bhopal is Senior Lecturer in Employment Studies at the University of North London, where he teaches comparative employee relations. He has maintained an active interest in multinationals, trade unions and the electronics sector in Malaysia. He has previously published in *Asia Pacific Business Review* and *Economic and Industrial Democracy*.

Michael Hitchcock holds a professorship in the Business School of the University of North London. He is Director of the International Institute for Culture, Tourism and Development and is a former chair of the Association of South East Asian Studies, UK. He has written and edited numerous books on South East Asia including *Tourism in South-East Asia* (ed. with V.T. King and M.J.G. Parnwell) and *Bali: The Imaginary Museum* (with L. Norris). He has often appeared in the media as a South East Asia analyst.

Anne Booth is Professor of Economics (with reference to Asia) at the School of Oriental and African Studies, University of London. Prior to taking up her appointment at SOAS, she held appointments at the Australian National University and the University of Singapore. She has published extensively on the economic development of the ASEAN region, with special reference to Indonesia.

Andrew Harding researches and teaches Comparative Public and South East Asian law at the School of Oriental and African Studies, University of London. He is interested in law in the context of development and his publications include *Law, Government and the Constitution in Malaysia* (1996), and 'Comparative Law and Legal Transplantation in South East Asia: Making Sense of the "Nomic Din"', in D. Nelken and J. Feest (eds), *Adapting Legal Cultures* (forthcoming).

Len Holmes is Acting Director of the Management Research Centre, the Business School, University of North London. He has previously published in the field of skills, and he is currently exploring the relational perspective on organization and management as affected by the potential and affordance of the new Internet technology for promoting social inclusiveness and widening participation.

Margaret Grieco is Professor of Transport and Society at Napier University, Edinburgh and Senior Visiting Fellow at the Institute for African Development,

Cornell University. She has published extensively on gender and development and has a particular interest in electronic ontologies.

Pavida Pananond is Lecturer in International Business at the Thammasat Business School, Thammasat University in Thailand. Her research interests include the emergence of developing-country multinationals and business strategies of South East Asian firms.

Tim G. Andrews is Senior Lecturer in International Marketing at Bristol Business School, University of the West of England. He is working on a body of research on Western multinational corporations in South East Asia, including a forthcoming book, *The Changing Face of Multinationals in Southeast Asia* (2002).

Abstracts

Introduction: The Culture and Context of the ASEAN Business Crisis: *by Mhinder Bhopal and Michael Hitchcock*
The Asian economic crisis heightened tensions within South East Asia and provoked considerable commentary on and analysis of the region. While there is already a burgeoning literature on the crisis, multi-disciplinary approaches offer richer and local insights into what is largely seen as an economic and political phenomenon. In this introductory essay, we stress the need to consider the cultural context of the crisis and in particular the specific characteristics of business and politics in the South East Asian region. Our aim is to provide a critical backdrop to the events of 1997 and to evaluate the substance of the associated Asian values and crony capitalism discourse.

The Causes of South East Asia's Economic Crisis: A Sceptical Review of the Debate *by Anne Booth*
This contribution argues that the crisis in South East Asia was due to a number of causes, often interacting with one another, and that these causes varied across countries. It is explained how domestic policy weaknesses interacted with external factors to produce the severe contraction in national product in 1998 in Thailand, Indonesia and Malaysia. Particular attention is given to the decline of technocratic influence especially in Indonesia and Thailand, the role of the IMF, and changing public tolerance for corruption and cronyism in the worst affected countries.

The Economic Crisis and Law Reform in South East Asia *by Andrew Harding*
The crisis has widely been seen as an economic one, but this crisis was no mere economic downturn, such as has occurred before in South East Asia; its origins and its effects are clearly political and institutional in character. The impact of the crisis has also varied from country to country reflecting the different political and institutional circumstances; it seems unlikely that a single batch of remedies will help solve the region's problems. Despite this variety the lessons to be learned are broadly similar and this essay argues that the legal systems will have to respond strongly and much more swiftly for the situation to improve; the economic and political crisis is also fundamentally a legal one. In this context the imperatives of commerce and investment have to contend with those of democracy and the rule of law. However, in the current situation, most states in the region are weak, with the exception of Singapore, in precisely these areas; unfortunately they have a great deal of catching up to do. This piece does not suggest that Singapore's system

can simply be copied; the whole point of Singapore's success is that the institutions and the legal culture have been developed over 30 years in a highly premeditated fashion. The other South East Asian nations need much faster solutions in the short term as well as much deeper reforms in the longer term, because they are not starting from the same vantage point as Singapore.

The Internet, Email, and the Malaysian Political Crisis: The Power of Transparency *by Len Holmes and Margaret Grieco*

The case of the arrest and imprisonment of Anwar Ibrahim in Malaysia has exposed a dilemma for governments attempting to exploit the commercial use of new communication technologies for economic development. While necessary for such development, the same technologies are available for political challenge and contestation. This contribution examines examples of how the Internet and the Web enable the transformation of traditional forms of political opposition, for the building of solidarity and the evasion of state efforts to neutralize opposition voices. A tool, originally adopted by the government for matters of economic policy, becomes an instrument for subversion, a dilemma yet to be resolved.

Malaysian Unions in Political Crisis: Assessing the Impact of the Asian Contagion *by Mhinder Bhopal*

The Asian economic crisis led to the rupture of underlying pre-crisis pressures and tensions in Malaysia and gave rise to a new rupture in the heart of Malaysian politics. In the field of industrial relations the events are testing and, potentially, (re)forging the relationship between the state and labour, which has been assumed to be one based on suppression arising from the economic imperatives of the dependent state. This contribution, focusing on the Malaysian Trade Unions Congress (MTUC), outlines the historical antecedents and contemporary changes in analysing the 'choice' exercised by key actors in constraining the labour movement's response to the economic and ensuing political crisis. It is argued that while Malaysian trade unionism has been historically hampered by ethnicity, these factors are changing. Trade union divisions during the economic and political crisis, while constraining the labour movement's political involvement, hold out the possibility for future material gains.

Tourism and Total Crisis in Indonesia: The Case of Bali *by Michael Hitchcock*

In a joke circulating in Bali in 1998 the term 'total crisis' (kristal) was used to refer to the impact of the financial crisis upon Indonesia. The joke not only referred to the constant stream of bad news, but also was an ironic commentary on the state of affairs in Bali: the crisis did not appear to be as severe on the island as elsewhere in Indonesia. During the crisis the island was not as peaceful as it appeared to be on the surface, but nonetheless managed to retain a relatively stable tourism industry. The island's comparative peacefulness is attributable to various intersecting interlocutors: Bali's well established international identity, the all-important tourism, the vested interests of the Chinese and other powerful Indonesian investors. These outside interests are also closely interwoven into the island's economy via well-connected islanders. These interest groups were also able to persuade the media that Bali remained safe, despite the international attention focused on Indonesia's troubles between 1997 and 1999. The prevailing view that security is a prerequisite for the maintenance of a successful tourism industry needs to be qualified, but it remains unclear whether or not any general conclusions can be drawn, since Bali remains an island with many special attributes.

The International Expansion of Thailand's Jasmine Group: Built on Shaky Ground? *by Pavida Pananond*

Exploring how Thai telecommunication firms are able to expand internationally given that they still depend largely on foreign technology, this contribution addresses specifically how the Jasmine group develops its competitive advantages in domestic and international markets. It argues that the Jasmine group's competitive advantages were based mainly on its vast connections with state agencies, politicians and financial sources rather than its technological expertise. Concluding that these types of advantage are short-lived and hard to sustain once the competition intensifies, it is pointed out how the rapid growth of the Thai economy and the inclination toward market protection has led to the emergence of domestic firms that are large in size but have yet to match their international competitors in expertise.

Downsizing the Thai Subsidiary Corporation: A Case Analysis *by Tim G. Andrews*

The unprecedented severity of the Asian economic recession in Thailand came as a shock to the indigenous corporate sector. Businesses long habituated to record levels of growth were suddenly confronted with spiralling costs and declining sales. In response to this crisis a number of powerful Western corporations began 'downsizing' their Thai operations in order to boost profitability levels via the reduction of staff. Adopting a processual approach, this article seeks to explore the role of 'corporate' and 'national' cultures in the local employee reaction to these externally imposed directives. Drawing on years of participative experience, the author presents a rare internal case study tracing the initiation and progression of one revelatory programme of downsizing throughout its year-long phase of implementation. Initial findings point to the dangers of Western management underestimating the strength and resilience of indigenous Thai business culture. Implications for Western MNCs and future research are outlined, along with some tentative recommendations for practice.

Conclusion: ASEAN Economic and Institutional Development in Perspective *by Mhinder Bhopal and Michael Hitchcock*

The authors concur with the argument that the roots of the Asian economic crisis are political and institutional as well as economic and consider the possibilities of reform in this context. They suggest that reform requires an underpinning legal structure but this in itself requires a change of political will or a change of regime. Both changes point to the need to reconfigure the institutional structures. However, such prescriptions not only ignore the impact of institutional sedimentation and the great social disruption that such change would cause but also fail to consider the sustainability of institutional restructuring and modification as short-term economic pressures recede. As a result the authors argue that while the crisis has induced change and created new opportunities, we should remain uncertain, uncommitted and unconvinced about the possibility for fundamental change in this region.

Index

Abdullah Yusuf Ali, 65
ABIM [Islamic Youth Movement of
   Malaysia], 64
Aceh (Sumatra), 105
ACeS (Asia Cellular Satellite System), 130,
   141, 143
Acumen (subsidiary of Jasmine Group),
   129, 135, 136, 137
Aditjondro, George J., 115–17, 119
Adler, Mortimer, 66
Administrative Court (Indonesia, 1990-), 54
administrative staff, 128, 162
Advance Info Service (AIS), 127
affirmative action, 78, 80, 81, 114
agriculture, 27, 80, 108
air travel: flights to Indonesian
   destinations, 104
airports, 106, 109, 145(n9)
Amalgamated Steel (Malaysia), 84
Anees, Munawar, 62, 63
Aquino, Corazon, 141
ASEAN (Association of South East Asian
   Nations), 2, 13, 19, 25, 63, 168, 174,
   181–2;
   banking, 35
   capital outflow (1997), 36
   effects of globalization, 10–11
   financial sector reform, 31
ASEAN economic and institutional
   development in perspective,
   culture, identity and politics, 176–7
   economic debates, 174–5
   economic growth: extent and
   implications, 170–1
   global discourse and local realities,
      174–80
   limits of reform, 179
   model crisis, 173–4
   states and markets, 172–3
   sustainability of South East Asian
      business, 177–9

Asia Cellular Satellite System (ACeS), 130,
   141, 143
Asian:
   government, 61
   growth: 'murkier side', 12
   management, 10–13, 61, 72
   miracle, 21, 36, 124
   model, 3, 13–14
Asian Crisis, 9, 82, 145(n11);
   Asian model, 13
   debate about causes, 174–5
   fears of recurrence, 16
   law reform, 49–58
   'political and institutional' causes, 49
   political ruptures and trade unions
      (Malaysia), 83–6
   recovery, 49
Asian values, 2–10, 81, 177, 180;
   and Confucianism, 3–4
   crony capitalism, 13–16
   cultural heterogeneity, 6
   culture and identity, 6–7
   'diversity', 8
   economic growth and social
      (dis)integration, 5–6
   managing through cultures, 7–10
Association of South East Asian Nations,
   see ASEAN

Badung (Denpasar, Bali), 105
Bagus, Professor I. Gusti Ngurah, 119
baht, 36;
   appreciation against Asian currencies,
      22, 23
   exchange rate to US dollar (1999),
      145(n7)
   fall, 15
   flotation (2 July 1997), 1, 2, 24, 29, 30,
      102, 135, 158
   US dollar peg, 22, 24, 29
Bakrie brothers, 116, 117

balance of payments, 21, 24–6
Bali: communications, 106, 109, 111, 114
cultural peak, 106–7, 108
cultural rejuvenation (1930s), 105–6
foreign visitors (1996–98), 110
haven, 9, 103, 104, 113–14, 118, 178
'Hindu, peace-loving', 102, 112, 117
image of stability, 102, 103, 109–12,
117, 119, 178
impact of Asian monetary crisis on
tourism (1997–), 102
indigenous ownership, 115, 117
interest groups, 118–19
religion, 104, 110
security, 118–19
tourism boom, 105–6, 107–9
violence, 105, 106, 111, 112, 117–18,
119
Bali Merdeka (Hindu political party), 112
Balisering (Balinization), 105–6
Bangkok, 22, 35, 126
Bangkok International Banking Facility
(BIBF 1993–), 23, 34–5
Bangladesh, 22, 85t
banjar ('tightly-knit residential units', Bali),
111, 118
bankers: foreign, 26
banking, 50, 51, 130, 145(n8)
bankruptcies: corporate, 38
bankruptcy law, 52–5
banks, 25, 43, 50, 56, 142;
closure (Indonesia, November 1997), 38
Indonesia, 26, 31–4, 35, 38, 54
loan portfolios, 31
Malaysia, 34
Philippines, 35
political connections (Malaysia), 34
'politically motivated lending'
(Indonesia), 26
South Korea, 38
state-owned, 32, 33, 35, 45(n13)
Thailand, 34–5, 38
Barisan Alternative, 90
Barisan Nasional (Malaysia), 77–8, 87
Bhagwati, Jagdish, 37, 46
Bimantara Group, 116, 118
Bodharamik, Adisai, 128, 129, 138–9,
145(n12)
borrowing, 23–4, 25, 30, 175
Brazil, 122, 181
Bretton Woods institutions, 37, 40, 43
Brittan, Samuel, 13–14
Brunei (Negara Brunei Darussalam), 6, 11,
181
Buddhism, 6, 103
bunkhun (psychological bond arising from
reciprocated favours), 164, 168

Bureau of Religious Affairs (Bali), 104
bureaucracy/civil servants, 6, 14, 27, 43,
50, 81
Burma/Myanmar, 11, 66
business, 59, 63, 70, 71, 177–9
class (Malaysia), 80
groups, 28
interests: represented by UMNO, 78–9
leaders: parodied (Malaysia), 68
practice, 9, 12, 83, 176

capital, 74, 122, 123, 126, 129;
controls, 36–7, 55
deregulation, 83
flight, 26, 43, 54, 175, 178
flow, 20, 31, 35, 37, 43, 83, 144
formation, 44(n5)
Jasmine Group, 128
markets, 11, 28, 37
outflow (from ASEAN economies), 36
private inflows, 14
'unregulated global flow', 12
Western, 176
capitalism (types), 11
CAT (Communications Authority of
Thailand), 125, 126, 127
Central Bank of Thailand, 52
central banks, 27, 29, 33, 34, 45(n13,
n19), 50, 52, 53
Charoen Pokphand (CP) Group, 127, 137n
Chat Pattana Party (CPP), 138–9
Chatichai Choonhawan, 139
Chile, 37, 45(n13), 145(n4)
China (pre-1949), 4, 12, 15
China, People's Republic (1949–), 22, 41,
44(n8), 156
Chinese (overseas), 4, 23;
categories, 113
control of domestic capital (Indonesia,
1974, 1999), 113
Indonesia, 9, 90, 104, 113–14, 118,
119, 178
majorities, 15
Malaysia, 76, 78, 90, 93, 98
political gains (Malaysia, 1969), 78
refugees, 113–14
trade unions (Malaya, 1940s), 77
victims of riots (1965, 1998), 113–14, 118
Christians, 6, 23
Cojuangco family (Philippines), 141
commerce, 49, 70
Commercial Court (Indonesia), 53–4
Communications Authority of Thailand
(CAT), 125, 126, 127
communism, 12, 77, 106, 182
communitarianism, 8, 174
competition, 8, 33, 35, 141, 173

competitive advantage, 121, 155, 177
confidence, 8, 26, 30, 39, 42–3, 44
Confucius/Confucianism, 4–5, 6, 66
conglomerates, 32, 113, 115–17, 118,
    145(n8), 178
corporate:
    bankruptcies, 43
    foreign borrowing, 44
    governance, 43, 45(n17), 50
    headquarters, 153, 159, 162, 164, 165,
        167–8
    restructuring, 16
corporations, 11, 16, 25, 26, 151, 174
corruption, 3, 14, 15, 16, 20, 28, 36, 39,
    41–2, 45(n15), 50, 52, 54, 56, 59, 64,
    65, 67, 71, 110, 124, 175, 178, 180
Corsetti, Giancarlo, 20, 45(n13), 46
courts, 52, 56, 57
crisis predictors, 24, 44(n2)
cronyism, 3, 13–16, 28, 29, 32, 39, 41, 54,
    64, 73, 124–5, 144(n2), 178;
culture, 76, 124, 176–7, 179;
    Bali, 105
    context of 'Asian Crisis', 1
    corporate, 57, 152, 155–6, 163, 166–7
    global corporate, 152, 154–5, 168
    headquarters v subsidiary, 160–61
    hybrid, 154–5
    and identity, 6–7
    industrial, 5
    Indonesia/Bali, 102
    national, 152–3, 154–5, 163–7
    organizational (Thailand), 151–5
    'Thai way', 161, 163–6
    Thai business, 153–4
currency, 43, 45(n19), 142
currency controls: Malaysia, 95
currency crises: Latin America and Western
    Europe (early 1990s), 37
currency falls, 40
current account:
    deficits, 24–5;
    surplus (Singapore), 50

debt, 15, 22, 25, 35
'delayering' systems, 151, 164
democracy, 49, 52, 54, 97, 181;
Democratic Action Party (DAP), 90
Denpasar (Bali), 104, 105, 112, 114
dependency theory, 74
deregulation, 30, 31, 34, 51, 83
developing countries, 31, 37, 42, 63,
    122–5, 133–4, 139, 140, 141–2, 144,
    145(n4), 168
development agencies, 27, 31, 36
dollarization, 43, 45(n19)
downsizing/layoffs, 155, 161–2;

implications, 166–8
'job-shedding', 51
local response to multinational, 176
organizational, 150–51
separation programme, 161–3, 163–6
'Thai values', 163–6, 168
Dutch East Indies, 104, 105

economic:
    development, 2–3, 56
    growth, 2, 8, 11, 13, 14, 45(n11), 50,
        60, 82, 150, 171–2, 174, 176, 177
    recovery, 22–3, 49, 52–3, 56–7, 83, 98,
        179
    shocks, 29, 175, 179
The Economist, 19, 21, 44(n2)
economists, 19, 26, 27, 28, 29, 30, 31, 37,
    43, 45(n16);
education, 22, 23, 27, 172, 173, 174;
efficiency, 6, 42, 151–2, 159, 167
electronic:
    mail, 59–72, 82, 161
    commerce, 62, 71
elites, 10, 76, 112, 174, 177, 178, 180
employees, 153, 161–2, 162–3
employment, 80, 83, 108
engineers, 128, 134, 141–2
environment, 13, 55, 114, 117
ethnic restructuring (Malaysia), 91
ethnicity, 73, 75–6, 96–7, 107, 109
exchange controls: Malaysia, 55
exchange rate, 23–4, 25–6, 43, 45(n11)
exports, 12, 14, 24, 28, 38, 80, 113, 171,
    177

'face', 8, 13, 151, 162, 168
factionalism, 10, 14, 89, 90, 180
FDI, see foreign direct investment
finance, 139, 142, 145(n8)
Finance and Development (IMF journal),
    45(n17)
financial:
    crises, 43, 45(n18)
    information (disclosure), 44–5(n10)
    institutions, 36, 56, 139, 142;
    liberalization, 30–5, 44(n8)
    markets, 83
    regulation, 20, 54
    sector, 22–3, 39, 43, 50, 51, 54;
Financial Times, 13–14, 22, 37
foreign direct investment (FDI), 16, 21, 23,
    31, 55, 74, 79, 88, 90, 121;
    see also investment

gender, 75, 76
globalization, 10–11, 50, 83, 174
Goh Chok Tong, 50, 51

Golkar, 117
Gomez, T., 14, 17
governance, 42, 43, 45(n15, n17), 50
government, 14, 15, 27
government bonds (Indonesia), 33
government concessions (Thailand), 135, 139
government expenditure (Indonesia, 1996), 23
Gramsci, Antonio, 64
group identity, 6, 154, 159, 176, 177
Guoco Holdings (Philippines), 130, 131

Habibie, B.J., 29–30
hedge funds, 36, 57(n2)
Hill, Hal, 14, 17, 41, 47
Hindus/Hinduism, 6, 103
Hobday, Michael, 122, 132, 146
Hofstede, G., 152, 153, 154–5, 169
Hong Kong, 2, 5, 15, 23, 123, 156, 171–2, 173
Hong Kong Telecom, 132
hotels, 115, 116–17, 118
Huntington, Samuel P., 6–7
hydroelectric power, 131t, 140

Ibrahim, Anwar, 55, 57(n1), 59, 62–71, 72(n18), 86, 87, 89–91, 93–8
ILO [International Labour Organization], 88
image, 101–2, 105–6, 107; see also Bali
IMF, see International Monetary Fund
India, 41, 44(n8), 130, 131, 132, 140, 142–3, 145(n11)
Indian values, 6
Indians (in Malaysia), 76, 92, 93
Indonesia:
  economy, 1, 2, 4, 15, 16, 20–21, 23–6, 28, 30, 36, 38–40, 44, 44(n9), 45(n12, n18), 85, 94, 107, 131t, 140, 141, 156, 171–2
  finance and banking, 25–6, 26, 31, 32–3, 34, 39, 40, 44(n8), 45(n10–11, n13–14, n19), 51, 102, 175
  government and politics, 7, 9, 10, 14, 15, 23, 28–9, 30, 33, 41, 42–3, 44, 51, 53, 54, 104–5, 107–8, 114, 175, 177, 178, 179
  history, 7, 11, 113
  IMF, 19, 20, 30, 38, 54
  religion, 5, 6
  technocrats, 15, 27, 28, 29–30, 44(n5)
  tourism, 101, 102, 108–9, 110
Indonesian Tourism Promotion Board, 109–10
industrial relations (Malaysia), 73–100

industrialization, 5, 75, 78, 81, 174
  late industrializing countries, 123–4, 144(n1)
inefficiency, 14, 16, 56
inflation, 23, 45(n11)
information technology, 1, 164
infrastructure, 114, 145(n8), 176
Ing Baring (Philippines), 131, 143
institutional:
  reform (essential to prevent economic instability), 51
  restructuring, 181
  theory, 152
  weakness, 83
institutions, 50, 174
intellectuals: Muslim (Indonesia), 114
international:
  agencies, 43
  financial markets, 44(n9)
  financial transactions (suggested tax), 37
  investment agencies, 14
  investors, 42
  labour system, 11
  markets, 30, 36, 123
  military order, 11
International Monetary Fund (IMF), 16, 19, 20, 29, 30–31, 37, 43, 45(n11), 52, 54–5, 56, 158, 165;
  behaviour, 21, 38–40, 41
  critics of, 31, 35
Internet, 10, 38, 82, 179–80;
Internet, email and the Malaysian political crisis;
  client-counting techniques, 69–71
  electronic challenge on hegemony, 64–9
  prison notebooks, 64–9
investment, 23–6, 49, 52, 54, 56, 57(n5), 60, 61, 114, 119, 124, 125, 138, 140, 158, 172, 173, 180;
  see also foreign direct investment
Islam, 6, 64, 104, 113, 177
Ital-Thai (Development/Group), 129, 130, 131, 132, 137, 145(n8–9)

Jakarta, 105, 114, 115–17, 118
Japan, 5, 6, 11, 12, 15, 25, 27, 129, 172, 173, 177
Japanese tourists, 112
Jasmine Group (Thailand, 1982–):
  debt-to-equity ratio (1994–97), 139
  debt-financing, 142–3
  employees (1996), 128
  growth and development, 128–32, 145(n6)
  international expansion (1994–97), 130–32, 145(n9)
  international investments (1994–99), 131

managerial capabilities, 137, 140
ownership advantages, 132–9
see also Thai Telephone &
    Telecommunications
Jasmine International (JI), 128, 129, 136,
    145(n9)
Jasmine International Overseas (JO, 1994–),
    130, 136, 138
'Jasmine Submarine Telecommunications'
    (JSTC), 129, 135, 136, 137
Java, 3, 23, 103, 104, 112, 114, 118
Johnson, Chalmers, 27, 41, 47, 125, 146
joint ventures, 130, 131, 135, 138, 140,
    141, 142, 145(n9, n11)
Jomo, K.S., 14, 17
JT Mobiles (India), 130, 131, 143, 145(n11)

Keadilan (opposition party), 90, 98;
Kenward, Lloyd R., 23, 24, 47
KKN (Korupsi, Kronisma, Nepotisma /
    'corruption, cronyism, nepotism'), 14, 20,
    40–44, 89, 178
Klungkung (Bali) 'hall of justice', 108
Korea, see South Korea
Krugman, P., 14, 17, 36–7, 47, 83
Kurikural, 66

labour, 12, 22, 28, 74, 75, 77, 78, 80,
    90–96, 123, 156, 173, 180
Lamsam family, 139, 145(n8)
language, 69–70, 103, 113, 153, 157
Laos, 11, 125, 131, 140, 143
Latin America, 25, 37, 40, 45(n18)
Laurent, A., 155, 169
law, 6, 49–58, 126, 151, 161, 180–1;
Lee Kuan Yew, 3, 4, 50, 51, 53
Lembaga Ilmu Pengetahuan Indonesia
    (Indonesian Institute of Sciences), 111
liberalization, 14, 20, 30–5, 44(n8), 125,
    132, 142, 175
Lim, Linda Y.C., 124, 147
Lingle, Christopher, 13–14, 17
Lloyd, David (pseudonym), 160–8, 169(n1);
loans, 30, 33–4, 35, 44–5(n10), 53, 53, 142
Lockheed Martin, 131, 143
Loxley Group, 127, 129, 139, 145(n8)

McLeod, Ross, 41, 47
macro-economic perspective, 14, 23, 28, 29,
    176
Mahathir Mohamed, 1, 3, 5–6, 9, 36, 55,
    63, 64, 86–7, 98, 176;
Malaysia:
    economy, 1, 5–6, 14, 20–1, 23, 24, 25,
        26, 28, 34, 36, 45(n12), 55, 81, 83,
        84, 85, 96, 97, 98, 145(n4), 156,
        171–2, 175

finance and banking, 31, 34–5, 37,
    44(n8), 55, 64, 83, 175
government and politics, 6, 10, 14,
    28–9, 42, 53, 55, 59–72, 78, 81, 82,
    86–90, 92, 95–6, 97, 98–9, 177, 178
history, 7, 11
IMF behaviour, 38
labour, 80, 83, 84, 97
Malaysian Labour Organization (MLO,
    1988–), 81, 87, 91
Malaysian Trade Unions Congress (MTUC),
    73, 79–80, 81, 82, 87–96
Malaysian unions in political crisis, 73–100;
    financial crisis, political ruptures and
        trade unions, 83–6
    impact of Asian contagion, 73–100
    Malaysian labour in the political crisis,
        90–6
    political ruptures past and present, 86–90
    pre-crisis trade union development and
        political economy, 76–82
    trade unions and political structure,
        74–6
MalaysiaNet, 62–3, 70, 72(n15)
management, 2, 13, 122, 125, 133, 135,
    145, 152–3, 156–7, 163, 168, 173, 174,
    179;
    Asian, 7, 8, 10–13
    Chinese, 153
    through cultures, 7–10
    'internal cost', 160
    Japanese, 153
    Malaysia, 79
    'professional', 159
    Thai, 159, 162
    Thai downsizing case-study, implications
        of 166–8
    Western, 7, 8, 153, 165, 166, 179
manufacturers/manufacturing, 22, 24, 80,
    122, 123
Mar'ie Muhammad (Minister of Finance,
    Indonesia), 30
Marcos, Ferdinand, 141
market:
    criteria, 176
    information, 124
    mechanism, 11, 21, 74
    orientation, 172, 177, 182
    supremacy, 174
marketing, 134, 145(n11), 157, 158, 160,
    163, 164, 165, 167
markets, 11–12, 139, 172–3, 174, 177;
    global, 12, 155
    semi-protected, 134–5, 143
    telecommunications, 141
    Thai, 157, 159
    uncontrolled, 174

media, 42, 117, 112, 119, 176, 178;
    academic press, 13, 14
    government-controlled (Malaysia), 65
    international, 38
    Internet newspaper, 82
    mass, 10, 181
    nationalistic, 165
    new forms of communication, 67
    newspapers, 66–7
    popular, 13
    press, 36, 53, 62, 90, 95, 101, 111, 118
    print and broadcast (Malaysia), 59
Megawati Sukarnoputeri, 112, 118
Merrill Lynch, 131, 143
Microsoft, 60
migrant labour (in Malaysia), 84, 85, 85
MLO (Malaysian Labour Organization, 1988–), 81, 87, 91
MNCs/MNEs, see under multinational enterprises
mobile telephones, see telecommunications
motor lubricants, 155, 156, 158
MTUC, see Malaysian Trade Unions Congress
Mugwanya, Dennis, 144, 145(n10);
Multimedia Super Corridor (Malaysia), 55, 60, 62–3
multinational enterprises (MNEs)
    ('MNCs'; 'multinational companies'; 'transnational corporations'), 5, 74, 79, 98, 122–5, 127, 132, 133, 140, 141, 155, 177
Myanmar/Burma, 11, 66

Nair, C.V. Devan, 79
Nasution, Anwar, 44(n9), 48
nation-building, 10, 56
nation-state/s, 11, 83, 176
nationalism, 7, 10, 107, 165, 177
Natthapong, Thongpakdi, 133, 147
neo-liberalism, 8, 10, 172, 174
Nepal, 130, 131, 132
nepotism, 3, 12, 15, 28, 39, 159, 178
Netherlands, 11, 104, 105
networking, see cronyism
New Economic Policy (NEP, Malaysia 1970–), 78, 80, 87–8
newly-industrialized countries (NICs), 5, 123
newly-industrializing economies (NIEs), 11, 177
NGOs, 89, 96
Noland, Marcus, 20, 48
Nusa Dua (beach resort, Bali), 108, 115, 117
Nusa Dua Beach Hotel, 116
Nusantara, 113

ownership-specific (O) advantages, 122, 132, 138–9
PAKTO reforms (Indonesia, 1988), 33
pancasila ('five principles', Indonesia), 5, 7
Paquin, Bob, 59–60, 61, 72(n1)
Partai Demokrasi Indonesia Perjuangan (Indonesian Democratic Party Struggle), 112
Parti Rakyat Malaysia (PRM) [People's Party of Malaysia], 90, 98
PAS [Pan-Malaysian Islamic Party], 90
Pasifik Satelit Nusantara (PSN) of Indonesia, 130, 131, 141
patronage, 86, 87, 154, 179
Patten, Chris, 173
Paz, Octavio, 64
PDIP (Partai Demokrasi Indonesia Perjuangan / Indonesian Democratic Party Struggle), 112
Pecatu Graha project, 116
Pehl, Lothar, 111
performance, 156, 160, 163, 164, 167
peso (Philippines): depreciation (1997–98), 35
petrochemicals, 24
petroleum, 34
Phatra Thanakit, 131, 139
Philippine Long Distance Telephone (PLDT), 130, 131, 141
Philippines, 6, 11, 20, 22, 27, 44(n5), 131, 132, 140, 145(n9);
    central bank (1993–5), 35
    economic recovery, 22–3
    crisis, 20
    martial law era, 44(n5)
    need for legal reform, 51
Picard, Michel, 103, 108, 119, 120
PLDT (Philippine Long Distance Telephone), 130, 131, 141
policy mistakes, 36, 39
policy-makers, 20, 26, 28
political parties, 74, 76, 77, 78, 79, 80, 82–3, 86
politicians, 3, 16, 28, 29, 36, 81, 89, 110
politics, 2, 13, 59–72, 76, 118, 173, 176–7, 179
Prabowo, General, 114
privatization, 126, 127, 128, 132
PRM (Parti Rakyat Malaysia), 90, 98
public:
    expenditure, 56, 172, 174
    opinion, 42, 43, 45(n15), 112
    services, 42

Rahim Nor, Tan Sri (Inspector-General of Police, Malaysia), 65
Ramos, Fidel, 22–3, 141

rating agencies, 24, 36
Razaleigh, Tengku, 87
real estate, 24, 34, 130, 145(n9)
reformasi (Malaysia), 59, 60, 61–2, 64, 67, 63, 71, 72(n2), 87, 97
Reformasi Nasional (website), 70
regulation, 33, 34, 35, 41, 43, 51, 52, 54, 56–7, 57(n2), 180
research and development, 60, 133, 137, 145(n10)
ringgit (Malaysia), 36, 55
riots, 23, 103, 104, 109, 113–14, 118
Rock, Michael, 28, 48
rupiah, 1, 30, 36, 38, 45(n11–12)

SAC (Thailand) Co. Ltd:
    cultural make-up, 156–7
    economic meltdown (1997–98), 158
    post-crisis (1997–98), 160–61
    pre-crisis (1996–97), 159–60
Sachs, Jeffrey, 38
savings, 24–5, 33, 175
Schein, E.H., 154, 170
Securities Commission Act (Malaysia), 55–6
Semangat '46 (Malaysia), 87, 90, 91
Shell, 158
Sheraton Nusa Indah, 111, 116
Shin Corp, 126, 127, 145(n5)
Shinawatra, Thaksin, 145(n5)
Shinawatra Group, 127
Siam Teltech, 135, 136, 137
Siamwalla, Ammar, 29, 48
Singapore, 5, 6, 7, 11, 12, 15, 21, 23, 44, 50–52, 56, 123, 156, 171–2, 181, 182;
Singapore Telecom, 132
South East Asia, 1, 3, 4, 6, 8, 11, 16, 62, 124, 157–8, 175, 176, 180;
    domestic firms (sustainability), 177–9
    financial system, 30
    heterogeneity, 10
    law reform, 49–58
    limits of reform, 179
    political corruption, 42–3
    social protection ('weak' legal provision), 56
South East Asia's economic crisis:
    behaviour of IMF, 38–40
    causes, 19–48
    fear of further financial crises, 43
    financial sector liberalization, 30–35
    'interacting causes', 20
    'internal causes' v 'external contagion', 20
    role of foreign speculators, 35–7
South Korea, 1, 4, 5, 7, 11, 12, 15, 19, 27, 29, 30, 34, 38, 41, 44(n6), 94, 123, 171–2, 173, 177
speculation/speculators, 20, 32, 175

Spies, Walter, 106
state, 8, 74, 75, 79, 81, 173, 174, 180
State Airplane Enterprise (Bandung), 30
Stiglitz, J., 35, 37, 48, 83
Stock Exchange of Thailand, 145(n3, n6), 146
subsidiary corporations, 153, 154–5, 159–62, 164–8
Suharto, President, 3, 23, 29, 30, 39, 42, 44, 44(n5), 45(n11), 86, 102, 106–7, 113–14, 179
Suharto family, 9, 30, 32, 38, 39, 45(n11), 113, 115–16;
    Ari Haryo Wibowo, 116
    Bambang Trihatmodjo/Trihatmojo (b 1953), 116, 117, 118, 141
    Hutomo Mandalaputra Suharto ('Tommy'), 115, 116t, 116–17
    Probosutejo, 116
    Sigit Harjojudonto (b 1951), 115, 116
    Siti Hardiyanti Rukmana ('Tutut'), 116
    Sudwikatmono, 116, 116
    Sukamdani S. Gitosarjono, 116
Sukarno, President, 3, 106, 171
Sumatra, 57(n6), 104, 105

Taiwan, 2, 5, 7, 12, 15, 27, 29, 44, 44(n8), 123, 171–2, 177
Tanah Lot (temple, Bali), 108, 116, 117
technocracy/technocrats, 20, 24, 27–30, 43, 44(n5), 52, 175, 181;
technology, 122–5, 132–4, 137, 140–42, 145, 156, 157, 171, 177, 179–80
TelecomAsia (TA), 126–7, 137, 137n
telecommunications:
    government support (Thailand), 177
    liberalization, 132
    'politicized' industry, 138, 141
    privatization, 132
    research and development, 133, 137
    see also Jasmine Group
Telephone Organization of Thailand (TOT), 125, 126–7, 128, 129, 131, 132, 135, 137, 145(n11)
temples (Bali), 104, 108
terrorism, 101
Thai subsidiary corporation: downsizing, 149–70;
    conclusions, 168
    contents, 150
    downsizing in Thailand, 151
    further research, 168
    implications for management, 166–8
    organizational culture, 151–5
    organizational downsizing, 150–1
    'Project Delta': SAC separation programme, 161–3, 163–6

SAC and 'Thai values', 163–6, 168
SAC (Thailand) Co. Ltd: case study,
    155–68
Western-corporate and Thai-societal
    elements, 149
Thai Telephone & Telecommunications
    (TT&T), 126, 127, 129, 135–7, 137n,
    145(n8);
'Thai values', 163–6, 168
Thailand:
    economy, 1, 2, 4, 16, 20–1, 21–2, 23,
        24, 26, 28, 38, 44(n3), 45(n12),
        52–3, 56, 125–6, 142, 145(n3), 149,
        153–4, 155, 158, 171–2
    employment, 85t, 94, 149
    finance and banking, 28, 29, 31, 34, 35,
        36, 44(n8), 51, 53, 102, 175
    government and politics, 23, 28–9,
        42–3, 44(n5), 51, 52, 53, 57(n3), 132
    history, 151, 153
    IMF, 19, 20, 38, 39–40
    military, 14, 29, 52
    religion, 6
    telecommunications, 14, 125–7, 129,
        135, 145(n4), 177
    tourism, 101–2, 109
Time Switch Investment Ltd, 117
TJP Engineering, 136t, 137
TNT UK, 110
Tobin, Professor James, 37
Toffler, Alvin, 62, 72
torture, 65, 66
tourism (in Bali), 1, 101–20, 178
    Chinese refugees, 113–4
    cultural peaks, 106–7
    foreign visitors (Indonesia/Bali 1996–8),
        110
    Jakarta- and foreign-based
        conglomerates, 115–17
    tourism boom, 107–9
trade, 27, 60, 61, 71, 171
trade unions, 1, 73–100, 186;
    and political structure (Malaysia), 74–6
    pre-crisis development and political

economy, 76–82
see also MLO; MTUC
training, 134, 173, 174
transparency, 50, 53, 59–72, 174, 176, 180

Ubud hills (Bali), 106, 108
UEM ('UMNO-linked engineering
    company'), 55
unemployment, 56, 83–4, 84, 85, 86, 112,
    172;
United Communications Industry (Ucom),
    126, 127
United Kingdom, 4, 7, 11, 154, 155, 168,
    173
United Malays National Organization
    (UMNO), 9, 55, 77, 78–9, 81, 82, 86,
    87, 88–9, 91, 92, 96–7, 97–8
United States of America, 11, 12, 27, 35,
    52, 173;
    US dollar, 22, 23–4, 29, 36, 43, 45(n12,
        n19), 55

Valenzuela, Jaime, 74, 100
Vietnam, 4, 6, 11, 12, 22, 130–32, 156

wages, 22, 51, 56, 78, 82, 84–5, 86, 95,
    96;
    salaries, 29
Wallerstein, Immanuel, 11, 18
Wang An Shih, 66
Weber, Max, 4
Western:
    financial institutions, 40
    government, 40
    'industrial decline', 8
    values, 5, 6–7
    world, 11, 69
Western Europe, 37
workforce, 5, 77, 80
World Bank, 21, 31, 40, 43, 45(n17), 48,
    57(n6)

Yogyakarta (Java), 105, 114
Yoshihara, Kunio, 44(n5), 48, 144(n2), 14

Printed in the United Kingdom
by Lightning Source UK Ltd.
107014UKS00003B/85-90